The Trouble With Passion

The Trouble With Passion

POLITICAL THEORY
BEYOND THE REIGN OF REASON

Cheryl Hall

ROUTLEDGE
NEW YORK AND LONDON

Published in 2005 by
Routledge
Taylor & Francis Group
711 Third Avenue
New York, NY 10017

Published in Great Britain by
Routledge
Taylor & Francis Group
2 Park Square
Milton Park, Abingdon
Oxon OX14 4RN

© 2005 by Taylor & Francis Group, LLC
Routledge is an imprint of Taylor & Francis Group

International Standard Book Number-10: 0-415-93405-2 (Hardcover) 0-415-93406-0 (Softcover)
International Standard Book Number-13: 978-0-415-93405-3 (Hardcover) 978-0-415-93406-0 (Softcover)
Library of Congress Card Number 2004027358

No part of this book may be reprinted, reproduced, transmitted, or utilized in any form by any electronic, mechanical, or other means, now known or hereafter invented, including photocopying, microfilming, and recording, or in any information storage or retrieval system, without written permission from the publishers.

Trademark Notice: Product or corporate names may be trademarks or registered trademarks, and are used only for identification and explanation without intent to infringe.

Library of Congress Cataloging-in-Publication Data

Hall, Cheryl Ann, 1963-
   The trouble with passion : political theory beyond the reign of reason / Cheryl Hall.
       p. cm.
   Includes bibliographical references and index.
   ISBN 0-415-93405-2 (hb : alk. paper) -- ISBN 0-415-93406-0 (pb : alk. paper)
    1. Political psychology. 2. Emotions. 3. Plato--Contributions in political science. 4. Rousseau, Jean-Jacques, 1712-1778--Political and social views. 5. Feminism--Political aspects. 6. Political participation. 7. Liberalism--Psychological aspects. 8. Ideology. 9. Public opinion. I. Title.

JA74.5.H34 2005
320'.01'9--dc22   2004027358

Taylor & Francis Group
is the Academic Division of T&F Informa plc.

Visit the Taylor & Francis Web site at
http://www.taylorandfrancis.com

and the Routledge Web site at
http://www.routledge-ny.com

For Mara, Paige, and Eileen

Contents

Acknowledgments		ix
Chapter 1	What About All Those Flags? Passion in Politics	1
Chapter 2	The Passions and the Reasons: Conceptualizing Capacities	11
Chapter 3	Public Reason, Private Passion: The Trouble with Passion in Liberal Political Theory	21
Chapter 4	"The Madness of Eros Is the Greatest of Heaven's Blessings": Plato's Passion for the Good	39
Chapter 5	"A Man Who Had No Passions Would Be a Very Bad Citizen": Rousseau's Passion for Community	71
Chapter 6	"Our Erotic Knowledge Empowers Us": Passion and Action in Contemporary Feminist Theory	93
Chapter 7	Passion, Politics, and Democratic Education	121
Notes		135
Bibliography		149
Index		153

Acknowledgments

Many people helped me write this book. One of the best parts about publishing the book, for me, is the opportunity it provides to publicly thank them for their help. To begin at the beginning, then, I would like to thank Peter Euben, Donna Haraway, Valerie Hartouni, George Kateb, Elizabeth Kiss, Ann Lane, and Hanna Pitkin—teachers and mentors who long ago kindled my interest in many of the issues I take up in this book. Their superb intellectual guidance was matched only by the inspiring example of their passionate commitment to scholarship. I am especially grateful to George, Elizabeth, and Peter, all of whom gave extensive and invaluable comments on this work in its very early dissertation form. My graduate school comrades at Princeton were also a wonderful audience for trying out ideas in progress. For their feedback I am particularly indebted to Judith Barish, Sammy Basu, Joshua Dienstag, Roxanne Euben, Judy Failer, Cindy Halpern, Jamie Mayerfeld, Pratap Mehta, Sara Monoson, Natalie Stoljar, and Paul Vogt.

Several portions of this book were presented at annual meetings of the American, Southern, and Western Political Science Associations. Discussants, other panel members, and audience members all helped me to strengthen my arguments through their attentive responses. I am grateful in particular to Annalise Acorn, Cynthia Burack, Lisa Ellis, Stephen Engelmann, Christopher Kern, Peter Lawler, Brenda Lyshaug, Sara Monoson, Shane Phelan, Edward Portis, Patricia Sykes, Robert Bruce Ware, and Penny Weiss. At the University of Hawaii at Mānoa, where I spent a semester visiting, I benefited from suggestions and criticisms from faculty and students in the Department of Political Science, the Department of Philosophy, and the Office of Women's Research. I am also very grateful to

x • Acknowledgments

Annalise Acorn, Katharina Heyer, Kathleen Hurtubise, Chloe Jessen, Shane Phelan, and Decha Tangseefa, visiting faculty and graduate students who participated in my seminar on reason and passion, as well as to Kerry Burch for enthusiastically advocating for my visit and to Kathy Ferguson for facilitating it.

At the University of South Florida I have been extremely fortunate to have a number of people with whom to discuss both political theory and feminist theory. Kennan Ferguson, Mike Gibbons, and Steve Johnston have been everything one could wish for in colleagues: knowledgeable, generous, careful, critical, supportive and, not least, fun. Together they read and commented on virtually the entire book. Marilyn Myerson and Joanne Waugh gave their suggestions on sections of the text, and Carolyn DiPalma and Betsy Hirsh provided much stimulating conversation on topics in feminist theory. I am also thankful for the many undergraduates who have taken my course in Classical Political Theory, whose exasperated yet lively responses to encountering Plato have kept me excited about the *Republic* year in and year out.

A number of people served as anonymous reviewers of the arguments in this book, in part or in whole, and I am grateful for the help their reviews provided. In addition, Susan Bickford and Barbara Koziak both reviewed the entire manuscript, providing comments of such generous engagement that they helped to restore my faith in the possibilities of the academic enterprise. As with all of the feedback I received, the book would surely have benefited had I been able to take all of their advice. Finally, I would like to thank Eric Nelson for pursuing and signing the book for Routledge, and Robert Tempio, Angela Chnapko, and Jay Margolis for seeing it through to publication.

Financial support from the Andrew W. Mellon Dissertation Fellowship and the University of South Florida Research and Creative Scholarship Fund allowed me two rare and much appreciated time periods in which I could focus exclusively on this work. Further institutional support came from Delores Bryant and Doris Kearney, office managers extraordinaire, without whose generous help I would have had to spend even more time navigating the university bureaucracy.

As anyone who has attempted to write one knows, a book is more than an intellectual project: it is a life project. Thus, I end with those whose contributions to this project were less tangible but no less crucial to its completion. For listening, sympathizing, offering encouragement, and tending my spirit throughout the challenging process of writing this book, I owe thanks in particular to Carolyn DiPalma, Louise Graves, Betsy Hirsh, Steve Johnston, Susan Kattlove, Ann McDowell, Gail Miller,

Chris Otten, Polly Powledge, Natalie Stoljar, and Lee Talley. I especially owe thanks to my partner Denise Roemer, who has been in the unenviable position of living with me during the later stages of the process. Her loving humor, playfulness, intelligence, and passion continue to inspire, challenge, amuse, and sustain me. I deeply appreciate all of the support she has provided in order that I might do this work, and I am delighted to finally be able to say two magic words: it's done! Finally, I thank my parents, siblings, and siblings-in-law, Rascha Hall, David Hall, Laurie Hall, Darren Hall, Schuku Schabanpour, Ronna Harris, and Ian Harris, for their love, their support, and their reassuringly steady faith in me. I have dedicated the book to my nieces, Mara, Paige, and Eileen, whose developing forms of reason-passion have been a true delight to witness. May they grow up to be passionate, reasonable citizens of the world.

CHAPTER **1**

What About All Those Flags?
Passion in Politics

Right after the attacks, they were everywhere. On cars and homes, businesses and schools, street lamps and fences, churches, synagogues, and mosques: anywhere an American flag could be flown, it seems, one was. Within a few days of the September 11 assaults on the World Trade Center and the Pentagon, people all over the country were wearing flag t-shirts and lapel pins. Within months, the creative machinery of capitalism had multiplied the possibilities in mind-boggling ways. One could proclaim one's patriotism with flags on bathing suits, scarves, credit cards, tote bags, coffee mugs, blankets, lamps, clocks, lawn ornaments, bumper stickers… and the list goes on. From expensive jewelry to cheap key chains, the market for anything bearing the likeness of the American flag became impressively broad.

This profuse display expressed a range of emotions. Exhibition of the flag communicated, among other things, a shared grief for those killed in the attacks, sympathy and compassion for loved ones left behind, respect and appreciation for those who helped in rescue efforts, and pride in the nation's ability to cope with tragedy. It symbolized people's stronger tendency to feel solidarity with strangers who are nonetheless fellow Americans, their stronger commitment to the idea that Americans should care for each other and work together. And it demonstrated people's renewed appreciation for public servants such as firefighters, police officers, and even politicians, indeed, their renewed appreciation for the very concept of

2 • The Trouble With Passion

public service. All of these emotions were part of an increased sentiment that the nation is, and should be, a community—something more than just a collection of people who happen to live within certain geographical boundaries, an "us" that involves some level of shared perspective and mutual responsibility.

At the same time, display of the flag also expressed an increased sense of a hostile and terrifying "them." For some, the flag demonstrated a stance of defiance in response to the threat posed by "them," as conveyed by the occasional accompanying slogan "these colors don't run." It demonstrated support for retribution against those perceived to be responsible for the attacks, whether at home or abroad, often despite tenuous or nonexistent links to the actual perpetrators and "collateral damage" of unclear magnitude. It also communicated a more general message of support for the government and its actions, and sometimes even the idea that any dissent is inappropriate in such a time of crisis. As President Bush himself repeatedly proclaimed, "You're either with us or you're against us." This simplistic dichotomy reinforced the fears of many American citizens and residents—especially those who differ from the dominant majority in ethnicity or dress or culture or religious practice—that they would be considered suspect by their neighbors and other citizens. Many consequently felt compelled to display the flag to prove their membership in "us" rather than "them."

Clearly, the meaning of the flag varies. It can symbolize sympathy, respect, pride, solidarity, anger, defiance, thirst for retribution, support for political leaders, submission to conformity, or any combination thereof. Despite this variety of emotions, though, all but the last are part of one overarching emotion: a passion for the polity. A flag is a tangible symbol of political passion. When displayed according to the conventions of respect, especially by citizens under no obligation or pressure to do so, a flag is a sign of allegiance to a polity, its members, and the values for which the polity is believed to stand. When displayed with scorn or contempt (for example, when hung upside down or burned), it is a statement of outrage against that polity and its members, values, and actions, in the name of values one believes the polity has violated. In both situations, cognitive evaluation of the worth of the polity is accompanied by emotional enthusiasm, either for the polity or for something one believes the polity threatens. This cognitive/emotional nexus of evaluation and enthusiasm is what I mean by passion. The ubiquity of the American flag in the wake of September 11 was a particularly visible sign of political passion.

Flags raise many questions for political theorists. What are their political implications? What might be worrisome about them? What might be beneficial? Can or should a polity do without flags? What, if anything, should be done to discourage the worrisome aspects of flags and encourage their beneficial aspects? These are the questions this book addresses about passion.

The Trouble with Passion

As the example of the flag illustrates, there are some positive aspects to an abundance of passion in the public sphere. Flag-waving is, in some respects, an expression of solidarity, cooperation, *involvement* in the community. It is usually a sign that people *care* and, as such, might be said to bode well for democratic participation. But just as passion can contribute to a vibrant political community, it can also contribute to political violence and repression. For example, to the extent that flag-waving expresses jingoism—a passion for nationalist domination—it works against the possibilities of global peace and justice. To the extent that it expresses unquestioning support for political leaders and suppression of dissent—what might be termed a passion for conformity and compliance—it also works against the possibilities of freedom and democracy within the country. Even when flags represent freely chosen commitment to the community, the implications can be disturbing if the values for which the community stands are disturbing. In these ways, political passion can be quite troubling.

Many people who care about peace, justice, freedom, and democracy have thus been deeply discomfited by a landscape draped in images of the American flag. Such concerns are not new: political theorists have worried about passion in politics for a long time. Among liberal theorists, there has been a strong tendency to respond to the trouble with passion by trying to minimize it in the political realm. Some have even seen passion as the primary reason for political authority in the first place. "Why has government been instituted at all?" asks Alexander Hamilton in *Federalist #15*. "Because the passions of men will not conform to the dictates of reason and justice without constraint" (Hamilton et al., 1961, 110). Here Hamilton offers a classical liberal articulation in which passion is opposed to both reason and justice. Left to themselves, Hamilton claims, the passions of "men" lead to irrational and unjust behavior. Passion is thus identified as the problem for which government is the solution. Clearly, under this articulation government itself ought to remain as free from passion as possible. To suggest otherwise would be to sabotage its very purpose.

My intent, however, is precisely to suggest otherwise. I contend that the liberal mandate to keep passion out of politics is neither feasible nor desirable. It is not feasible because it relies on a dichotomy between reason and passion that is unsustainable. As I have already suggested, passion is not

4 • The Trouble With Passion

irrational but rather intertwined with reason; as a result, the attempt to include one but exclude the other in any enterprise is doomed to fail. Moreover, even if passion could be excluded from politics, doing so would not be desirable. For passion is indispensable to a fully democratic polity. Total political dispassion, were it actually possible, would result in a polity characterized by apathy, immobility, and, ultimately, disintegration. A vibrant democracy cannot exist without citizens who feel some connection to the political group and who care enough to participate in it, both of which depend on passion.

This, then, is the fundamental trouble with passion in politics: on the one hand, it can contribute to belligerence, intolerance, and persecution; on the other hand, it is both ineradicable and necessary for democracy. While many political theorists focus only on passion's potentially disturbing consequences (or ignore passion altogether), I find this one-sided focus disturbing in itself. The situation is far more complicated. So what is to be done? Rather than trying to find ways to minimize passion in the political realm, we should focus our attention on questions of how better to understand and develop constructive forms of the human capacity for passion. The best response to the trouble with passion is education. I argue that educating citizens' capacities for both reason and passion is a necessary part of fostering a fully democratic polity. To return one last time to the example of the flag: the question is neither "How can we get rid of all these flags?" nor "How can we get everyone to fly the flag?" but rather "What is the flag going to mean?" What can we do to increase the chance that the flag will symbolize neither chauvinistic pride nor silent obedience but rather a national passion for global justice and vigorous debate?

Political Theory Beyond the Reign of Reason

The purpose of this book is to argue, in contrast to prevailing liberal approaches, that passion is crucial to politics. The first part of the book thus investigates how passion is commonly treated in liberal political theory and examines the theoretical and political consequences of these approaches. The remainder of the book explores what I contend are better ways of thinking about passion and politics, drawing on resources from Plato, Rousseau, and contemporary feminist theorists. Although liberal political theory is scarcely the only school of thought wherein the treatment of passion is problematic, it provides the closest articulation of the current political ideology and practice of the United States, where the condition of democracy might be described as anemic at best. To argue for new approaches to passion and a more democratic culture in this country thus requires critically examining treatments of passion in liberal theory. Despite my engagement with liberalism, however, it is not my purpose to try to salvage it from the problems I identify. I am not persuaded that liberalism can seriously incorporate passion without a fundamental transformation in some of its defining features, especially its Enlightenment-based privileging of reason and its frequent commitment to excluding visions of the good (which are integral to passion) from the realm of politics. As a result, I make no attempts in this book to envision a reconstructed liberalism.[1] Rather, I attempt to envision a democratic politics enlivened by passion.

In order to do so, I turn to some thinkers from outside of the liberal tradition. While their writing is vastly different in numerous respects, Plato, Rousseau, and contemporary feminists of eros all offer theories identifying passion (or eros) as a key component of a just political community. All argue that their contemporaries misconceive the human capacity for passion and consequently undervalue it, or value it for the wrong reasons. Accordingly, all offer alternative conceptions of passion and assert its political and ethical significance. Interestingly, Plato, Rousseau, and contemporary feminists even see passion as being valuable in some of the same ways, for each contests existing views of passion as irrational (opposed to reason), debilitating (opposed to power), and a prime source of immoral or at least selfish acts (opposed to justice or virtue). Thus, they argue that passion may be deeply thoughtful, insofar as it is tied to our sense of meaning and value in life. They argue that passion may be a crucial source of power, insofar as it provides the motivation for action. And they argue that passion may be profoundly concerned with justice, insofar as it is the source of our connection to others and our imagination of a better world. Given these arguments, it should not be surprising that passion or eros is frequently presented by these authors as one of the most important things in the world. "Eros," says Plato, "interprets between gods and men…he is the mediator who spans the chasm which divides them, and therefore by him the universe is bound together" (1953B, 202e). "If we love the world," says feminist theologian Carter Heyward, "we matter. Lovers make all the difference in the world. Lovers recreate the world" (1984, 85). Passion is one of the most important things in the world because it can inspire people to act, to reach "across the chasm" to the gods/the good, to make a difference in the world. I argue that this ability makes passion a crucial political resource.

Of course, Plato is no democrat, or at least not in any straightforward way. On the other hand, Rousseau is perhaps too much of a democrat, or at least he pays insufficient attention to voices that deviate from the general will. Both Plato and Rousseau privilege masculinity in significant ways, while contemporary feminist theorists of eros privilege passion's beneficial potential in problematic ways. These features of the theories I

6 • The Trouble With Passion

explore present obstacles for envisioning a fully democratic politics enlivened by passion. But in considering these works I am not looking for theories that can be applied wholesale; rather, I am looking for questions, frameworks, suggestions, and cautions that may be useful for thinking about passion and politics. Such questions and frameworks are valuable resources that each body of literature can offer, despite the obstacles.

As liberals are not the only theorists whose treatment of passion is problematic, so Plato, Rousseau, and feminist theorists of eros are not the only theorists who can help us think beyond liberal rationalism. Certainly there are others who argue for the importance of passion or the closely related phenomena of emotion, desire, affect, and sentiment. One might wonder, then, why I have turned to these authors, rather than, for example, Aristotle, Hume, and feminist psychoanalysts. To a certain extent, the choices are a consequence of my own passion: these are authors I find particularly engaging and inspiring. But my choices also stem from my specific focus on and understanding of passion. In the next chapter I discuss my understanding of passion in more detail; for now, I have briefly defined it as enthusiasm. Although passion is often used as a synonym for either emotion in general or sexual desire in particular, I am most interested in one specific sense of passion: the experience of caring about something one perceives to be deeply valuable. This experience may or may not include a sexual component, but it is not reducible to sexual desire. Because of my focus on this sense of passion, then, I make use of Plato, who writes two dialogues about eros, but not Aristotle, who writes more broadly about many kinds of emotions. Because of my understanding of passion as mutually intertwined with reason, I make use of Rousseau, who argues that reason and passion influence each other, but not Hume, who famously argues that "reason is, and ought only to be, the slave of the passions" (1978, 415). And finally, because I am most interested in nonsexual passion, I make use of feminists who write about a broadly defined eros, but not psychoanalysts (feminist or otherwise), who theorize about a desire that is primarily or at root sexual.

My focus on passion as enthusiasm will not be exclusive, however. A number of the discussions to follow will necessarily draw upon, involve, and apply to arguments about "the passions"—that is, all strong emotions—as well. I say "necessarily" for several reasons. First, as I will argue in Chapter 2, there is an important connection between enthusiastic caring and the rest of the passions. Second, in part due to this link, many arguments about passion mix together these two senses of the term, "a passion (for x)" and "the passions," making it difficult to limit the topic to the former. And third, there are also many arguments about emotion in general that are useful to an investigation of passion. In the next chapter, then, I use cognitive theories of emotion for help in thinking about passion. And in Chapter 3 my analysis of liberal theory will largely refer to passion in its broader sense, since this is the sense used by most of the theorists I cite. Beyond my discussion of liberal theory, though, I concentrate as much as possible on passion as an explicit enthusiasm for and commitment to something valued, because this is an emotion that is crucial to politics and yet much overlooked, even by those who generally pay attention to emotions. As I argue in the concluding chapter, passion plays a key role in shaping political choices, forging political community, and motivating political action. While other emotions, such as grief, or envy, or anxiety certainly play roles in politics as well, the role that passion plays seems absolutely central.[2] Thus, this book concentrates on passion as enthusiasm, ardor, zeal.

To be more specific, this book concentrates on relationships between passion, reason, and politics. Considerable attention has been paid to relationships between any two of these elements, especially if passion is taken in its broader sense of emotion in general. Even in this case, however, little attention has been paid to the intersection of all three. Many political theorists, for example, have debated the relationship between reason and politics, but mostly not discussed passion. In their powerful challenges to the privileged status of reason in political theory, they have focused not on the attendant devaluation of passion but rather on the devaluation of such things as authority, tradition, custom, qualitative knowledge, the will to power, or the unconscious.[3] On the other hand, a number of philosophers have argued for the close connection between reason and passion/emotion, but mostly not discussed politics. While criticizing both the overvalorization of reason and the neglect of passion in philosophy, they have largely left aside the political implications of this value system.[4] Finally, many feminists, psychoanalysts, and postmodernists have analyzed the relationship between "desire" and politics, but mostly not discussed reason. They have emphasized the deeply political implications of desire and other emotions, yet tended to underemphasize the role of reason (as well as frequently overlooking nonsexual passion). I have learned a great deal from all of these thinkers about the relationships between various pairings of passion, reason, and politics. But I have also learned that there is a need to explore a confluence of relationships between all three elements.

Structure of the Argument

In the next chapter I focus on the concept of passion that underlies the argument of this book. The first part of the chapter discusses some historical and contemporary senses of the term, and explains how and why I

8 • The Trouble With Passion

depart from these senses. I argue in particular that passion is not irrational and not overpowering. It is not an alien force poised to take over the self, any more than reason is. Indeed, passion is linked to reason because it incorporates cognitive judgments about value. To say that passion is linked to reason, however, is not to say that it is inherently good or even wise, for not all reasons are good reasons. Like passion—in fact, together *with* passion—reason has the potential to be used for good or for evil. In the remainder of the chapter, I discuss the relationship between "sentiment" and passion, explaining why I do not argue for the former over the latter. I also identify the ways in which my concept of passion bears the influence of the Platonic conception of "eros," and the ways in which it departs from that influence.

Chapter 3 examines how classical and contemporary liberal political theorists treat passion. I argue that there are two main approaches. Classical theorists often pay quite a bit of attention to passion, but see it as a threat to peace and justice, and therefore argue that it should be kept out of the political realm. On the other hand, contemporary theorists rarely discuss passion, viewing it as already private and largely irrelevant to politics. Both approaches, I argue, stem from problematic conceptions of passion. Both approaches also ultimately rely on passion to make politics work, despite the theorists' intentions and recognition. In other words, the attempt to eliminate passion is unsustainable even in theory. I use the work of John Rawls as a case study to illustrate these points. The chapter concludes with a summary of the price of liberal treatments of passion.

In the fourth chapter I begin my exploration of alternative perspectives on passion. Here I take a close look at three of Plato's dialogues, the *Republic*, the *Symposium*, and the *Phaedrus*, each of which is centrally concerned with the dangers and benefits of passion and desire. The chapter pays special attention to the distinction in Plato's work between two different kinds of passion and desire: *eros* and *epithumia*. These concepts are distinguished precisely in that *eros* is defined as the desire for the good, and thereby linked to reason, whereas *epithumia* is presented as having no necessary relationship to the good because it is devoid of reason. I argue that this distinction helps explain why the *Republic* emphasizes the great dangers of desire (as *epithumia*) while the other two dialogues celebrate *eros* as "the greatest of heaven's blessings." Together the dialogues illustrate how passion can be employed in the service of justice or injustice. They also present a highly developed model of how to educate *eros* by learning to "channel" one's passions and desires away from false, harmful goods and toward those that are more worthy. The chapter ends by identifying two aspects of Plato's theory with which I especially disagree: the association of *eros* with the one, true good, and the association of *eros* with a disembodied masculinity. But I contend that, in spite of these aspects, Plato's work on passion is still useful in emphasizing the relationship between passion and reason and the importance of educating both capacities.

In the fifth chapter I turn to Rousseau for another perspective on passion and politics. Like Plato, Rousseau sometimes speaks of passion as profoundly harmful and sometimes as indispensable to justice. And even more than Plato, Rousseau sometimes speaks of *reason* as profoundly harmful and sometimes as indispensable to justice. These variations seem especially sharply opposed if we compare the *Second Discourse*, where Rousseau often argues quite passionately on behalf of passion, with the *Social Contract*, where he often argues rather coldly for the value of reason. Under the circumstances, it may appear that Rousseau believes the political realm must transcend passion. But with help from a few of Rousseau's other political texts, I demonstrate that this is not so. Even in the *Social Contract*, passion remains a key capacity. What *is* missing from this text, though, is a sufficient theory of the education of passion, an omission that I argue is instructive. As with the previous chapter, I conclude Chapter 5 by discussing two aspects of Rousseau's theory with which I especially disagree: his presentation of communal desires as unambiguous goods and his exclusion of women from the public realm. What I think remains useful about his work is its illustration of the role that passion plays in political community and its illustration, even if through omission, of the need to educate both passion and reason.

Chapter 6 explores the third and final body of literature on passion and politics considered in the book. Here I synthesize and analyze the central argument of nine feminist theorists who have written about "eros" or a similar concept of passion. According to these authors, eros has conventionally been perceived as a threat to masculinity, rationality, power, and justice. The logic of this view has led people to deny or repress eros, which in turn has led to violence and alienation. The authors argue that a better understanding of, and relationship with, eros would help to address these problems by empowering people both personally and politically. Most significantly, it would motivate grassroots struggles for justice. I conclude the chapter with an extended critique of the feminist literature on eros, focusing especially on its continued association of eros with women and its significant tendency to idealize eros. Despite these problems, however, I argue that this literature is useful in challenging dominant conceptions of passion as debilitating and demonstrating the important role of passion in motivating political action. As with Rousseau's *Social Contract*, it is also useful as an illustration of why a theory of passion must include a theory of the education of passion.

10 • The Trouble With Passion

Chapter 7 returns to the larger issue of how best to think about relationships between passion, reason, and politics. Liberal political theorists tend to either fear or ignore passion. In the former case, they argue that passion poses a danger to politics and is best eliminated from the public realm. In the latter case, they seem to simply consider it politically irrelevant, or, at best, a phenomenon that the political process exists to manage. In neither case, though, is the *capacity* for passion treated as an important part of politics—as the capacity for reason always is. My first purpose in the concluding chapter is to explore some of the political significance of the capacity for passion. In particular, I draw upon the discussions in Chapters 4, 5, and 6 to argue that passion is crucial for making political choices, creating political community, and motivating political action. The second purpose of the concluding chapter is to explore some important elements of educating passion for democracy. I discuss two elements in particular: learning to work with one's passions, and developing a passion for democracy itself. I acknowledge that there are some legitimate concerns about the prospect of educating passion, but I conclude that there is no better alternative to educating citizens' passions in and toward democratic skills and values.

CHAPTER **2**

The Passions and the Reasons: Conceptualizing Capacities

A Passion Is Not a Storm

When we say "she is passionate about her work" or "he has a passion for art," what do we mean? We mean that she is devoted to her work, that he is enthusiastic about art. We mean that these people want to put time and energy into work or art. This is the sense of passion that I emphasize in this book. To have a passion is to be keenly drawn toward something—be it a person, object, activity, or concept—and, consequently, to be committed to pursuing and supporting that thing. A passion for a person implies attraction (sexual or otherwise) to that person, appreciation of him or her qualities, and, usually, a desire for some kind of relationship. A passion for an object implies regard for its beauty and/or function, and usually a desire to have use of or possess it. A passion for an activity implies enjoyment in its practice, and usually a desire to engage in or observe it. And a passion for a concept implies belief in its rightness or usefulness, and usually a desire to defend or promote it. What all of these passions have in common is the finding of value in the object of passion and a corresponding desire to create or preserve that value in one's life and (perhaps) the world at large.[1]

Clearly, this sense of passion differs somewhat from other senses of the word, both historical and contemporary. Passion is a Middle English word originating in the Latin root *pati*, meaning "suffer." Initially it denoted the

12 • The Trouble With Passion

suffering of pain, most specifically the suffering of Jesus on the cross. *Pati* is also the root for the word passive, a link that illustrates passion's original and often current sense as something that happens *to* us, something we do not control, something that, in short, we suffer. In later usages passion came to denote, more broadly, (an) emotion, especially (a) "strong barely controllable emotion" or (a) feeling that is "intense, driving, or overmastering." References to "the passions," meaning the entire set of strong emotions, convey this sense (James 1997, 4). And in recent times especially, passion is often virtually equated with sexual desire or "ardent affection."[2] As Peter Stearns points out in *American Cool: Constructing a Twentieth-Century Emotional Style*, in the last century "passion itself was redefined, becoming suspect unless it was sexual" (1994, 4). Note that these definitions offer propositions about both the *range* of emotional experience conveyed by the term "passion" and the *characteristics* of that experience. The range varies from quite broad (including all strong emotions) to rather narrow (including only sexual desire), but in either case the dominant characteristic remains the same: a strength or intensity of emotion that is virtually overpowering. My use of passion departs to some extent from all of these propositions.

With respect to range, passion as enthusiasm is neither as broad as all emotion nor as limited as sexual desire. I emphasize this sense of passion because I believe that enthusiasm deserves more attention from political theorists. When passion is used as a synonym either for emotion in general or for sexual attraction in particular, it becomes difficult to talk about the specific experience of nonsexual desire, enjoyment, and devotion. Lacking a precise name of its own, this set of feelings becomes obscured by a focus on the other forms of feeling.[3] I aim to reduce this obscurity with my focus on passion as enthusiasm.

At the same time, there are connections between passion as enthusiasm and "the passions" that will lead me to talk about the latter as well as the former. What are these connections? To begin with, and turning to the issue of defining characteristics, both terms do imply a certain level of intensity. Emotions such as love, hate, anger, joy, and fear are sometimes called passions; emotions such as like, dislike, annoyance, amusement, and mild concern, on the other hand, are not. The difference between the two is the depth of feeling involved. Similarly, to have a passion for something also involves depth of feeling. This is why, despite my use of the term enthusiasm for shorthand, the word is not an entirely effective substitute for passion: it does not resonate in the same way. Passion connotes a stronger, more powerful feeling. So both of these senses of passion are defined in terms of intensity. There is, however, an even deeper way in which "the passions" and "a passion (for x)" are linked, because the former necessarily involve the latter. The most obvious example is that of love: the passion *of* love implies a passion *for* the object of love. But so, too, the passion *of* hate implies a passion *for* something: specifically, something that one values and believes is threatened by the object of hatred. In the case of hatred, then, the objects of the two senses of passion are different, but there is a necessary link between them. There would be no motivation to hate were there not something one cared about, passionately. Likewise, there would be no motivation for anger, joy, or fear were there not something valued on behalf of which one might become angry or joyful or fearful. Enthusiastic caring thus lies at the core of any kind of strong emotion. As a result, talking about *the* passions means implicitly talking about *a* passion as well.

While I agree that intensity of feeling is central to the definition of both "the passions" and "a passion (for x)," though, I contend that such intensity need not, and indeed should not, be interpreted as "overmastering." Despite its common inclusion in definitions of passion, subjection is not intrinsic to strong feeling. To make this point, let me begin by surveying the logic of the claim that passion is overpowering. First, as we have already seen, passion is conceptually opposed to agency. We are not the instigators of our own passions; rather, we are their passive objects, their victims even. They are not *us* but an alien force. Common metaphors of the passions as natural disasters (storms, torrents, tempests) that befall us illustrate this perspective well (James 1997, 13). Second, and clearly following from this opposition to agency, passion is seen as opposed to self-possession and self-control. When beset by strong and intense storms of feeling, the argument goes, we may be buffeted along with these feelings despite our best attempts to resist. Like natural disasters, passions are tempestuous, unpredictable, and wild, and they can make our behavior tempestuous, unpredictable, and wild. This is the idea behind the notion of a "crime of passion": the person was overcome by passion, not in control of her own actions, and therefore arguably not responsible for them. Finally, passion is considered to be opposed to reason. It is blind to consequences and impervious to logic. It makes us do "crazy" things. Accordingly, passion is sometimes explicitly defined as "the emotions *as distinguished from* reason." This opposition of passion to reason is linked to the first two oppositions. For it is reason most of all that is presumed to provide a person with both agency and self-control. Unlike our passions, in this view, our reason is civilized and civilizing. Indeed, unlike our passions, our reason *is* us; it is the core of our personhood and independence.

The claims above are frequently made about such emotions as love, hate, anger, fear, and envy, (i.e. "the passions" in general) but they are also made about the specific emotions of enthusiasm, ardor, fervor, and zeal. Consider, for example, the nationalism I discussed in the previous chapter,

14 • The Trouble With Passion

or sports fandom, or religious fervor. Each form of passion is commonly viewed as stemming from emotion *rather than* reason. Moreover, in each case, the influence of a group, charismatic leader, star, or even deity is thought to sway people into doing things they would not otherwise do, or would not do in their more rational moments. At the extreme, devotions of these sorts are viewed as fanatical, beyond the pale of the reasonable. One is considered virtually possessed by the object of one's ardor. In this way, passion as strong enthusiasm is also seen as opposed to reason, agency, and self-possession.

There are two main problems with these presumptions. The first is precisely that they treat passion (whether broadly defined or not) as if it were an alien force that operates independently of the psyche. While passions may sometimes be experienced this way, there is no reason to believe that our feelings are any more imposed on us than our thoughts. What about the times when thoughts come into our heads unbidden, as if from nowhere? Or when our minds wander from the topic we intended to think about? Or when we find it difficult to *stop* thinking about something, despite our best attempts? In all of these cases, the workings of reason can be seen as both anarchic and commanding, in tension with personal agency and self-control. And yet few have concluded that reason is a strange power that overmasters the self. My purpose here is not to argue that reason is in fact such a force. Rather, my purpose is to question the dichotomization of these capacities on the basis of identification with the self. Passion and reason are both "us." They are both native to the self, both part of the workings of the psyche. Neither is a foreign power poised to take over the self.

Of course, our thoughts and feelings are influenced in many ways by the world around us. Having taken up the language of "native" and "foreign" to challenge the opposition of reason and passion, I want now to challenge that language, for these metaphors imply a clearly discernible distinction between self and other that has been much disputed. As our surroundings affect us, so they affect our experiences of passion and reason. For example, different cultures have different "feeling rules" about how emotions of all kinds are to be expressed and even understood.[4] As a consequence, the kind and intensity of emotions that individuals report having, the meaning they ascribe to those emotions, and the goals they set for working with specific emotions (acceptance, denial, modification, encouragement, resistance, and so forth) have all varied. Despite the common perception that reason is universal, different cultures also have different rules about how reason is to be expressed and understood, a point that is perhaps most clearly evident in the contrast between the Western emphasis on pursuing noncontradiction and the Eastern emphasis on embracing paradox.[5] Because the self does not exist in isolation from others, then, the capacities of the self are not developed and expressed in isolation from others. But even so, neither passion nor reason is an independent force that acts upon us or befalls us the way a thunderstorm does. Neither is an agent in its own right, capable of possessing us. These capacities are our own.

A Passion Has a Reason—and a Reason Has a Passion

The second problem with the conventional presumptions about passion (again, whether broadly defined or not) is that they neglect the interconnectedness of passion and reason. Up until this point, although I have argued that passion is not *opposed* to reason, I have still been speaking of passion and reason as separate capacities. Indeed, in arguing that *one* is not more alien or imposed than *the other*, I have actually reinforced the idea that each is distinct. Ultimately, however, I want to argue that the two are deeply tied, perhaps to the point of being effectively indistinguishable.[6] Here I follow cognitive and evaluative theorists of emotion such as Cheshire Calhoun (1984), Ronald de Sousa (1987), Martha Nussbaum (1990), Amélie Rorty (1980), and Robert Solomon (1993) and apply their argument to passion as enthusiasm in particular.[7] Now, much like the words emotion and passion, the word reason carries many potential connotations. To give but a few examples, it may refer to the capacity for thinking in general; the capacity for thinking in a connected or logical manner; the ability to use concepts; and/or "the mental faculty which is used in adapting thought or action to some end" (what is often called "instrumental reason"). Additional senses of reason are apparent in the adjective "reasonable," which may describe a person who can provide reasons (explanations or justifications) for what she does; who is open to persuasive argument; and/or who is sensible and moderate, not extreme or excessive. For my purposes, however, it is helpful to distinguish primarily between two main senses of reason: first, the capacity for any kind of thought, and second, the capacity for careful and reflective thought (see Calhoun 1984).

With this distinction in mind, cognitive theorists of emotion contend that all emotions involve reason in at least the first sense; that is, all emotions necessarily entail such basic, fundamental forms of thought as conceptualization, interpretation, evaluation, and the formulation of purposive behavior (Solomon 1993). I believe this argument is well illustrated by the case of passion as enthusiasm, for implicit in any enthusiasm about an object is, first, a *concept* and interpretation of the object's nature and qualities; second, a *judgment* that the object is valuable in some way;

16 • The Trouble With Passion

and third, an *intention* to pursue the value of that object in one's life. Consider the persistence of a passion over time—even in the physical absence of its object—and the need for a stable concept of the object becomes obvious. Nor can one sustain a passion without the belief that the object in question is worthy of one's commitment, particularly in view of competing alternatives. Such a belief requires judgment. Hence, passion is not "mindless" or "blind"; rather, it entails a *vision* of a good. Moreover, as with all emotions, passions have a logic to them: specific passions require specific beliefs, and a change in our knowledge or belief about the object of passion sooner or later results in a change in the passion (Nussbaum 1990, 41; Solomon 1993, 254). Finally, passion not only entails a vision of the good, but also, generally, some idea of how to pursue or sustain that good. As Robert Solomon describes emotions in general, "emotions are purposive, serve the ends of the subject, and consequently can be explained by *reasons* or 'in-order-to' explanations" (1993, 262–63). In all of these ways, passion necessarily involves basic forms of thought.

The implicit contrast between a passion and a basic appetite may help to explain further. There are probably few human desires that could truly be called basic appetites. But however few there may be in reality, the *concept* of an appetite implies a physical impulse requiring little to no discernment about the value of the desired object. Simple hunger, for example, can be satisfied by food of any quality. A gourmet's passion for culinary specialties, on the other hand, certainly cannot. The difference between the two is precisely that a gourmet's passion incorporates and depends on a cognitive ideal of what constitutes *good* food, as well as a judgment about whether a particular food lives up to this ideal. That is, the passion depends on the use of reason, whereas the appetite does not.[8]

While all passions entail thought, however, not all passions entail careful and reflective thought. Calhoun and Solomon's argument about emotions in general certainly applies to passions: "because they are, in part, 'cognitive' and 'evaluative' phenomena, emotions presuppose rationality in the psychological sense—the ability to use concepts and have reasons for what one does or feels. Whether these reasons are good reasons, however, is another matter" (Calhoun and Solomon 1984, 31). The belief that an object of passion is worthy of commitment may be the result of painstaking reflection, or unconsidered assumptions, or anything in between. Particularly when they are based on unconsidered assumptions, judgments about value may be poor ones. They may even be in tension with other beliefs that we hold more self-consciously. In these cases, passions will certainly seem irrational. But it would be better to say that they are unwise—that they do not reflect *careful* thought—since, as I argued above, all passions have a rational component. In Solomon's words, "It is in this sense that emotions [including passions] are 'blind'; more accurately, they are *myopic*. Emotions serve purposes that are rational; but because the purposes emotions serve are often short-sighted, they appear to be non-purposive and irrational on a larger view" (1993, 265). Some passions involve careful, reflective reasoning, then, and some do not, but all of them involve reason in a general sense.

In turn, some of our reasoning involves deeply felt passions (or other emotions) and some of it does not, but at least in the realm of human affairs, good thinking requires feeling. As the neurologist Antonio Damasio has persuasively argued, people who suffer brain damage and a consequent decline in their ability to feel emotions lose the ability to make good decisions. They may still be able to perform any number of tasks requiring "intelligence," but they are no longer able to manage their time, effectively weigh alternative courses of action, choose wisely, and learn from past mistakes. In short, without an emotional investment in what happens to them—or anyone else—their rational judgment is seriously impaired. Damasio concludes that "We are faced by uncertainty when we have to make a moral judgment, decide on the course of a personal relationship, choose some means to prevent our being penniless in old age, or plan for the life that lies ahead. Emotion and feeling, along with the covert physiological machinery underlying them, assist us with the daunting task of predicting an uncertain future and planning our actions accordingly" (1994, xiii). So just as a *passion* for an object implies a *reason* for valuing that thing, a *reason* for choosing one thing over another implies at least some *passion* for the choice taken. In this way, reason and passion are inextricable.

But, some might say, feelings that involve careful and reflective thought are better called sentiments than passions. On this view, the word passion describes feelings that are intense, excited, erratic, and extreme—and therefore likely to be both irrational and unjust. Sentiment, on the other hand, describes feelings that are milder, calmer, more deliberate, and more moderate—and therefore likely to be rational and just. One might contend that such feelings offer the advantages of emotional attachment and investment without the dangers posed by stronger emotions. If, then, my intention is to argue for the value of emotion in the political realm, shouldn't I focus on sentiment?

Let me be clear at the outset that I am not arguing *against* sentiment in politics. What I am arguing against is a distinction between passion and sentiment that is oversimplified, and therefore misleading. The distinction is oversimplified because it groups together characteristics that are not necessarily linked and then assumes the best of one set (sentiments) and the worst of the other (passions). In particular, mildness, calmness, moderateness, reasonableness, and justness are all associated with each

18 • The Trouble With Passion

other, giving the impression of sentiments as gentle, thoughtful, equitable feelings. While this is certainly true of some sentiments, it is not true by definition. The mildness, calmness, or moderateness of a feeling bears no necessary relationship to its content. One can, for example, be mildly racist. Likewise, one can be calmly and deliberately racist (whether mildly or not), for it is possible to be calm and deliberate in pursuit of any end. On the other hand, moderate, middle-of-the-road opposition to racism is not more reasonable or just than extreme opposition. In this way, the cluster of characteristics associated with sentiments disaggregates. Feelings can be mild without being calm, calm without being moderate, and so forth. Moreover, even feelings that are mild *and* calm *and* moderate are not necessarily gentle, thoughtful, equitable, or just. For these reasons, sentiments are not necessarily better than passions.

Of course passions are not necessarily better than sentiments either. The difference between passion and sentiment is one of intensity, not ethical value. Again, my argument is not a criticism of sentiment per se. I focus on passion, though, because I am especially interested in exploring the value of strong feelings. I think we need more than sentiment in politics; I think we need passion. At the same time, insofar as emotions are troubling, it is strong emotions that really press the issue. This book concentrates on passion, then, because passion is the harder case of emotion in politics.

Passionate Debts and Departures

Clearly, my argument about passion owes a strong debt to cognitive theories of emotion (which, in turn, owe a strong debt to Aristotle). My argument also owes much to Plato's concept of *eros*, especially as developed in the *Symposium* and the *Phaedrus*. This concept will be discussed in more detail in Chapter 4, but its basic meaning can be summarized here. According to the *Symposium*'s culminating definition, *eros* is "the [desire] for the everlasting possession of the good" (1953B, 206a).[9] Although desire is not precisely the same as passion (see note 1), as with my use of passion, the Platonic *eros* conveys an affective attraction toward and longing for what is (perceived as) good. Moreover, in the *Symposium* and the *Phaedrus eros* is specifically presented as a kind of desire that is distinct from appetite (*epithumia*). Both dialogues include central arguments against the conventional understanding of *eros* as appetitive sexual desire, a desire essentially of and for the body. According to the *Phaedrus*, when a true lover looks at a beloved, what he sees is an image of a god (1953A, 251a). The lover perceives the beloved to be just, or wise, or strong—or at least potentially so—and pursues a relationship with him because he admires these values and wants to encourage them in others and himself (253a). It is the god, or the good, embodied in the beloved that is the ultimate object of attraction and desire. Thus, the Platonic *eros* is defined as an orientation toward a normative ideal, not a bodily appetite for pleasures independent of their ethical value. As an orientation toward an ideal, *eros* necessarily depends on both affective and cognitive capacities within the soul. It also extends beyond not only sexual desire but even the desire for another person, for, as the *Symposium* makes clear, the attraction to values embodied in various objects and activities is not fundamentally different from the attraction to values embodied in a person (205d).

As employed in this book, passion contains many echoes of *eros*. At the same time, it departs from the concept of *eros* found in Plato's dialogues in at least one key way. *Eros* is the desire for the good, and in Platonic ontology, "the good" exists in the realm of the universal, uniform, and unchanging *eide*. There is a single objective truth to what is good, and, ultimately, only one desire for that good, although expressed in different forms. My use of passion does not rely on this ontology. I accept the perspective shared by moderns and postmoderns alike that there are multiple and diverse visions of the good, and no authoritative truth as to the correctness of these visions. When I say that passion entails a vision of a good, then, I do not claim that the goodness or rightness of any particular vision is thereby guaranteed. There is always the possibility that a passion for a specific person, object, activity, or concept may be harmful or unethical if pursued. Rather than assuming that passion is by definition either good or bad, I assume that the value of each specific passion, along with the value of its object, is a subject for debate. I hasten to add that the same holds true for reason: the value of each specific reason, along with the value of its aim, is also a subject for debate. Indeed, since the two capacities are not separate but operate together, questioning one must entail questioning the other.

It is in part in order to reinforce this departure from Platonic epistemology (as well as to avoid strong associations with sexual desire) that in my own argument I do not use the term "eros," meaning the one true desire for *the* good, but rather passion, meaning the myriad desires for and commitments to *envisioned* goods, whatever those visions may be. Given this objective, though, one might still wonder why I so often refer to passion itself as singular. Speaking of passions, or even "the passions," has the advantage of emphasizing the multiplicity of possible passions, magnificent and mundane, heartwarming and chilling, personal and political. However, no one speaks of "the reasons." Reason is usually presumed to be a singular, unified faculty within the psyche, not a capacity that has a variety of incarnations. I have argued above that there are many kinds of

20 • The Trouble With Passion

reason and many kinds of passion, and, furthermore, that these faculties are interwoven; thus, neither reason nor passion are unified. But my primary focus is on the human *capacity* for both passion and reason, not a list of specific passions or reasons. It is in order to highlight this focus that I refer to both in the singular.[10]

Conclusion: Passion, Reason, and Fanaticism

In this chapter I have discussed several senses of the word passion and emphasized an understanding of passion as enthusiasm. I have also argued that, like other emotions, passion is not opposed to reason or agency. People who boisterously cheer for sports teams, proudly sing national anthems, enthusiastically embrace their work, or devoutly practice their religious faith are not irrational and they are not possessed. As strong as their feelings may be, it is not the case that these people are not thinking. They *are* thinking: about how this team is better than that team, about what their nation stands for, about why their work is important to them, about what they believe to be their purpose in the universe. It is precisely because they are thinking in these ways that they feel the way they do. Of course, people are not always able to identify their thoughts clearly, even to themselves, and others frequently find their thoughts disagreeable or mystifying—but that does not make their thoughts any less thoughts. Even those who have been called fanatics are thinking: the problem is not that their reason has been overtaken by their passion; the problem is that they are thinking and feeling very differently about the world than those who charge them with fanaticism.[11]

None of this is to say that passion is never involved when people behave irresponsibly, aggressively, and violently, as some fanatics (but not only fanatics) do. What I have argued, and will continue to argue throughout the book, is that such actions are never the consequence of passion *alone*. They are the consequence, rather, of a combination of both reason and passion. So, too, noble, steadfast struggles against injustice are the consequence of a combination of both reason and passion. What, then, is the distinguishing factor between ethical and unethical behavior? Not the presence or absence of either reason or passion, but only the specific content of both the reason and passion involved. How might this understanding of passion and its relationship to reason improve our thinking about politics? In chapters to come I explore this question through readings of three very different bodies of literature. Before doing so, however, I take a closer look at the trouble with passion in liberal political theory.

CHAPTER **3**

Public Reason, Private Passion: The Trouble with Passion in Liberal Political Theory

Writing in the wake of the Enlightenment, liberal political theorists have put their faith in the saving grace of reason perhaps more earnestly than any of their predecessors. Interpretations of what constitutes "reason" may vary and faith in its powers fluctuate, but the conclusion that the activity of politics would benefit from greater or more refined use of the human capacity to reason is virtually unanimous amongst liberal political theorists. What, then, about passion? Do liberal political theorists argue that the activity of politics would also benefit from greater or more refined use of the human capacity to feel? Do they argue that passion does or should play an important role in the public realm? The fundamental answer to these questions is no. While generalizations are always oversimplifications, I think it is safe to say that positive arguments on behalf of passion are scarce in liberal political theory. Rather, liberal theorists work to marginalize passion, either through explicitly arguing that it is best kept outside the margins of the public sphere, or by speaking of it only marginally, if at all. My purpose in this chapter is to criticize both of these attempts to marginalize passion in liberal political theory. I argue that these approaches stem from an impoverished interpretation of passion. I also argue that passion is actually at the heart of these arguments, despite the theorists' intentions and recognition. In other words, the attempt to eliminate

22 • The Trouble With Passion

passion is unsustainable even in theory. Since passion is no *less* relevant or valuable—and no *more* dangerous—to politics than reason, I conclude that the liberal strategy of encouraging reason while attempting to privatize (or simply ignoring) passion is neither possible nor desirable.

When liberal political theorists use the word passion, they usually mean the entire class of strong emotions ("the passions"). Accordingly, much of this chapter is concerned with claims about passion in its broader sense. However, because enthusiastic caring lies at the core of any kind of strong emotion, passion as enthusiasm will remain central to the argument. The chapter begins with a discussion of the two ways in which liberal political theorists attempt to marginalize passion. Next, I trace the source of these approaches to the theorists' problematic assumptions about passion. To illustrate further the tendencies I address in the chapter, I provide a case study of the place of passion in John Rawls' theory of justice. The chapter concludes with a discussion of the harmful consequences of liberal treatments of passion.

The Trouble with Passion: Approaches to Passion in Liberal Political Theory

Of course, one chapter can scarcely claim to characterize liberal political theory in its entirety. I do aim to show, however, that a broad spectrum of liberal theorists work to marginalize passion. For reasons that will be explained shortly, explicit arguments that passion should be confined to the private sphere occur more often in classical liberal theory, while inattention to passion occurs more frequently in dominant versions of contemporary liberal theory. I discuss each case in order.

The roots of the argument that passion is best kept out of the political realm lie in the classical liberal view of human nature. As Stephen Holmes shows in his study of the foundations of liberalism, the charge that liberal theory generally posits "men" as rationalists is inaccurate: the presumption of rationalism only begins with neoclassical economic theorists. Classical liberals such as Locke, Mill, Smith, and Madison in fact demonstrate an "acute awareness of human irrationality," of the possibility that human beings will often be motivated by "irrational desire" (Holmes 1995, 43, 267). Indeed, Holmes contends, prior to the 19th century, "most human behavior was understood to spring from unthinking habit or irrational passions. Rational choice of action was exceptional" (24). This understanding is in many ways the foundation for liberal theory. Or as Holmes puts it, the "psychological premise" of liberalism is "the fragility of reason" (267).

Starting from this premise, classical liberal theorists develop strategies for coping with the perceived problem of the passions.[1] Although rationalism is not their starting point, it is their final goal. Thus, they argue for the establishment of rational public institutions to control passions. "Why has government been instituted at all?" asks Hamilton. "Because the passions of men will not conform to the dictates of reason and justice without constraint" (Hamilton et al. 1961, 110).[2] Using similar logic, Madison contends that frequent constitutional conventions should be avoided because "The *passions*, therefore not the *reason*, of the public would sit in judgment. But it is the reason, alone, of the public, that ought to control and regulate the government. The passions ought to be controlled and regulated by the government" (1961, 317, his emphasis). Analyzing classical liberal arguments for why a democratic citizenry would be willing to limit its own actions by establishing a constitution, Holmes argues that it is "in order to ensure that its reason will outweigh its passion in the public realm" (272). Indeed, this explanation for the phenomenon of citizens limiting their own behavior is perhaps most evident in social contract theories. Overwhelmingly, liberal arguments about how citizens could or should handle the fundamental challenge of making (or acknowledging) the social contract rely on citizens' capacities for reason, seen as the corrective to their individual passions.[3] As Robert Solomon suggests, "in many versions of [social contract] theory, justice becomes a matter of reason whose purpose is to counter and control the unruly and usually selfish dictates of our natural passions" (1995, 55). In other words: passions are the problem and reason is the solution.

But *why* are passions so problematic and reason such a salvation? The answer lies in the characteristics attributed to passion and reason in classical liberal theory. Already it is clear that classical liberals conceive of passions as the polar opposite of reason, that is, as inherently irrational. Other assumptions about passion and reason become evident once we look more closely at the consequences they fear passion will bring. One of these consequences is injustice. On this view, partiality, selfishness, and arbitrariness are all considered to stem from passions. Locke, for example, argues that government is necessary in part because "everyone in that state [of nature] being both judge and executioner of the law of nature, men being partial to themselves, passion and revenge is very apt to carry them too far, and with too much heat, in their own cases" (1980, 66). And Madison argues that passions are the primary root of factions, which in turn are the primary root of injustice in popular governments. As he writes in Federalist #10, "By a faction I understand a number of citizens, whether amounting to a majority or minority of the whole, who are united and

24 • The Trouble With Passion

actuated by some common impulse of passion, or of interest, adverse to the rights of other citizens, or to the permanent and aggregate interests of the community" (1961, 78). Considering such arguments against passions in politics, Nancy Rosenblum concludes that

> liberalism requires people to inhibit the full range and force of their personal judgments and affective ties. In a heterogeneous society cooperation depends on indirectness and impartiality, which in turn requires deliberate indifference to one another of the sort encouraged by market and contractual relations.... Abstract individualism does not deny eroticism, comradery, ideological affinity, and so on; liberalism asks men and women to ignore all the other things they are in order to treat one another fairly in certain contexts and for certain purposes (1987, 161–62).

Here dispassion is seen as a prerequisite for fairness. Implied in this argument that passions lead to injustice are several conceptions of the passions: first, that they are egoistic and self-regarding, second, that they are necessarily biased towards one's "near and dear," and third, that they are capricious and unstable. Reason, on the other hand, is considered the sole source of universalist, impartial moral behavior (particularly for those who follow Kant) (Spragens 1981, 243, 245).

Another consequence of passion, in the classical liberal view, is political instability. According to this argument, the diversity of people's passions is what makes it difficult for them to reach agreements with each other; thus, the more passions are allowed to play a role in politics, the more fragmented and divisive the political realm will be. The more reason plays a role, on the other hand, the greater the chance for concord and peace. Perhaps the most glaring example of this perspective can be found in Hobbes' argument that civil war is caused, in great part, by the inability of citizens to agree on the meaning of those most basic of words, good and evil.[4] For "whatsoever is the object of any man's appetite or desire, that is it which he for his part calleth good; and the object of his hate and aversion, evil" and "because the constitution of a man's body is in continual mutation, it is impossible that all the same things should always cause in him the same appetites, and aversions: much less can all men consent, in the desire of almost any one and the same object" (1994, 28). It is only through the correct use of reason that this dilemma can be solved and civil strife be averted through the establishment of a Sovereign Definer. "For all men reason alike, and well, when they have good principles" (25). Implied in this argument that passions threaten divisiveness is a conception of them as subjective and idiosyncratic and a corresponding conception of reason as (at least potentially) objective, general, and unifying.

Finally, passions are thought to pose a third main threat: that of intolerance, violence, and tyranny, in leaders and/or citizens. According to Locke, the passions of those who govern carry the greatest risk. For tyranny

> is the exercise of power beyond right.... And this is making use of the power any one has in his hands, not for the good of those who are under it, but for his own private separate advantage. When the governor, however intitled, makes not the law, but his will, the rule; and his commands and actions are not directed to the preservation of the properties of his people, but the satisfaction of his own ambition, revenge, covetousness, *or any other irregular passion* (1980, 101, my emphasis).

Focusing instead on the passions of the people, Rosenblum argues that for liberals "everything personal is irrational and dangerous, a potential source of unsafety, cruelty, and repression.... Liberalism's task is to protect against personal politics and the chaos of unconstrained self-expression" (1987, 36). That is why liberals are "reluctant to arouse public spirit": because it is "not just undependable" but "dangerous." One danger here is that "competing ideologies of the public good can threaten liberty" (128), as in the case of religious intolerance. Another danger is that there may be too *much* agreement about the supposed public good, agreement that is fanatical and in truth misplaced. (Interestingly, this argument challenges the previous one that passion leads to division.) In its starkest terms, the contention is that there is a deeply passionate quality to the politics of "the masses." As Madison puts it in Federalist #55, "In all very numerous assemblies, of whatever characters composed, passion never fails to wrest the scepter from reason. Had every Athenian citizen been a Socrates, every Athenian assembly would still have been a mob" (1961, 342). Implied in this last argument that passions threaten individual or mass tyranny is a conception of the passions as irrational, cruel, and extreme. Reason, in turn, is considered the source of moderation.

The classical liberal perspective just described, where passion is seen to pose important dangers for politics, follows from a sharply dichotomous model in which reason and passion are opposed. In contrast, the contemporary liberal approach, which rarely mentions passion, follows from a unitary model in which passion has been conceptually absorbed by (private) reason or rationality. The shift towards this second model is traced in Albert O. Hirschman's influential book, *The Passions and the Interests* (1977).[5] As Hirschman shows, in the 18th century theorists began to

26 • The Trouble With Passion

argue for the promotion of "interests" over passions. Although considered to be as subjective and egotistical as passions, interests were also presumed to be much more rational, moderate, and predictable (33, 50, 58). The hope, then, was that the passions of both citizens and leaders could be tamed or reduced through a countervailing emphasis on interests. As Holmes writes, "the principle aim of liberals who wrote favorably of self-interest was to bridle destructive and self-destructive passions, to reduce the social prestige of mindless male violence, [and] to induce people, so far as possible, to act rationally, instead of hot-bloodedly or deferentially" (1995, 4). I would add that the aim was also to transform potentially political, and therefore disruptive, passions of the populace into more predictable and manageable private interests. One might object that passion is not privatized if politics is conceived in terms of individuals or groups fighting for their interests. Yet the point is that the political institutions themselves are supposed to be above the private interests of citizens in order to mediate between them. Or as one major strand of liberal theory might put it, government ought to remain neutral between individual conceptions of the good.

The success of the transformation of passions into interests is evident in the contemporary dominance of the discourse of interests. The model of human motivation has shifted: following the liberal economists of the 19th century, contemporary liberals tend to operate with a model of men, and sometimes even women, as motivated primarily by rationally pursued self-interest, rather than irrational passions. (It is important to note that, coincident with this shift in the model of human motivation, the concept of rationality also shifted. Here rationality is understood in solely instrumental terms, having lost the moral weight that it held before. See Spragens [1981] for an extensive discussion of this shift.) The consequence is that liberal theorists today simply do not discuss passion as much as their forebears did.[6] This is the second way in which liberals work to marginalize passion: through largely omitting it as a topic in political theory.[7]

Many contemporary liberal theorists do continue or even intensify the classical liberal focus on reason, positing the promotion of reason as the defining characteristic of liberalism, its primary purpose, and the source of its superiority over other political systems. For example, in a book entitled *Reason and Democracy*, Thomas Spragens argues that "the idea of politics as a rational enterprise provides an appropriate framework for rendering the best accounts of liberal democracy, both traditional and contemporary, philosophically perspicuous and coherent" (1990, 9).[8] In a book entitled *Free Public Reason*, Fred D'Agostino argues that providing public reasons for embracing principles and committing to the requirements of "reasonableness" are the fundamental bases of liberal political theorizing and the primary condition for successful politics (1996, 6, 24). The concepts of public reason and reasonableness of course form the theoretical heart of John Rawls' *Political Liberalism* (1993). Finally, according to Charles Anderson, the fundamental purpose of liberal politics is "the promotion of collective rational action" (1990, 31), while according to Rogers Smith, it is to defend "rational liberty," the most distinctive and important human capacity (1985, 5).

Contemporary theorists also occasionally echo classical theorists in identifying passion as the specific problem that reason must correct. In Spragens' argument, institutionalized rational discourse provides both "a useful corrective to the myopia induced in human beings by their immediate passions and interests" and "an important centripetal counterforce against the fissiparous effects of individual passions and interests" (1990, 136, 9).[9] In Smith's argument, the capacity for rational liberty or reflective self-determination explicitly involves "governing" passions (1985, 28–30). And for Anderson, rationality "is understood precisely as the capacity for *dispassionate* examination of established usage, custom, and tradition" (1990, 193, my emphasis). But more often than they speak of reason countering passion, contemporary liberals tend to speak of public reason as the tool for mediation between private interests (or individual conceptions of the good). From this perspective, the problem is not so much that people are not (yet) rational as that they are not (yet) reasonable. Reason, contemporary liberals argue, transcends rationality; it is what brings neutrality, consistency, generality, and fairness in the face of citizens' differing and competing interests. What happens to the subject of passion under this formulation? I would argue that it is essentially subsumed under the rationality of interests. Even though the concept of interests obviously incorporates desires, attachments, and preferences, the overwhelming emphasis is on individuals' rational (and equally valid) pursuit of such things. The emotional component of interests is virtually ignored. Meanwhile, the term "passion" itself is often linguistically pushed even farther outside the realm of politics, into the realm of intimate relationships (recall the modern equation of passion with sexual ardor).

The result of the model of interests is that passion becomes a nonissue for many contemporary liberal theorists. There is little talk of passions posing a threat to the political realm, but there is also little talk of them offering any benefit.[10] If passions are discussed at all, it is usually as a subject matter that politics exists to manage. They are an *object* of the political process, not one of its components. In this way, silence about the potential role of passion in politics works to marginalize passion just as much as explicit arguments against it. In the latter case, politics is intended to overcome and contain passions, and in the former case it is

28 • The Trouble With Passion

intended to create a context in which different passions (as incorporated in interests) can be fairly and peacefully maximized, but in neither case is the *capacity* for passion treated as an important part of politics—as the capacity for reason always is. Speaking, in effect, of both forms of marginalization, Rosenblum writes:

> When everything personal and affective is perceived as disturbing and potentially despotic and cast outside the bounds of political thought, certain experiences are left out of the official subject matter of political theory though they continue to have a bearing on political life. Liberalism has difficulty assigning a place to the family, for example, or patriotism, or the politics of personal leadership—except to warn against it. There is no intellectual justification for ignoring these elements of experience.

Despite this statement, Rosenblum goes on to suggest that "there are good reasons for valuing legal formalism" although "these traditional reasons may not always be strong enough to convince romantic sensibilities that for many purposes individuality is safely ignored" (1987, 37). But one need not have a romantic sensibility to find Rosenblum's initial argument more persuasive: there is indeed no intellectual justification for political theorists to ignore everything affective.[11]

The Trouble with Liberal Approaches to Passion

My argument is that both of the common liberal approaches to passion (explicit rejection and tacit exclusion) are inadequate because they stem from impoverished characterizations of passion and, as a consequence, lead to impoverished approaches to politics. If we think about passion more carefully, neither the calls for its exclusion from politics nor the presumptions of its political irrelevance are persuasive. Let us consider the calls for exclusion first. I argued above that when liberal theorists see passion as a threat to the polity, it is because they believe passions lead to injustice, instability, and/or violence. Whether they think such outcomes are inevitable or merely probable, all seem to agree that the danger is high enough to warrant reducing passion as much as possible. Certainly political theorists ought to be concerned about the sources of violence and injustice. But designating passion as the preeminent source of these problems is a faulty argument. As I argued in the previous chapter, the presence of feeling—even intense feeling—does not, in itself, tell us anything about the ethical quality or political consequences of that feeling. Rather, the character of a passion depends on the character of the object that it values.

Although some passions do not have just objects, others do. So it is a mistake to generalize that passion will be a political problem rather than a benefit (or, perhaps most likely, some of each). Moreover, since all passions involve the use of reason, even those passions that do contribute to violence and injustice do not do so single-handedly. It is also a mistake, then, to name passion alone as the source of the trouble, leaving reason out of the equation.

To elaborate on the first point, let me return to the specific characteristics that classical liberal theorists have associated with passion. Are passions egoistic, partial, and capricious? Are they subjective and idiosyncratic, cruel and extreme? In all cases, the answer is: some are and some are not. It is not difficult to think of passions that have contributed to war and oppression, in part because we have heard so much about them. Passions that have contributed to cooperation and liberation get far less attention, but that tells us more about the nature of our attention than it does about the nature of passion. For even a committed liberal such as Rawls acknowledges that people may well have desires for the good of others or for such principles as justice and tolerance. In his own words, "once we grant—what seems plainly true—that there exist principle- and conception-dependent desires, along with desires to realize various political and moral ideals, then the class of possible motives is wide open.... How is one to fix limits on what people might be moved by in thought and deliberation and hence act from?" (Rawls 1993, 85). Indeed, how is one to fix limits? And if we cannot, then it seems we must take account of those passions that can contribute to peace and justice in the political realm as well as those that can contribute to injustice, divisiveness, and/or violence.

Now, one might acknowledge that such passions exist, and still argue that passion in general is best kept out of politics. If one's priority is preventing worst-case scenarios,[12] then the benefit of minimizing potentially harmful passions may seem worth the sacrifice of also minimizing potentially constructive passions. This strategy might be prudent if one further presupposes that educating citizens' passions is either impossible or an unacceptable infringement of individual liberty, so that the sole choice lies between encouraging all passions and discouraging them all. But citizens' passions not only *can* be educated, they *will* be, whether that education is intentional or not. The only question is *how* they will be educated. Under these circumstances, encouraging the development and expression of potentially constructive passions is a better alternative.

The other side of the issue, as I have already suggested, is that even those passions that do contribute to political problems such as violence and injustice do not do so single-handedly. Because all passions involve some form of judgment, reason is always involved. Of course, the judgments

30 • The Trouble With Passion

implicit in some passions are poor ones. For example, people may well be devoted to prejudicial, repressive causes, as when they support ultra-nationalist and fundamentalist regimes. But the problem here is not *that* people have brought their passions into politics: the problem is that the passions they have brought are for specious ideas. The ideas of national purity and superiority are as much to blame for ultra-nationalism as the passions they inspire. Likewise, the ideas of religious purity and superiority are as much to blame for religious fundamentalism as the passions they inspire. As we have seen, arguments for the exclusion of passion tend to cast passion as the source of the problem and the use of reason as the solution. Passion is considered subjective, partial, and selfish while reason is considered objective, impartial, and just. But these formulations of the problem are inaccurate. One can use one's reason to be selfishly calculating; one can be motivated by one's desire to be giving and just. The examples of ultra-nationalism and religious fundamentalism illustrate that dangerous political circumstances stem from passionate commitments to unjust concepts, that is, from a specific use of both reason and passion.[13] Guarding against such circumstances, then, does not call for drawing a line between reason and passion. Rather, it calls for discussing ways to encourage more generous forms of reason-passion.

To say all of this is also to say that passion should be given a good deal more attention than it has been given, especially in contemporary liberal theory. When liberal theorists ignore passion, it is because they assume that it is politically irrelevant, that is, *already* limited to citizens' private lives. It should be clear by now that such is not the case. The "goods" that people enthusiastically desire and commit themselves to include goods that involve and affect the communities in which they live. Passions of this kind are deeply political. In the concluding chapter I explore three ways in particular that passions play a role in politics: first, as key components of political values and choices; second, as bonds of political community; and third, as motivators of political action. Such roles are underexplored in contemporary liberal theory precisely because of its tendency to privatize passion.

The Passion Within: Passion's Inescapability in Politics and Political Theory

I have argued that liberal arguments against, and inattention to, passion in politics are problematic in that they overstate the dangers and/or understate the value that passion brings to the political realm. But there is a further point. Whether one explicitly attempts to exclude passion from the public sphere or simply assumes it is already private, passion remains in politics. Put another way, even as they argue for excluding passion or simply overlook it, liberal theorists still rely on passion to make politics work.[14] Recall, for example, Madison's argument in *Federalist #49* that "it is the reason, alone, of the public, that ought to control and regulate the government. The passions ought to be controlled and regulated by the government" (Hamilton et al. 1961, 317). Recall as well that Madison considers passion-driven factions to be the primary danger facing popular governments. Analyzing his treatment of passion and reason in *The Federalist Papers*, Richard Matthews notes that out of thirty-one separate uses "there does not appear to be a single positive reference to passion in Madison's arguments." Conversely, "while he did not view reason as unproblematic...it nonetheless unlocked the door to the Muse of political science" (1995, 81). Madison's explicit position against passion would appear to be quite stark. Yet in explaining why the solution to the problem of factions lies in a representative form of government, he writes that having representatives works "to refine and enlarge the public views by passing them through the medium of a chosen body of citizens, whose wisdom may best discern the true interest of their country and whose patriotism and love of justice will be least likely to sacrifice it to temporary or partial considerations" (1961, 82). In other words, countering the passions of factionalism requires, among other things, the passions of patriotism and love of justice.

Madison is not an anomaly. Liberal theorists consistently rely on some kinds of political passion in their theories, even though they often do not acknowledge this reliance or even use the terminology of passion. The work of John Rawls, arguably the preeminent theorist of contemporary liberalism, can serve as a more extended example of this phenomenon.[15] As with many other contemporary liberals, Rawls presumes that people are basically rational individuals, incorporates desires primarily under the category of rational interests, and pays far more attention to reason than to passion in his writing. Yet he also echoes classical liberals in explicitly arguing that virtually all desires ought to be limited to the private sphere. Finally, the primary exception to this rule, his "sense of justice," illustrates the way in which passion remains at the heart of his theory without being acknowledged as such. Rawls thus amply embodies the paradoxes of liberal theory.

The importance of reason to Rawls' theory of "justice as fairness" is emphasized everywhere in his work. There are innumerable references to citizens' capacities for rationality (the capacity to "advance one's interests") and reasonableness (the willingness to "propose and honor fair terms of cooperation") (1971, 142; 1993, 49). Indeed, these qualities of mind are presented as the key to establishing a just society. The *Theory of Justice*'s

32 • The Trouble With Passion

central device of the original position, through which the fundamental principles of justice are determined, uses rational deliberation to accomplish its task. *Political Liberalism* continues this emphasis, devoting an entire chapter to what Rawls terms "Public Reason." Public reason is the way a political society makes its decisions, as well as its capacity to do so (212–13). In Rawls' argument, to abide by public reason is akin to affirming the value of justice in the political realm. It is clear, then, that reason plays an indispensable role in the just society Rawls is attempting to theorize. The question is: What is the role of passion in the just society?

The answer to this question is somewhat difficult to determine, for compared to Rawls' frequent references to the capacity of reason, his references to any kind of emotional capacity are relatively rare. Still, he occasionally speaks of "desires," and, to a lesser extent, "affections," "devotions," "sentiments," and "passions." The primary context in which Rawls speaks of these emotions is his argument about conceptions of the good. The *Theory of Justice* establishes an understanding of "goodness as rationality," according to which a thing is good for people if it is rational for them to desire it, given their overall aims (407). Conceptions of the good are thus defined in terms of rationality, but also in terms of desire. In *Political Liberalism*, Rawls is especially concerned to argue that such conceptions include not only the ends people want to attain for their own sake, but the flourishing of those people and groups they feel attached to as well. Conceptions of the good incorporate "ideals of friendship and of familial and associational relationships" and "attachments and loyalties giv[ing] rise to devotions and affections" (13, 19). Despite his persistent language of rationality, then, Rawls does not imagine that people are without desires, affections, and loyalties; on the contrary, such emotions are described as playing a significant role in people's sense of themselves and their choices in life.

The crucial point, though, is that for Rawls these conceptions of the good have no place in the creation and functioning of a just political system. On the contrary, he proposes creating basic institutions designed precisely to transcend such conceptions. For Rawls, the fact that citizens have differing conceptions of the good is the primary dilemma facing political society. He sees only two plausible responses to this dilemma: "tolerance" of different conceptions or domination of one conception over others. Needless to say, his purpose is to defend tolerance, and to delineate its conditions. The essential step to creating a just and tolerant society is the veil of ignorance in the original position, which prevents any particular conception of the good from affecting the deliberation about principles of justice. Principles arrived at in this manner, Rawls hopes, will not only be fair for all but can be agreed upon by all, regardless of differences. In effect, public agreement on a conception of "the right" is achieved through keeping (almost all) conceptions of "the good" outside of the public realm.[16]

To debate whether this solution to the problem of difference is an effective one is not my purpose here. What I want to point out is the implication of this argument with respect to what I have called passion, the enthusiasm for and devotion to an envisioned good. If conceptions of the good must be kept outside of the public realm, then the passions they incorporate must be kept out as well. As noted above, Rawls most often mentions emotions in the context of people's conceptions of the good. (An important exception is the sense of justice, which will be discussed below.) He then argues that the political realm must be constructed to transcend such conceptions. The effect is to say that the political realm must be constructed to transcend most of emotional life as he recognizes it. Indeed, not only are emotions not seen as part of the solution to creating a just and stable society, they are to a certain extent cast as the problem threatening such a society. Perhaps the most extreme case of this is the danger that "the convictions and passions of the majority" (about, for example, minority religious or sexual practices) may lead to serious injustice. Justice as fairness combats this possibility by excluding such convictions and passions: "we may think of the principles of justice as an agreement not to take into account certain feelings when assessing the conduct of others" (1971, 451, 450). But as we have seen, the argument goes beyond a specific set of feelings: all desires associated with conceptions of the good are to be kept private.

Now, there is one significant exception to this exclusion of passion from the political realm. Although most desires in Rawls' theory are associated with conceptions of the good, a few are mentioned in the different context of his discussion of "moral sensibility," which includes conceptions of the right as well as the good. What is this sensibility? In discussing morality, Rawls specifies that he will use "the older term 'sentiment' for permanent ordered families of governing dispositions, such as the sense of justice and the love of mankind, that have a central place in a person's life." Moral sentiments for Rawls are inherently rational, and may be reasonable as well, insofar as they are based on intelligible moral concepts and principles. He distinguishes sentiments from attitudes, which are "not… so regulative or enduring," and from feelings and emotions, which "we experience on particular occasions" (1971, 479–80). He does not explicitly distinguish sentiments from passions, but his references to passions indicate that he likely considers them to be less reasonable than sentiments. While these are understandable distinctions from Rawls' perspective, I am interested in the place in his theory of justice of any kind of emotional commitment to an ideal (that is, any kind of passion in my definition). Thus, for my purposes

34 • The Trouble With Passion

his concept of moral sentiment qualifies as a form of passion. Indeed, passion might be a more appropriate word than sentiment to describe Rawls' "sense of justice" insofar as it must be quite strong to serve the function that Rawls assigns it.

Moral sensibility, then, includes most importantly a sense of justice, which Rawls describes as the desire to comply with rules perceived to be fair (1971, 148), or the desire to be a "fully cooperating member of society," provided others are as well (1993, 81). Rawls considers such desires to be part of a "reasonable moral psychology" (1993, 82). Although they are clearly higher-order desires[17] that may not be developed in everyone, he thinks it is plausible to assume them under positive circumstances. In fact, in *A Theory of Justice* Rawls attempts to delineate the circumstances under which moral sensibility can develop, tracing three key stages: the morality of authority, the morality of association, and, finally, the morality of principles. Interestingly, experiences of love, affection, trust, and friendship all play crucial roles in one's ability to develop the first two kinds of morality, which together provide a foundation for the third and highest kind (1971, 462–79).

In these ways, Rawls does provide a political role for at least some kinds of passion. Moral sensibility entails enthusiasm for principles of justice and cooperation, and this sensibility is critical to the functioning of a just society, for it ensures that citizens will follow the principles of justice once they are established. The problem Rawls is addressing here is what he sometimes calls the problem of "free riders": outside of the artificial constraints of the original position, what is to prevent individuals from taking advantage of a cooperative society? His answer to this problem is to point to citizens' *desire* to be fair, under the right conditions. He thus acknowledges the unavoidable necessity for an emotional commitment to the principles and ideals he is setting forth in his theory. He goes so far as to argue that a "correct" theory of politics "presupposes a theory of justice which explains how moral sentiments influence the conduct of public affairs" (1971, 493). Clearly, he has endeavored to contribute to such a correct theory in delineating the importance of the sense of justice.

As it turns out, then, Rawls' theory of justice actually depends on the development of a certain passion. The human capacity for reasonableness is the linchpin of the theory. Simply put, without it there could be no justice. But reasonableness requires the willingness, the commitment—the desire—to engage in fair cooperation. To be reasonable *is* to have a "sense of justice." In this way, it is a capacity constituted as much by passion as by reason. Looked at from another angle, reasonableness and the sense of justice are not distinct; rather, they are but two ways in which Rawls describes the same quality. If reasonableness is the linchpin of the theory, then the passion for justice is also the linchpin of the theory.[18]

In spite of the importance of passion or sentiment to Rawls' theory, though, sentiment does not begin to approach the status that reason has as a category of analysis for him. In *A Theory of Justice*, "sentiment" only comes up in the latter part of the book, long after the principles of justice are supposed to have been established. It is presented as an important component of the stability of a just society, but explicitly denied as a component of the original position. In *Political Liberalism*, Rawls includes a chapter entitled "Public Reason," but none entitled "Public Sentiment" or even "Public Reason and Sentiment." Indeed, even though Rawls specifies that both reasonableness and rationality involve (different forms of) passion, he spends little time discussing the relationship between reason and sentiment. In both of these cases, sentiment is essentially subsumed under the category of reason, leaving the misleading impression that reason is the only quality involved. The point is that Rawls does not explicitly *focus* on passion in the way that he focuses on reason. As we have seen, his argument relies on a theory of desire, but this theory is relegated to an auxiliary position, usually discussed under a separate section on "moral psychology." In contrast to his arguments about reason, which are highly developed, well integrated, and clearly central to the overall theory of justice, Rawls' arguments about desire and sentiment are scattered throughout his writing in isolated sections that are not always tied to each other or to the overall theory.[19] The consequence is that Rawls simultaneously presupposes and denies the importance of sentiment. The passion for justice lies at the heart of his theory of justice, yet holds only a marginal place in Rawls' purview.

The Price of Liberal Approaches to Passion

What is wrong with the liberal approaches to passion I have explored in this chapter? To begin with, as discussed above, liberal theorists undermine their own theories by ignoring or attempting to exclude passion. Whether or not it is acknowledged in liberal theory, passion plays a role, including a positive one, in politics. Liberal theorists who see only danger in passion cannot adequately address important political problems because they misdiagnose the cause of those problems and overlook potential solutions. Liberal theorists who ignore passion altogether are also unable explicitly to address and theorize important components of political life. In Chapter 7, I will argue that making political choices, creating political community, and motivating political action all depend in part on passion. If this is so, then liberal theorists are constrained from

36 • The Trouble With Passion

thinking productively about political choices, communities, and actions because they are not prepared to think about passion.

While ignoring the passion that exists in political *life* creates weaknesses for liberal political *theory*, it is also possible that the marginalization of passion in liberal political *theory* may contribute to problems in political *life*. It would be simplistic to posit a direct causal relationship between political theory and political life, but it seems reasonable to say that liberal theory has contributed and continues to contribute to the ideological foundations of Western political structures, processes, and cultures in a myriad of ways. What are the potential consequences of failing to identify the positive roles that passion plays in the political realm? Two of the most prominent consequences, to my mind, are the perpetuation of gender inequality in politics and the stifling of political innovation.

Gender inequality is hardly unique to liberalism. Virtually every existing political system has excluded—and continues to exclude—women from participation, at least to some extent. But liberalism is relatively unique in that it has often been presented as if it were gender-neutral. And indeed, once women gained the right to vote, to speak in public, and to run for political office, one could arguably claim that formal political equality had been largely attained. Formal equality, however, is a long way from actual equality. Consider but one example. In the United States women are still a distinct minority amongst those with political power in all branches of government, a minority whose percentage shrinks in direct relationship to the increase of power involved. Why, in the 21st century, is this so? No doubt there are many reasons, but one is surely a continued cultural perception of politics as a properly masculine activity. My point is that this perception is reinforced and perpetuated by the association of reason (seen as a political resource) with men and the association of passion (seen as a political liability) with women. Marking reason as public and male and passion as private and female contributes to a culture in which women are seen as out of place in politics unless they conform to standards of masculine comportment—in which case they are promptly vulnerable to accusations that they are somehow (as women) unnaturally cold and hard.[20]

Turning to the stifling of political innovation, while I have argued that passion cannot be eliminated from political life, this is not to say that it may not be *minimized* to some significant extent. Citizens and political leaders may be discouraged from honoring, expressing, and working with their passions and desires in political contexts. A cultural focus on the legal formalities and power dynamics of politics may make sentiment seem irrelevant, and provide little acknowledged opportunity for its use. But where there is little passion and desire, political life becomes dull and stagnant. Discouraging a role for passion in politics fosters apathy (literally, "lack of feeling"), passivity, and privatism among citizens; it reduces the conditions for citizen involvement in public life. Perhaps most importantly, it blunts the key force for improving political life. As Anne Carson, in a book called *Eros the Bittersweet*, points out, when we desire, "the difference between what is and what could be is visible" (1986, 17). When we desire, "we reach out from what is known and actual to something different, possibly better, desired" (71). Minimizing passion in politics means minimizing this process of reaching out for new and better political possibilities. It means limiting political interactions to an endless repetition of the same ideas. In this respect, to the extent that the call to rationalize politics is successful, it is quite counterproductive.

Conclusion: Passion, Politics, and Political Theory

My purpose in this chapter has been to explore attempts to marginalize passion in liberal political theory, and to argue that these attempts, while ultimately unsuccessful, are nevertheless unjustified and damaging to political theory and political practice. The fundamental problem is the impoverished character of liberal conceptions of passion. Conceptualizing passion as inherently irrational, egoistic, partial, erratic, idiosyncratic, cruel, extreme, and/or private does not allow liberal theorists to recognize important dimensions of emotional life. Such conceptions of passion are not useful for exploring the full complexity of actual and potential human experience. They frequently do not account for the inevitable interweaving of reason with passion. Finally, such conceptions of passion are incoherent in that they do not acknowledge the passion that exists within liberal theory itself.

If liberal conceptions of passion are the fundamental problem, then it is important to explore alternative conceptions of passion and theories of its potential role in politics. Rather than trying to find ways to banish passion from politics, or perhaps ignoring it altogether, I argue that political theorists need to focus on better ways to understand and develop the human capacity for passion. This is what I aim to do in the remainder of the book, through exploring and building on the work of Plato, Rousseau, and contemporary feminist theorists.

CHAPTER **4**

"The Madness of Eros Is the Greatest of Heaven's Blessings": Plato's Passion for the Good

Although political theorists tend to focus primarily on the arguments about justice, power, and knowledge in Plato's work, the subject of passion and desire is in fact central to several of his dialogues, particularly the *Republic*, the *Symposium*, and the *Phaedrus*. Just how central *eros*, in particular, is to Plato's thought is demonstrated by a brief comment that Socrates makes in the *Symposium*. Whereas in other dialogues Socrates consistently claims to understand nothing except that he is ignorant (and only in this sense to be wiser than others), in the *Symposium* Socrates claims to understand nothing except matters of *eros* (1953B, 177d). This is a striking exception, and one that ought to convince political theorists to pay more attention to this subject in Plato's work. If we do, we will find a fertile collection of arguments about passion and desire. Unlike liberal theorists, Plato does not cast passion as necessarily irrational, egoistic, erratic, or extreme. Rather, he presents a complex picture that accounts for many possible forms of, and relationships between, the capacities of passion and reason.

I contend that this picture can be useful for thinking about the significance of passion for politics. In this chapter, I explore Plato's thinking about passion and desire through a reading that integrates arguments from the *Republic*, the *Symposium*, and the *Phaedrus*. It is important to

40 • The Trouble With Passion

look at all three dialogues because there are some significant differences among them. While the *Republic* generally presents passions and desires—including *eros*—as a threat to both justice and happiness, the *Symposium* and the *Phaedrus* each present *eros* as a crucial guide to a just and happy life. At the same time, while the *Republic* pays a great deal of attention to the political significance of passion and desire, the latter two dialogues focus far more on individual, private concerns. Accordingly, a good portion of the chapter will be concerned with making sense of the various arguments about passion and desire in Plato's work and teasing out some of the political implications of passion. The ultimate purpose of the chapter is to investigate the resources that Plato has to offer for thinking about passion and politics. I argue that, despite some of Plato's own ontological and political standpoints, his writing can help us to imagine a democratic political realm animated by passion and reason.

The chapter begins with a discussion of two different concepts of desire in Plato's dialogues: *eros* and *epithumia*. The latter is seen in opposition to reason, while the former is not. The second and third parts of the chapter are a close examination of the treatment of desire in the *Republic*, the *Symposium*, and the *Phaedrus*, detailing Plato's arguments about both the dangers and the blessings of this human capacity. Since the *Republic* concerns itself primarily with *epithumia*, the dominant argument in this dialogue is that desire must be heavily controlled by reason in order to prevent madness, slavery, and tyranny. But since the other two dialogues are focused primarily on *eros*, a profoundly reasonable desire for the good, the argument here is that this kind of desire is a crucial component in living a good life. The fourth section addresses the question of why the dialogues focus on these two different forms of desire. Here I argue that the difference is at least partly explained by the different political projects of the dialogues. The fifth section draws out of Plato's explorations of passion some resources for thinking about passion and politics. I conclude the chapter by discussing where I depart from Plato's theories in constructing my own argument about the political significance of passion.

Eros and *Epithumia*: Two Conceptions of Passion and Desire

How does Plato talk about passion and desire? The words that figure most prominently in his discussions are *philia*, *epithumia*, and *eros*.[1] *Philia* is usually translated as "love," and carries similarly broad applications as the word does in English. It includes familial love, friendship, love of objects, and possibly what contemporary English-speakers might call romantic love. As an adjective, *philos* means "dear (to)" or "close (to)"; as a noun, it means friend, relative, or dear one. Although *philia* (along with its compounds)

"The Madness of Eros Is the Greatest of Heaven's Blessings" • **41**

certainly appears frequently in the *Republic*, the *Symposium*, and the *Phaedrus*, it is not closely examined and evaluated there in the way that *epithumia* and *eros* are. For this reason, my focus is on the latter two terms.

Epithumia is usually translated as "desire" or "appetite." Like *philia* it is a broad category: it includes desires for all sorts of things, from food to money to sex. Importantly, in Plato's dialogues *epithumia* is specifically defined in opposition to reason. In the *Republic*, Socrates argues that the soul is composed of three parts, *logistikon* (the rational part), *thumoeides* (the spirited or angry part), and *epithumetikon* (the appetitive part). These parts are not only distinct from each other but engaged in struggle, with the primary struggle being between reason and desire. Indeed, Socrates contends that this very struggle is evidence that the *epithumiai* are irrational:

> Doesn't that which forbids in such cases come into play—it if comes into play at all—as a result of rational calculation, while what drives and drags them to drink is a result of feelings and diseases?.... Hence it isn't unreasonable for us to claim that [these parts] are two, and different from one another. We'll call the part of the soul with which it calculates the rational [*logismos*] part and the part with which it lusts, hungers, thirsts, and gets excited by other appetites the irrational [*alogiston*] appetitive part, companion of certain indulgences and pleasures (1992, 439d).

This same opposition between desire and rationality is echoed in the *Phaedrus*, where Socrates originally argues that there are two separate and distinct principles in us, "desire of pleasure" and "acquired opinion which aspires after the best" (1953A, 237d). At this point in the argument, the word used for desire is *epithumia*, and desire is quite explicitly described as "devoid of reason" (238a). The consequence is that *epithumia* simply impels us toward whatever we desire, regardless of its value. In other words, it has no necessary relationship to the good.[2]

Eros, on the contrary, is specifically defined in the *Symposium* as the desire for the good. Now, this definition is a departure from the conventional meaning of *eros* in Plato's time, where *eros* signified a particularly sexual desire, or love where there is a sexual component, or "the passionate longing awakened in us by the appeal of physical beauty" (Halperin 1985, 163). But this is precisely the point of the *Symposium* as well as the *Phaedrus*: to argue for a new understanding of *eros* and its value.[3] As David Halperin explains it,

> The basic difference between *eros* and *epithumia* as Plato conceptualizes them...is the difference between a good-dependent and a

good-independent desire: erotic desire incorporates an implicit, positive value-judgment about its object, whereas appetitive desire expresses no such judgment—it merely aims at the gratification of a need…whether such gratification actually constitutes a good thing for the agent in the context of his present circumstances or not (1985, 171–72).

The reason erotic desire can incorporate a value-judgment is because, unlike *epithumia*, *eros* includes within itself or is linked to an ability to reason about the good.[4] As we shall see in the *Symposium* and the *Phaedrus*, with *eros* the faculties of desire and reason, far from being opposed, work together as closely as possible. Thus, in terms of both their relationship to reason and their relationship to the good, *epithumia* and *eros* are profoundly different conceptions of desire.

Because it incorporates reason and judgment about value, because it can be directed towards activities and ideas as well as persons, and because it is more about appreciation than acquisition, Plato's concept of *eros* is very close to the sense of passion I emphasize in this book.[5] Nevertheless, I investigate his comments about *epithumia* as well as his comments about *eros*, for two reasons. First, the two concepts are in many ways defined in terms of each other, so understanding one requires understanding the other. Second, passion as I conceive of it is open to both the possibilities Plato sees in *eros* and the dangers he sees in *epithumia*. In other words, although my understanding of passion is closer to *eros*, it includes elements of both of these concepts. Like *eros* it necessarily incorporates some form of reason and a positive value-judgment about its object, but like *epithumia* it may or may not actually be for the best. Thus I explore both the *Republic*'s arguments that *epithumia* is the source of injustice and the *Symposium*'s and the *Phaedrus*' arguments that *eros* is "the greatest of heaven's blessings."

The *Republic* on the Dangers of *Epithumia*

The *Republic* can be read, among many other ways, as a sustained argument about the dangers of desire. The most explicit goal of the dialogue is a search for justice. Yet it is desires that create the need for justice in the first place: it is when Glaucon wants relishes and couches in the imaginary city that the real search for justice begins. Although he makes it clear that the simple city is the true, healthy one, Socrates does not object to imagining a luxurious city, "For by examining it, we might very well see how justice and injustice grow up in cities" (372e). An exploration of justice apparently requires a more extravagant setting, because justice is not much

"The Madness of Eros Is the Greatest of Heaven's Blessings" • **43**

of an issue in a city where desires are minimal. Licentiousness—unrestrained desire—is thus presented as the ultimate source of the sickness of injustice. In a sense, then, the desires are the root of the problem in the *Republic*, and their proper control the solution.

Of course, the reference here is to the *epithumiai*. There are relatively few specific references to *eros* in the *Republic*, and most of these simply include *eros* in a group with other desires and passions. *Eros* appears as a distinct category only three times: in the discussion of "erotically inclined men" who love boys (474d–475a), in the discussion of philosophers who have an erotic love of truth (490b, 499b), and in the discussion of tyrants who are themselves tyrannized by *eros* (572e–579b). Aside from the passages on the philosopher, these references are decidedly negative, in keeping with the argument about *epithumia*. What this indicates, I would argue, is that in the *Republic* Plato presents *eros* largely in conventional terms, that is, as a particularly virulent form of *epithumia*.[6] Thus, in spite of occasional allusions to *eros*, the species of desire at issue in the *Republic* is *epithumia*.

Why is *epithumia* so dangerous? What are the problems it causes? As already mentioned, *epithumia* is the root of injustice (or tyranny), but it is also the root of slavery, madness, weakness, and profound unhappiness. It is important to note from the start that it is *unchecked* desires, and not simply desires per se, that pose these problems. However, as presented in this dialogue, the desiring part of the soul is incapable of self-limitation. In telling fashion, the subject of the desires is always discussed in a language of rule and mastery. There can be no peace between desire and reason without some form of dominance. The dominance of reason is healthy, as it allows the other parts of the soul to function within their proper places. But if reason is not in control, the desires, which in themselves are insatiable, will inevitably enslave the rest of the soul (442a–b). Victory of the desires turns out to be a form of enslavement. Indeed, the desire of *eros* (again, understood here in the conventional sense) so dominates the soul in which it resides that it is called a tyrant (573b). The need to restrain such desires is thus the need to maintain freedom.

But enslavement is only the beginning of the danger inherent in desire; madness follows as a direct result. Again this stems from the nature of the soul and its divisions as described in the *Republic*. As we have seen, *epithumia* and rationality are distinct and separate parts of the soul. From here it is only one step to madness, for if the desires are successful in their battle to take control of the soul, then rationality will be completely banished. When *eros* becomes a metaphoric tyrant in the soul, the soul goes mad. The example is provided by the real tyrant, who is completely mad with a "great winged drone" of *eros* (572e). Even the satisfaction of desires is to be

44 • The Trouble With Passion

suspected, because excessive pleasure "drives one mad just as much as pain does" (402e). The tremendous emphasis on a proper hierarchy within the soul is even more understandable in this light. The need to restrain desires is the need to maintain not just freedom but sanity.

The recurring image of the tyrant in demonstrating the danger of the desires is significant, for the tyrant is the example par excellence of the terrible effect of unchecked desires. He is tyrannized by his own desires, and therefore mad.[7] But he earns the name of tyrant because he tyrannizes others. The relationship between the two tyrannies is causal: "a man becomes tyrannical in the precise sense of the term when either his nature or his way of life or both of them together make him drunk, filled with erotic desire, and mad" (573c). In other words, the rule of desires leads to slavishness and madness, which in turn leads to domination and injustice in one's dealings with others. For the demands of the desires, if not restrained, are never-ending; consequently, one who is a slave to his desires exhausts his own resources to meet these demands and must appropriate more and more of the resources of others (573d–574b). Eventually he will do anything to get what he needs. Thus is a tyrant born.

> Now, however, under the tyranny of erotic love, he has permanently become while awake what he used to become occasionally while asleep, and he won't hold back from any terrible murder or from any kind of food or act. But, rather, erotic love lives like a tyrant within him, in complete anarchy and lawlessness as his sole ruler, and drives him, as if he were a city, to dare anything that will provide sustenance for itself and the unruly mob around it (574e–575a).

Once again we see that the root of injustice, the fundamental problem in the *Republic*, is uncontrolled desire.

It is worth a reminder here that although desires may lead to tyranny and domination, they are not therefore a source of power for the person. Indeed, precisely the reverse. Tyranny, in the analysis of the *Republic*, both stems from and creates weakness: the weakness of being a slave to one's own desires. The tyrant is actually the weakest person of all because he is the neediest, thus the least capable of satisfying his own desires. He is in direct contrast to the "decent" man (*epieikes*: the one who does what's fit) who is "most self-sufficient in living well and, above all other, has least need of anyone else" (387d). In this formulation, desires make people dependent. When one is ruled by desires, and dependent on others to meet those desires, one is free neither in one's own soul nor with respect to others. But freedom is necessary for true power. Only those who are

"The Madness of Eros Is the Greatest of Heaven's Blessings" • **45**

self-controlled, then, can be truly powerful. This is the case for groups and cities as well as individuals. When the unit as a whole is not just—that is, when reason is not properly employed, whether internally or externally, to control desires—then there will be hatred and factions amongst the members or parts. A group so divided will be unable to accomplish anything, effectively powerless (351e–352a). Again, licentiousness is weakness.

The final and in a sense most important consequence of the rule of desires is unhappiness. Socrates' task here is most difficult, for it seems entirely counter intuitive to argue that refusing to fulfill all of one's desires would lead to happiness. Plato's contemporaries apparently thought, much as many people do today, that the road to happiness involves satisfying as many desires as possible. But building on the other arguments he has made regarding the effects of the rule of desires, Socrates paints a picture of those who live their lives in this way as miserable. The key to happiness lies not in satisfying desires but in properly limiting them.

Again we return to the tyrant as the final test case of such an argument. If happiness involves acquiring things and having one's way, the tyrant ought to be the happiest of anyone. But as Socrates describes him, the tyrant is a lonely, fearful, wretchedly unhappy man. He is driven by a never-ending stream of needy desires, and his relationships to other people are dictated by these needs. In his quest for the power to obtain what he desires, he must flatter those above him and accept the flattery of those below him. "So someone with a tyrannical nature lives his whole life without being friends with anyone, always a master to one man or a slave to another and never getting a taste of either freedom or true friendship" (576a). Once the tyrant has attained a position of power, he must guard it jealously. He must live in fear of everyone, having behaved unjustly to everyone. His dominion becomes a prison in which he himself is bound (579b). In the end, Socrates evaluates the quality of the tyrant's life by calling on his analogy between the soul and the city. When one considers a city under a tyranny, including all of its members and not just the ruler, it is easy to see that this city is the least happy of all. Similarly, the tyrant is the least happy of people, if one takes account of all the parts of the soul and not just the "great winged drone" in charge. The tyrant is unable to see this, for he is a slave to the drone and mad. But a good observer who can see into the whole soul can see how unhappy he is: "And isn't the enslaved and tyrannical city least likely to do what it wants?" "Then a tyrannical soul—I'm talking about the whole soul—will also be least likely to do what it wants and, forcibly driven by the stings of a dronish gadfly, will be full of disorder and regret" (577d–e). "And do you think you'll find more wailing, groaning, lamenting and grieving in any other city [than the tyrannical one]?" "Then, are such things more

46 • The Trouble With Passion

common in anyone besides a tyrannical man, who is maddened by his desires and erotic loves?" (578a). The final conclusion leaves no room for ambiguity:

> In truth, then, and whatever some people may think, a real tyrant is really a slave, compelled to engage in the worst kind of fawning, slavery, and pandering to the worst kind of people. He's so far from satisfying his desires in any way that it is clear—if one happens to know that one must study his whole soul—that he's in the greatest need of most things and truly poor. And, if indeed his state is like that of the city he rules, then he's full of fear, convulsions, and pains throughout his life (579de).

We come full circle in the description of the dangers of desire: the tyrant is in truth unhappy—and a mad, powerless slave.

Such is the status of unchecked desires in the *Republic*. They loom ominously, threatening to plunge a soul into slavery, madness, and wretchedness. They sap the power of an individual or group and feed injustice in the world. Whether in the city or the soul, the image of the "many-headed" or "mob-like beast" (588c, 590b) is symbolic of the degrading demands of the desires that must be restrained by that which is supposed to be more human in us. So far, one could hardly imagine a more dangerous capacity. But before moving on to the *Symposium* and the *Phaedrus*, it is important to complicate this picture. While desires are treated as a relatively monolithic category for much of the *Republic*, eventually, when speaking of the democratic man, Socrates begins to distinguish between "necessary" and "unnecessary" desires. Necessary desires are desires that are impossible to deny and/or for things that benefit us. Unnecessary desires are desires that may be controlled with training and that are for things that do not benefit us and may even harm us (558d–559a). For example, hunger for basic food is a necessary desire; hunger for elaborate foods is an unnecessary desire (559a–559c). The problem with the democratic soul, and the democratic state, is that it does not distinguish between these different kinds of desires and thinks that all desires must be honored equally (561b–c). This is the kind of freedom that may end up turning into tyranny in both the soul and the city.

The way to guard against such tyranny is, of course, moderation (*sophrosyne*): a harmony between parts of the self or city, an "agreement between the naturally worse and the naturally better as to which of the two is to rule both in the city and in each one" (432a). Clearly, the better should rule the worse. But though this principle is generally interpreted to mean that reason should rule desires, in fact the situation is more

"The Madness of Eros Is the Greatest of Heaven's Blessings" • **47**

complex. In addition to reason, "the better" includes within itself the better, necessary desires. The best class of people, according to Socrates, have "desires that are simple, measured, and directed by calculation in accordance with understanding and correct belief" (431c). Moreover, these are the people who rule in a well-ordered, moderate city: "the desires of the inferior many are controlled by the wisdom *and desires* of the superior few" (431c–d, my emphasis). At least within the city, then, if not the soul as well, necessary desires appear to play some part in the achievement of controlling unnecessary desires.

Moreover, although Socrates spends most of the time in the *Republic* discussing desires that are harmful, there are a few key sections where he indicates what kinds of desires might be beneficial. Many of these desires are simply necessary for survival, such as that for basic food. But there is one positive desire that goes beyond such basic needs: the desire for wisdom. In Book VI, Socrates describes the philosopher as one who is in love with learning the truth (485b). (Here Plato would seem to be moving towards the understanding of *eros* developed in the *Symposium*.) Such a desire for the truth helps control other desires, for desires are like a stream: when they are channeled strongly in one direction, the flow becomes correspondingly weak in other directions. "Then, when someone's desires flow towards learning and everything of that sort, he'd be concerned, I suppose, with the pleasures of the soul itself by itself, and he'd abandon those pleasures that come through the body—if indeed he is a true philosopher and not merely a counterfeit one" (485d–e).

In Book IX, Socrates elaborates further on the beneficial desire for wisdom. Here he argues that the desire for wisdom is the best of all desires, not only because it leads to justice and virtue, which has already been established, but because it brings the most satisfaction. He offers three proofs that the just man, that is, the one whose strong desire for wisdom diminishes his other desires, is happiest. The first proof relies on the counterexample of the tyrant, the most unjust man, who is assumed to be happiest but whom Socrates demonstrates to be most unhappy. The second proof is an argument that those who love wisdom have experienced the other types of pleasures and can adequately judge that the pleasure of wisdom is best, whereas those who love other things have not tasted the pleasure of wisdom and cannot know that their preferred pleasure is best (581c–583a). In the third proof, Socrates supports the conclusion that the pleasure of wisdom is best by arguing that it is the only one based on truth rather than illusions. Most so-called pleasures are really just forms of relief from pain, and they feed the transitory part of us with transitory things. But wisdom, because it feeds the part of us that "is" with things that "are," brings a complete and permanent satisfaction. In a long but evocative

48 • The Trouble With Passion

passage, Socrates sums up the difference between the lower and higher forms of desire and pleasure:

> Therefore, those who have no experience of reason or virtue, but are always occupied with feasts and the like, are brought down [into pain] and then back up to the middle [relief from pain], as it seems, and wander in this way throughout their lives, never reaching beyond this to what is truly higher up, never looking up at it or being brought up to it, and so they aren't filled with that which really is, and never taste any stable or sure pleasure. Instead, they always look down at the ground like cattle, and, with their heads bent over the dinner table, they feed, fatten, and fornicate. To outdo others in these things, they kick and butt them with iron horns and hooves, killing each other because their desires are insatiable. For the part that they're trying to fill is like a vessel full of holes, and neither it nor the things they are trying to fill it with are among the things that are (586a–b).

To take account of this complexity within the desires, our earlier perspective on the *Republic* as a warning against the dangers of the desires needs to be modified. In fact the warning only applies to certain kinds of desires. The problem, then, is to be able to distinguish between harmful and beneficial desires, and to prove that the former lead not only to injustice but to unhappiness, while the latter are at least compatible with, and perhaps an important component of, happiness and justice. Fundamentally, Plato wants us to learn how to desire the right things in the right measure. He therefore aims to convince us that our basic desire for happiness cannot be satisfied by unlimited attainment of all the things commonly considered desirable: primarily, money, sex, and power. Rather, if we truly want happiness we must control our excessive desires for these things and limit ourselves to moderate desires for only that which is necessary and beneficial. Although the *Republic* does not emphasize it, the *Symposium* and the *Phaedrus* show that this process also involves the proper cultivation of *eros*.

The *Symposium* and *Phaedrus* on the Blessings of *Eros*

The *Symposium* and the *Phaedrus* provide a dramatically different perspective on desire than the *Republic*. Instead of the constant specter of danger, the constant worrying about what will happen if desires are not controlled, here we have imaginative and enthusiastic—indeed, passionate—discussions of the possibilities of desire to enrich people's lives. Of course in these dialogues the specific subject is not *epithumia* but *eros*.

"The Madness of Eros Is the Greatest of Heaven's Blessings" • **49**

In both cases, though, *eros* is initially identified with or defined as a species of *epithumia* (1953A, 238b–c; 1953B, 200a–e). Eventually, however, *eros* is distinguished from *epithumia*, and given a ringing defense. What are the reasons for this defense? Why is *eros* so valuable?

Let us begin with the *Symposium*. A symposium is, of course, a drinking party; to set a discussion of *eros* in this context is thus already to establish a festive mood. Moreover, the explicit goal at this symposium is to offer speeches in praise of the god Eros, whom Phaedrus complains has never yet been given a worthy tribute. Through this structure of tributes to a god, the *Symposium* investigates the nature of the human quality of *eros* and its benefits to humanity. Despite the accused neglect of *eros*, the members of the party all take for granted at the outset that it is deserving of praise. Nor is this judgment ever refuted, although it is certainly refined as the dialogue proceeds. Plato uses the strategy of the different speakers, each offering a different description of *eros* and its value, to eventually compose his own unusual and even radical tribute to *eros*. He extracts the important insights from the more common views expressed by each of the speakers and weaves them into Socrates'/Diotima's final resounding argument for the value of *eros*.[8] While the earlier speeches are seemingly lavish in their praise of *eros*, in the end Diotima's praise is the most comprehensive of all.

The value Plato places on *eros* in this dialogue (and in the *Phaedrus*) is inseparable from the special way in which he understands this term. The key beginning point is Socrates'/Diotima's emphasis on the source of *eros* as lack. Aristophanes originally brings up this theme with his fanciful tale of humanity's fall from the blessed state of wholeness. Once people are cut in two, they are terribly unhappy and desire to be one again. This "desire and pursuit of the whole is called [*eros*]" (193a). Socrates picks up this theme of incompleteness in his questioning of Agathon, who has attributed to the god Eros nearly every positive quality existing. Through this exchange, Socrates establishes that if Eros is desire, he (or it) cannot possess any of these things, for we do not desire what we already have (200a–b). The consequence is that Eros cannot be divine after all, for he is lacking in precisely the fair things that gods must have to be gods (202c–d).

And yet *eros* is not the complete absence of these things either: Diotima reproaches Socrates when he assumes that what is not good is therefore evil. Eros, she argues, is a mean between good and evil, fair and foul, and so forth. What is at stake here? The problem is that one who lacks something completely may have no *vision* of what is lacking and therefore no motivation towards attaining it. Lack may be a necessary condition of desire, but it is not sufficient. Diotima offers the case of wisdom and ignorance as an example. On the one hand, the wise do not desire wisdom, because they already have it. But on the other hand, the foolish do not

50 • The Trouble With Passion

desire wisdom either, because they are not even aware that they lack it. "[T]here is no desire when there is no feeling of want" (204a). In other words, there is no desire without awareness and imagination as well as lack. Thus, it is crucial that one be situated between the two extremes of complete possession and complete lack for the dynamics of desire to operate. This point is conveyed through the mythical genealogy of Eros, making him the child of both Poverty (*Penia*) and Plenty (*Poros*). From his mother Poverty comes Eros' actual lack of things, the first requirement for desire. But from his father Plenty comes his awareness of what he lacks, the second requirement for desire. Eros is a mean between poverty and plenty.

At this point we have only established that *eros* is the desire for whatever we lack (plenty). Implicit in the argument, though, is the most important point: that *eros* is the desire specifically for the good. Again this is not an entirely new idea: the association of *eros* with fair things is a running assumption in most of the speeches. Agathon finally articulates the theme, stating that *eros* is the desire of beauty, having no concern with deformity (197b). There is no explanation for this claim; it is simply taken as obvious. But Socrates, following Diotima, identifies the good with the beautiful ("Is not the good also the beautiful?" [201c]), and in so doing provides a logical explanation for why people desire the beautiful/good.[9] The key conversation with Diotima begins with her question "When a man loves the beautiful, what does his love desire?" Since Socrates is unable to answer this question, Diotima substitutes the good for the beautiful:

> "Then let me put the word 'good' in the place of the beautiful, and repeat the question once more: If he who loves loves the good, what is it then that he loves?"
>
> "The possession of the good."
>
> "And what does he gain who possesses the good?"
>
> "Happiness…"
>
> "Yes, the happy are made happy by the acquisition of good things. Nor is there any need to ask why a man desires happiness; the answer is already final" (204e–205a).

It is obvious that we want happiness, thus we must desire the good, which will bring us happiness. *Eros* is the desire for the good.

Indeed, *eros* is the desire for the good alone. For, it is implied, only the good will bring us happiness. The argument here depends on a conflation

"The Madness of Eros Is the Greatest of Heaven's Blessings" • **51**

of "the good" with "good things" (or, as Diotima puts it at one point, "[our] own good" [205a]). Thus the rather tautological point that to want happiness is to want good things in one's life is indiscernibly transformed into an argument that to want happiness is to want goodness in one's life (notice that this assertion bypasses the crucial argument of the *Republic* that what people *perceive* to be "good things" may be very different from "the good"). The result is that Diotima explicitly contradicts Aristophanes:

> [Y]ou hear people say that lovers are seeking for their other half; but I say that they are seeking neither for the half of themselves, nor for the whole, unless the half or the whole be also a good; men will cut off their own hands and feet and cast them away, if they think them evil... for there is nothing which men love but the good (205d–206a).

Another way to put this is to say that people really only lack the good, therefore they really only desire the good. Finally, then, we arrive at the definition of *eros*. It is "the [desire] of the everlasting possession of the good" (206a). (Everlasting because we want the good not just for a moment but for all time.)

Despite the earlier point that those who are completely lacking do not desire what they lack, here Diotima argues that a desire for the good is common to everyone: "all men always desire their own good" (205a). Again, the identification of the good with happiness makes this seem obvious. The consequence, though, is that *eros* is present in all of life, not just the narrow range it has been accorded. As Socrates notes, conventionally only some people are said to love: those who are "lovers." That is, the word *eros* is used to describe only sexual desire for another person. But this is because a particular example of love/desire has, unfairly it is implied, taken over the general sense of the word:

> For you may say generally that all desire of good and happiness is only the great and subtle power of [*eros*]; but they who are drawn towards him by any other path, whether the path of money-making or gymnastics or philosophy, are not called lovers—the name of the whole is appropriated to those whose desire takes one form only—they alone are said to love, or to be lovers (205a–d).

Plato wants to restore (or create) a broader meaning to *eros*. For him, we are all lovers to the extent that we all want happiness and desire the good. *Eros* is ubiquitous, a pervasive phenomenon in our lives.

52 • The Trouble With Passion

And this phenomenon is something very special, as the mythology of Eros reveals. Recall that Eros is not a god—he cannot be, because he lacks the good. But he is not entirely human either. As he is midway between poverty and plenty, evil and good, ignorance and wisdom, so is he also midway between the mortal and the immortal: hence a daemon. His role is to serve as a mediator between the human (that which lacks) and the divine (that which is). As we have seen, *eros* is not plenty/good/wisdom itself, but the awareness of the lack of these things and the desire that moves us toward them. This awareness and desire is what brings the divine in reach of humanity. The allegory shows just how crucial a role this is:

> [Eros] interprets between gods and men, conveying and taking across to the gods the prayers and sacrifices of men, and to men the commands of the gods and the benefits they return; he is the mediator who spans the chasm which divides them, and therefore by him the universe is bound together (202e).

By now we can begin to see why *eros*, as conceptualized in the *Symposium*, is so important and so valuable. As the desire for the good, *eros* turns out to be responsible for whatever measure of wisdom, virtue, and happiness people are able to achieve in their lives. It is the impelling force, and therefore the cause, of these achievements. Explaining the process by which this happens, Diotima switches back to beauty as the quintessential object of desire. In the well-known passage on the ascent, desire for one beautiful person leads step by step to the desire for—and understanding of—beauty itself. One is led up the steps by making the connections between particular examples of beauty and the general form; in other words, by realizing that all kinds of beauty actually share something in common and that this larger commonality is the true object of desire and appreciation. Hence one gains entry into the world of the *eide*, the only world of which one can have true knowledge. Although we originally begin with beauty, the most obvious object of desire (along with the good), in the end it seems clear that beauty is just an example of what desire can lead to: knowledge of the *eide* (all of which are, of course, beautiful). The process of coming to know the *eide* is begun by *eros*, and *eros* is in turn carried along by this process until it is directed solely towards the *eide*. From the perspective of the *Symposium*, then, *eros* is a momentous force toward the highest of ends. "This...is the life above all others which man should live, in the contemplation of beauty absolute" (211d) and "in the attainment of this end human nature will not easily find a helper better than [*Eros*]" (212b).

"The Madness of Eros Is the Greatest of Heaven's Blessings" • **53**

It is important to note the ways in which *eros* is presented as closely tied to, and even incorporating, reason in the *Symposium*. Recall that Diotima describes *eros* as midway between poverty and plenty, ignorance and knowledge. Her point was that *eros* requires not just lack but an awareness of lack: an awareness that there is a good that one does not (yet) have, and thus an incipient *understanding* of that good. Already *eros* appears to be a cognitive as well as emotional faculty. And this picture is further developed in the *Symposium*'s description of the ascent, where *eros* and reason are deeply intertwined in the steps toward knowledge of the form of beauty. One begins by *desiring* one beautiful body, then comes to *perceive* that the beauty of one body is akin to the beauty of another, at which point one's *desire* is broadened to include all beautiful bodies, and so forth.[10] Far from being opposed, the faculties of *eros* and reason work together as closely as possible in enabling the soul to make the ascent. But this should not be surprising, since in a sense the whole point of the *Symposium* is that *eros* and reason actually share the same goal: apprehension of the good.[11]

The *Phaedrus* echoes this positive evaluation of *eros*, although its exploration of the subject touches on some points that the *Symposium* does not. Unlike the *Symposium*, the *Phaedrus* does not begin with the assumption that *eros* is to be praised—quite the reverse. As a result, its position on *eros* is initially much more in line with that of the *Republic*. Nevertheless, the *Phaedrus* ultimately offers a defense of *eros*, a defense that is all the more powerful since it directly counters some of Plato's own arguments against *eros* in the *Republic*. That this dialogue addresses opposing positions on *eros* makes it particularly interesting in a consideration of the status of the desires in Plato's work.

The specific issue in the *Phaedrus*, at least in the first part, is whether a youth ought better to "accept" and "grant favors" (*kharizesthai*) to a lover or to a nonlover; in other words, whether he benefits more (and suffers less) from the attentions and patronage of a man who is passionately in love with him or one who is not. Lysias has made what is on its face a controversial speech, arguing that in fact a nonlover is to be preferred, but in so doing has actually called on quite common opinions about the ways in which *eros* influences a lover's behavior. Socrates criticizes the speech for its poor rhetoric and offers his own speech for why the nonlover is to be preferred. He deepens the argument by providing a more theoretical account of the problems *eros* causes, starting with an explicit definition of its nature and power. After making his speech, however, Socrates is visited by his familiar inner voice, which chastises him for his "impiety" in criticizing *eros*, so that he must make another speech in praise of *eros*. In this way the dialogue repudiates the common, as well as some not so common, attacks on *eros* and takes a stand in its defense.

54 • The Trouble With Passion

The original argument against *eros* is familiar to us from the *Republic*: the problem with *eros* is that it makes people mad. Scattered throughout Lysias' arguments are statements that the nonlover is "more his own master" and "free," while the lover is under a "compulsion" and "ill advised about his own interests" (232a, 231a, 234b). Lysias' advice to the desired youth emphasizes the untrustworthiness of those who are not in their "right minds" (231c–d). Socrates explains the nature of this problem more fully:

> Let us note that in every one of us there are two guiding and ruling principles which lead us whither they will; one is the natural desire [*epithumia*] of pleasure, the other is an acquired opinion which aspires after the best; and these two are sometimes in harmony and then again at war, and sometimes the one, sometimes the other conquers. When opinion by the help of reason leads us to the best, and proves superior, its government is called temperance; but when desire, which is devoid of reason, rules in us and drags us to pleasure, that power of misrule is called excess (237d–238a).

Notice that here, as in the *Republic*, *epithumia* is explicitly defined in opposition to reason. Socrates goes on to explain that when a particular excess is very strong, it acquires its own name: such is that of *eros*.

> [T]he irrational desire which overcomes the tendency of opinion towards right, and is led away to the enjoyment of beauty, and especially of personal beauty, by the desires which are her own kindred—that supreme desire, I say, which by leading conquers and by the force of passion is reinforced, from this very force, receiving a name, is called [*eros*] (238b–c).

What follows from this desire that conquers rationality cannot be good. For Lysias, the result is that the lover is fickle and possessive, and therefore untrustworthy and damaging to the beloved's improvement. Not being in his right (rational) mind, the lover is likely to do things he will later regret. He may pick a beloved without knowledge of the beloved's character, so that when his passion subsides there is no basis for friendship (232e). He may neglect his own affairs and perform services for the sake of the beloved, but later repent of these kindnesses, holding them against the beloved (231a–b). Though his devotion may be strong at the time, there is no guarantee he will not simply transfer it to another in the future (231c). In essence, the rule of passion means that commitment for the future is sacrificed to the pleasure of the moment (234a). Moreover, the rule of passion makes the lover unreasonably jealous of his beloved. He tries to

"The Madness of Eros Is the Greatest of Heaven's Blessings" • 55

prohibit the beloved from having other friends, thus precluding the possibility that the beloved will benefit from associations with others (232c–d). At the same time, the lover himself does not help the beloved because he makes poor judgments about what is praiseworthy and what blameworthy in him, thereby obstructing his growth (233a–b). The lover's irrationality causes him, sooner or later, to harm his beloved; hence a beloved does not do well to enter into a relationship with him.

Socrates agrees that the lover harms the beloved. His central point is that the lover's passion makes him selfish: his treatment of the beloved is motivated by his own desires rather than a regard for the welfare of the beloved. The beloved is thus prevented from developing into a stronger, better, wiser man because the lover prefers him inferior and dependent. In order to maintain the beloved's "agreeableness," the lover will attempt to deprive him of friends and possessions, a strong body, and, most importantly, a strong mind (238e). The lover will even keep him from philosophy, the greatest injury of all (239b). In the end the lover's desire is bound to cease; he will then run from the beloved, selfishly breaking all of his promises to him and leaving him much the worse for the affair (240e–241b). Such a situation prompts Socrates to conclude that "in the friendship of the lover there is no real kindness; he has an appetite and wants to feed upon you: 'As wolves love lambs so lovers love their loves'" (241c).

But the conclusion is barely uttered before Socrates rushes to repudiate it. He fears he has blasphemed *eros* by speaking of a false imitation, rather than its true form. "For if [*eros*] be, as he surely is, a divinity, he cannot be evil" (242e). (Note that this assertion of *eros'* divinity stands in partial contradiction to the mythology given in the *Symposium*.) Interestingly, in moving to speak of true *eros*, Socrates does not dispute that it involves madness, but rather that madness is always bad. "'False was that word of mine' that the beloved ought to accept the non-lover when he might have the lover, because the one is sane, and the other mad. It might be so if madness were simply an evil; but there is also a madness which is a divine gift, and the source of the chiefest blessings granted to men" (244a). Socrates cites prophecy and the inspiration of the Muses as examples of beneficial madness. He means to argue that *eros* is in this category. The real question, then, is not whether a lover is mad or not, but whether his madness is of the right kind:

> [L]et us not be scared and confused by an argument which says that the temperate friend is to be chosen rather than the inspired, but let him further show that [*eros*] is not sent by the gods for any good to lover or beloved; if he can do so we will allow him to carry off the palm. And we, on our part, must prove in answer to

56 • The Trouble With Passion

> him that the madness of [eros] is the greatest of heaven's blessings, and the proof shall be one which the wise will receive, and the witling disbelieve (245b).

What, then, is the madness of eros, and how can it be a blessing? To answer this question, Socrates tells a parable of the journeys of the immortal soul. He explains that all souls in the beginning dwell in the realm of the gods and, to the extent they are able, behold the form of the divine: the true being of "beauty, wisdom, goodness and the like" (246e). Each soul is like a chariot with a pair of winged horses and a charioteer. The horses of the gods are both noble, but the human souls have one noble, obedient horse and one ignoble, insolent one. As a result, the human chariot is very difficult to manage, and eventually loses its wings and falls down to earth to inhabit a body (248a–e). But for some souls, the image of the upper world remains relatively fresh in mind. When such souls see someone beautiful on earth, they do not rush to give themselves over to "brutish" pleasures; rather, they stand in awe, for it reminds them of the divine beauty. Their wings begin to grow again, causing heat, perspiration, irritation, ebullition, and many other signs of joy and distress. "And this state... is by men called [eros]" (252b). Most people will misunderstand its true nature, though, thinking the desire is only for the beloved. In truth it goes far beyond, for when a lover looks at a beloved, he sees an image of a god (252c–253c). Eros is initiated by a beautiful person, but at base it is a desire for what the beloved recalls: the beauty of the eide.

Because its true source and object lie in the heavenly rather than earthly realm, eros is a form of madness. It is a supranormal phenomenon; it is not sensible within the bounds of ordinary life. One who is inspired by the divine—in love—loses interest in mundane things and therefore appears mad to the rest of the world. "[Eros] is...imputed to him who, when he sees the beauty of earth, is transported with the recollection of the true beauty; he would like to fly away, but he cannot; he is like a bird fluttering and looking upward and careless of the world below; and he is therefore thought to be mad" (249d). Notice that Socrates has quietly begun suggesting that one who is so inspired only *appears* mad to others ("the vulgar deem him mad, and rebuke him; they do not see that he is inspired" [249d]). Eros is not, in the end, truly irrational; it is simply not *exclusively* and narrowly rational. It is passionate, transporting, and somewhat mysterious.

Yet for the same reason that eros is a madness, it is also a blessing. As an inspiration from and toward the divine, it is not exclusively rational, but it is by definition for the best. The recollection of the eide, especially that of the good, inspires the lover to be virtuous (although not without some

"The Madness of Eros Is the Greatest of Heaven's Blessings" • **57**

struggle with the one ignoble horse). And because what the lover loves in the beloved is an image of a god/the good, he tries to bring out the god in his beloved as much as possible, encouraging him to be virtuous as well (253a). This virtuous influence is what makes true love so beneficial to the beloved. In Socrates' first speech, which upheld the nonlover, the argument rested on the ways in which a nonlover has the beloved's welfare more at heart. By now Socrates has made clear that it is the true lover who really has the beloved's welfare at heart. But he anticipated this conclusion all along, for the first nonlover was really a lover after all: "there was one special cunning [lover], who had persuaded the youth that he did not love him, but he really loved him more than any" (237b). In Socrates' second story, the beloved eventually returns the love of the lover, and the two inspired partners live out their lives together, encouraging each other in wisdom and virtue to the best of their ability. Whether or not they succeed in being entirely virtuous (in other words, in abstaining from sexual activity), they "obtain no mean reward of love and madness. For those who have once begun the heavenward pilgrimage may not go down again to darkness and the journey beneath the earth, but they live in light always" (256d). Thus, *eros* is a blessing for both the lover and the beloved, not in spite of but rather because of the inspired passion it involves.

It is important to note that Socrates has fundamentally departed from his original definition of *eros* here. In the beginning, he established two distinct principles, a natural, irrational desire [*epithumia*] for pleasure and an acquired opinion which aspires after the best, and argued that *eros* was a form of excess in which "the irrational desire...overcomes the tendency of opinion towards right, and is led away to the enjoyment of beauty, and especially of personal beauty, by the desires which are her own kindred." But now we see that the two principles of desire and opinion aspiring after the best need not be opposed. Indeed, they may be linked, for if *eros* is a recollection of and yearning for the divine, then it is certainly an aspiration after the best. Put another way, desire for beauty and a tendency toward right are not in conflict, so long as one remembers (or, as in the *Symposium*, begins by steps to understand) the true nature of beauty. True *eros* is both desire for beauty and tendency toward right. Thus *eros*—in contrast to *epithumia*—is not irrational.

This conclusion may seem suspect given that throughout the *Phaedrus* Socrates defends *eros* as a form of madness. One could certainly interpret the dialogue to be arguing that reason is not the only good; that desire is important too, *even if* irrational (madness is a blessing). But I would argue that although the *Phaedrus* praises madness, Plato's purpose is not to defend complete irrationality. Rather, his purpose is to criticize a form of rationality that is narrow and purely instrumental ("worldly prudence"),

58 • The Trouble With Passion

and therefore insufficient for the best life. This is the kind of rationality represented by the nonlover, against whom Socrates so passionately warns Phaedrus. For the friendship of the true lover will open up the possibility of a life in pursuit of true knowledge and excellence, and an ascent to the heavens when life is done,

> [w]hereas the attachment of the nonlover, which is alloyed with a worldly prudence and has worldly and niggardly ways of doling out benefits, will breed in your soul those vulgar qualities which the populace applaud, and will send you bowling round the earth during a period of nine thousand years, and leave you a fool in the world below (256e–257a).

In other words, the rationality of the nonlover is narrow and insufficient precisely because it excludes *eros*. Moreover, *eros* only appears irrational from the standpoint of *this* kind of rationality (recall that as the dialogue progresses Socrates begins suggesting that the true lover only appears to be mad from the perspective of the vulgar). The point of the *Phaedrus*, then, is that far from being irrational, *eros* actually incorporates or is tied to a higher form of reason.[12]

The distinction between the different kinds of reason as well as the different kinds of desire can be seen in the *Phaedrus'* use of the chariot as an image of the soul. The traditional interpretation of the image of the chariot is that the three members of the team—the charioteer, noble horse, and brutish horse—correspond to the same three parts of the soul as identified in the *Republic*: reason, spirit, and appetite. Given this model, it is easy to conclude that the struggle that occurs among the chariot team upon beholding the beloved is a struggle between reason and desire, and that the ideal outcome is for reason (the charioteer) to control desire (the brutish horse). But as Giovanni Ferrari shows, the interactions between the members of the chariot team are much more complicated than that, for in the struggle "it is the bad horse who adopts persuasive language and the methods of reason, while the charioteer maintains control by sheer strength and wordless violence" (1987, 186).[13] This apparent reversal suggests that the parts of the soul are not as separate and self-contained as they might appear. What, then, is the difference between the charioteer and the brutish horse, if not that between reason and desire? As Ferrari puts it,

> The essential point of contrast between the charioteer and rebellious horse is not that between a faculty of reason (without desire) and a faculty of appetite or desire (without reason) but…between that in us which aims at how best the life of the whole person

should go and that which looks only to as immediate a satisfaction as possible (201).

According to this interpretation, even appetites may command a certain form of reason, but it is a form of reason limited to prudential calculation. The brutish horse can *use* (a form of) reason to satisfy its desire; it can use reason as a means to a given end (190). (Notice that this form of reason bears a certain similarity to the reason of the nonlover.) But the charioteer can reason about the end itself; "he" can deliberate about what the best ends of the soul should be (191). One is clearly a much higher form of reason than the other. In the same way, the desire of the charioteer is a much higher form of desire than that of the brutish horse, for it is a desire for the good of the whole soul, whereas the horse cares only for the satisfaction of its own particular desire (191–92).[14] A better interpretation of the image of the chariot thus focuses not on the distinction between (and proper ordering of) reason and desire, but rather on the distinction between (and proper ordering of) forms of reason and desire that aim for the overall good and forms that aim for partial and potentially detrimental satisfactions.

Putting the Dialogues Together

Focusing on the differences between *epithumia* and *eros* helps to make sense of the contrast between the *Republic*'s heavy emphasis on reason controlling desire and the *Symposium*'s and the *Phaedrus*' celebration of the value of (erotic) desire. The different relationships of *eros* and *epithumia* to various kinds of reason and to the good explain why the dialogues differ so markedly on the need for rigid control of desires within the soul. The *Republic*'s central concept of desire is *epithumia*, which means that in this dialogue the desiring and calculating parts of the soul are viewed as distinct and relatively unmixed. As a result, desire in this dialogue is incapable of controlling itself or orienting itself toward the good, and must therefore be controlled by the external force of reason. Moreover, since *epithumia* is devoid of reason (or at least the higher forms of reason), there is no possibility that it can itself lead to a higher form of desire. The central concept of desire in the *Symposium* and the *Phaedrus*, on the other hand, is *eros*, which means that in these dialogues the faculties of desire and reason are seen as more integrated. *Eros* is not a danger to the soul because it is neither irrational nor unconcerned with true value, as *epithumia* is. Under the right circumstances its beginning stages can even lead to much higher stages. Thus, the more the faculties are integrated, the less the need for one to control the other. Indeed, the more reason and desire are

60 • The Trouble With Passion

interwoven, the less it is even possible for one simply to control the other. And this is how the *Republic*'s heavy emphasis on rationality can be directly challenged by the *Phaedrus*' defense of "madness."

Yet one might still wonder about Plato's choice to focus on these two different kinds of desire in these different dialogues. Why does he challenge the conventional understanding of *eros* in the *Symposium* and the *Phaedrus*, but not (for the most part) in the *Republic*? Why, especially, does he champion the potential of *eros* to guide a soul toward the good in the *Symposium* and the *Phaedrus*, but not (for the most part) in the *Republic*? Why does the *Republic* remain so worried by *epithumia* where the other dialogues are not?

One possibility is that Plato's views on the issue of desire simply changed. It is generally accepted that the *Republic* and the *Symposium* are roughly contemporaneous dialogues, while the *Phaedrus* is a later work.[15] It may be that Plato came to see his strict division of the parts of the soul as inadequate, that he came to see the faculties of reason and desire as more complexly interwoven than he had before. Later dialogues may have been written to develop a concept of desire only glimpsed in the *Republic*. Indeed, Martha Nussbaum argues that the *Phaedrus* constitutes a "recantation" of Plato's earlier position on desire.[16] She stresses the difference, much as I did in the early parts of this chapter, between the *Republic*'s disdain of appetite and emotion and the *Phaedrus*' appreciation of their potential value. On the one hand, she says, "it is unequivocally the view of the *Republic* that any state in which the non-intellectual elements dominate or guide will be characterized, no matter what we call it, by the defects of mania: the loss of true insight and a tendency towards excess" (1986, 204–5). On the other hand, the view advanced in the *Phaedrus* is that "Even [the intellect's] own aspirations are best advanced by a richer ferment of the entire personality, in which it is difficult to separate the contributions of one part from those of the others" (221–22). Nussbaum concludes that "There is little doubt that something new is here" (213). The *Phaedrus*, she argues, presents a new view of the cognitive capacity of some forms of passion, a new vision of the structure of the soul. At the same time, it makes a new argument about the psychic and interpersonal elements necessary for a good life, as well as the attitudes and actions that pose a danger to that life.

According to this argument, then, there is a fundamental change in the dialogues' pictures of how the parts of the soul are organized and interact. As we have seen, in the *Republic* there is a fairly rigid division between reason and desire, and in the *Symposium* and the *Phaedrus* the faculties are much more mixed. Another way to say this is to say that the concepts of *eros* and *epithumia* do not simply exist side by side; rather, the developed

"The Madness of Eros Is the Greatest of Heaven's Blessings" • **61**

concept of *eros* is a revision of the place and operation of *epithumia* in the soul. Thus, *epithumia* does not pose as much of a danger to the soul in the *Symposium* and the *Phaedrus* because in these dialogues there is the possibility that *eros* can supersede—as well as help to supervise—*epithumia*. The *Republic*, on the other hand, cannot rely on *eros* in this way because Plato had yet to fully distinguish between *eros* and *epithumia* in that dialogue.

But whether or not this is the case, one might also consider the different political contexts and aims of the different dialogues. Among its many other concerns, the *Republic* is concerned with whether and how an entire city could be just. Both the *Symposium* and the *Phaedrus*, on the other hand, are concerned primarily with the virtue of an elite class of men. This difference has several consequences. The *Republic* must take account of everyone in the city, the majority of whom are assumed to be incapable of coming to understand and desire what is truly valuable. According to Socrates, "it is impossible that a multitude be philosophic" (494a). To be philosophic is, by definition, to love wisdom, and thereby to channel one's desires toward wisdom and away from money, sex, and power. Most people, then, do not have the ability to develop true *eros* (together with reason), which would allow them to govern their own desires; instead, they remain governed by *epithumia*. Working from this assumption, the *Republic* must take tremendous pains to guard against unchecked *epithumia*, pains that include placing those who are ruled by *epithumia* under the governance of philosopher-guardians and ensuring that the guardians themselves do not turn into tyrants. In these circumstances, exploring the danger—and self-defeating nature—of *epithumia* would seem to be particularly pressing.

In the *Symposium* and the *Phaedrus*, the implications of the conversation are largely limited to the class represented by the dialogue participants, who seem to be given the benefit of the doubt as to their ability to come to understand and desire the good. Amongst this elite company, an exploration of what can happen when people at least know enough to know that they lack the good, and are therefore motivated to pursue it, may seem more appropriate. Indeed, since the participants in these dialogues lack the perfect education of the *Republic*'s ideal state, and must therefore find their own way to knowledge and virtue, an exploration of how the desire for the good (*eros*) can lead the way may be all the more necessary. In other words, outside of a well-ordered political regime, the importance of *eros* as an inspiration toward knowledge of the good becomes paramount. And such is the case even in the *Republic*, whose sole appreciation of the positive power of *eros* can be found in the discussion in Books V and VI of how a man who does not live in the ideal state might yet become a philosopher on his own. In this way, the different political

62 • The Trouble With Passion

contexts of the dialogues affect their different emphases on the problems and possibilities of desire.

Learning from Plato's Dialogues: *Eros, Epithumia,* Politics, and Democracy

Keeping all three dialogues in mind, what resources does Plato provide for thinking about passion and politics? As I suggested in the beginning of this chapter, in Plato's dialogues passions and desires are not presumed to be inherently irrational, egoistic, erratic, or extreme. At the same time, neither are they presumed to be inherently thoughtful and just. If we include both *eros* and *epithumia,* each in all of their forms, Plato has accounted for a wide range of possible passions. Having explored both appetites that people seek to satisfy without much thought about anyone's greater good and desires that are deeply interwoven with thoughts about what constitutes a good life, the dialogues illustrate both harmful and beneficial roles that passion may play in politics. The political harm that passion can cause is not hard to see. Passions for wealth or domination can easily motivate unjust behavior—especially among those who have access to power in the first place. But what about the potential benefits of passion? The *eros* developed in the *Symposium* and the *Phaedrus* may be a blessing for a lover and beloved, but is it a blessing for the polis?

Although I intend to argue that Plato's dialogues support the argument that it is, I want to acknowledge the force of various objections to this view. The mere fact that there is relatively little discussion of this higher form of *eros* in the *Republic* and, conversely, relatively little discussion of politics or even justice in the *Symposium* and the *Phaedrus* could suggest that even "true" *eros* is not politically helpful. Certainly in these latter two dialogues *eros* would appear to be primarily about private rather than public life. In both cases, the bulk of the discussion is about the dynamics of passionate relationships between lovers and beloveds, and the effects of such passion on their virtue. Comparing the dramatic contexts of each dialogue, Stanley Rosen notes that the dialogue of the *Republic* occurs during the day amidst a diverse, nonselect group, whereas the dialogue of the *Symposium* takes place at night, at a small private party, and that of the *Phaedrus* outside the city altogether. "*Eros,*" he concludes, "is an affair of privacy, either of the night or the countryside outside the city walls, of drunken enthusiasm which overflows into divine madness" (1965, 455).

Further objections to the notion that *eros* can be politically helpful follow from the much discussed tension between philosophy and politics in Plato's thought. As illustrated above, the *Symposium* and the *Phaedrus* draw a profound connection between *eros* and philosophy. Indeed, these

"The Madness of Eros Is the Greatest of Heaven's Blessings" • **63**

dialogues present philosophy as the supreme expression of *eros*, for the love of wisdom is the highest form of love there is. To the extent, then, that philosophers are drawn toward a contemplative life and away from political involvement—to that extent, the blessings of *eros* may not make their way into the political realm. On this view, *eros* leads people out of the cave, not back in. In Martha Nussbaum's explanation, to come to see the world as Diotima recommends in the *Symposium* "would erode the motivation for running after Alcibiades, for devoting oneself to a particular beloved person, even for loving one city above all other things…. A contemplative life is a natural choice" (1986, 181). Politics remains too particular to be the proper object of *eros*; ideally the philosopher will move beyond it. On the other side of the tension between philosophy and politics, as the philosopher may have a distaste for politics, so the political realm may have a distaste for philosophy. Again, what holds for philosophy holds for *eros*. If the philosopher questions and challenges the political order, it is *eros* that leads "him" to do so. "*Eros*, like tyranny, encourages the individual to disregard nomos, and so it encourages the individual to treason" (Rosen 1965, 460).[17] Of course, such a prospect could well inspire the political establishment to suppress *eros* in the name of order and stability, as did Athens with Socrates.

But this possibility of suppression is itself telling. To begin with, it illustrates that *eros* is not limited to the private realm, for if it were, why would it ever be considered threatening to the public realm? Despite the focus on personal relationships in the *Symposium* and the *Phaedrus*, the *Symposium* itself provides an explicit argument that the passion in such relationships is only one form of *eros*. Since "all desire of good and happiness is only the great and subtle power of *eros*," the desire for political goods (such as justice) also qualifies as *eros*. In fact, "seeing the beauty in institutions and laws" is a much higher form of *eros* than seeing the beauty in one person (1953B, 210c). True, it is not the highest form of all, which sees beyond any particular institutions and laws. But it is a significant expression of *eros* nonetheless. In addition, the possibility that *eros* could lead people to challenge the political order is quite plausibly one of its blessings for Plato. Political orders are often unjust, and therefore in need of challenge. An undue focus on the highly ordered and controlled *kallipolis* of the *Republic* may convey the notion that Plato sees the disruptive potential of *eros* as negative. But I believe this is a misinterpretation, for a number of reasons. First, it is *epithumia*, including its erotic version, that is to be controlled, or, better yet, appropriately channeled and educated whenever possible in the *kallipolis*. "True" *eros* would pose no danger to the just city, since justice is exactly (part of) what it desires. Second, the *kallipolis* is only a "theoretical model of a good city" (472c–e), and perhaps even more

64 • The Trouble With Passion

importantly a model of the soul. Existing cities, which do not approach its justice, do not call for quite the same obedient loyalty. Rather, they call for something like Socrates' response to Athens, as Plato depicts it in the *Apology*, the *Crito*, and the *Gorgias*—that is, for loyalty that is thoroughly imbued with passionate attempts to improve the city through disrupting the moral and intellectual obliviousness, self-satisfaction, and corruption of its citizens.

Of course these three dialogues remind us again of Socrates' fate. There is no doubt that Plato often portrays tension between philosophy and politics. Acknowledging tension, however, is not the same as claiming antithesis: pursuits that exist in tension may nevertheless have great need of each other. Whether Plato's dialogues convey that philosophy needs politics is open to interpretation; whether they proclaim that politics needs philosophy is not. As Socrates famously asserts in the *Republic*, "Until philosophers rule as kings or those who are now called kings and leading men genuinely and adequately philosophize, that is, until political power and philosophy entirely coincide...cities will have no rest from evils, Glaucon, nor, I think, will the human race" (473c–d). But if politics needs philosophy, it needs *eros*.[18] As the supreme form of *eros*, philosophy's contribution to politics is also *eros'* contribution.

What, then, is philosophy's contribution to politics? It is twofold. First, philosophy leads to wisdom about the good, which in turn provides guidance for the ship of state toward the good (and therefore justice). Second, philosophy replaces people's corrupting desires for such things as money, sex, and power with the noncorrupting desire for knowledge. The second contribution is, I venture to say, more important than the first, for even if perfect knowledge of the good is not attained, so long as people believe that the quest for knowledge will fulfill their souls more profoundly than anything else, they will not be interested in behaving unjustly even when they have the power to do so.[19] In this way, philosophy combats the temptation to tyrannize. And since it is the erotic desire for knowledge that both instigates the quest for knowledge of the good and channels the soul away from the epithumetic desire for power, it is *eros* that in many ways is responsible for leading the city to justice and protecting it from tyranny.

I have argued that the political contribution of *eros* is embodied in the political contribution of philosophy. But *eros* contributes one thing above and beyond that of philosophy: the desire to "beget" virtue in others. Recall that in the *Phaedrus*, *eros* inspires the lover not only to be virtuous himself but to try to bring out the god/good that he sees in his beloved as well. In the *Symposium*, Diotima explains that while those who are pregnant in body beget children, those who are pregnant in soul beget wisdom and virtue. Such is the case with poets and artists, "But the greatest and

"The Madness of Eros Is the Greatest of Heaven's Blessings" • **65**

fairest sort of wisdom by far is that which is concerned with the ordering of states and families, and which is called temperance and justice. And he who in youth has the seed of these implanted in his soul, when he grows up and comes to maturity desires to beget and generate" (209a–b). In this way, *eros* leads to public service, that is, to actions aimed at benefiting and improving the polis.

As examples of such public service, Diotima lists the laws that Lycurgus and Solon each provided for their cities. But the life of Socrates, as depicted by Plato, provides an even more interesting illustration. Although Socrates notes in the *Apology* that he has avoided participating in the formal political structures of Athens for his own safety, in the *Gorgias* he claims to be the only man in Athens to "practice politics" (521d). What could this claim mean? As Waller Newell interprets it,

> Socrates "practices politics" primarily by cultivating friendships. Although the *Republic* culminates in the lesson that one cannot impose the pattern of the good *tout court* on a city, one can begin to cultivate friends in one's actual city—friendships guided by the pattern of the good that one founds in the soul through philosophical investigations of politics and virtue of the kind that Socrates conducts with his partners. Beginning with these friendships mediated by the good, one can move outward gradually to effect larger reforms in the direction of the optimal politiea (2000, 71).

Or, as Newell puts it later, Socrates "practiced the art of ruling by compelling his friends to think about the meaning of virtue before presuming to rule over others" (84). His constant questioning of his friends and fellow citizens was a form of political action. And as both the *Symposium* and the *Phaedrus* amply convey, Socrates' questioning was motivated by *eros*. Socrates, who "profess[es] to understand nothing but matters of *eros*," is Plato's supreme example of a person imbued with true *eros*, and, not coincidentally, his supreme example of a person dedicated to promoting justice.[20]

Following from the political importance of passion and reason in Plato's dialogues is the political importance of the education of these capacities. No one is born inherently just: this cognitive/emotional capacity must be developed. Moreover, as the dialogues illustrate, selfish and/or unjust passions cannot simply be repressed or confined to some private sphere. The specter of a Thrasymachus or an Alcibiades always looms, even in a democracy. Hence, there is a tremendous emphasis on the education of passion and reason in Plato's dialogues. Books III, VI, and VII of the *Republic* are all devoted primarily to the proper education of a guardian or philosopher (or the harmful effects of a bad education). Likewise,

66 • The Trouble With Passion

the *Symposium* and the *Phaedrus* both illustrate a process by which lovers learn to develop *eros*. What is the nature of this education of passion and reason? Here Plato provides a thought-provoking model. Despite some impressions given by the *Republic*, it is not a matter of teaching reason to *control* or *suppress* passion. Rather, it is a matter of developing forms of reason and passion that together aim for an overall good instead of partial and potentially detrimental satisfactions. In Plato's argument, we must learn to investigate and evaluate the objects of our desire and to *channel* our desires towards objects that are worthwhile, redirecting misguided or self-defeating desires. The process is one of integration. Pointing to the common experience of being "at war" with oneself, of desiring something with one part and recoiling from it with another, the dialogues acknowledge the power of our passions for things that we realize we cannot have or that will not bring us satisfaction or happiness in the long run. The fundamental question is: How do we come to change what we want? The answer must involve getting the various parts of ourselves to work together, integrating our intellect and will and emotions so that the self as a whole comes to understand and desire what is truly valuable.[21] Here reason does not control passion; rather, the two work together.

Finally, I argue that Plato's dialogues illustrate that the education of citizens' passions is an important component of a just and vibrant democracy.[22] This argument may seem untenable given that there is no explicit depiction of a just democracy in the dialogues, nor much optimism that one could exist. But it is precisely the *Republic*'s infamous criticism of democracy that demonstrates my point. The problems with democracy identified in this dialogue have everything to do with the dangers of passion. As we have seen, in the argument of the *Republic*, those who have not developed a desire for the good and are dominated by *epithumia* are not suited to rule, whether in a monarchy or a democracy. The argument is self-evident in the case of monarchy, for a monarch driven by appetites would be a tyrant. Such a person would not be willing or even able to use his or her power for the good of the community (that is, to use power justly) and so should not be entrusted with power. The more difficult case is to show that this argument holds in a democracy as well. A democracy, as Socrates himself describes it, is characterized by great freedom and tolerance (557b, 558b). Since the citizens share power equally and allow each other equal freedom to pursue their own desires, nothing would seem to be farther from a tyranny. And yet Socrates places the democratic regime one step away from a tyranny. The reason is that the freedom to pursue all desires equally is in effect a rejection of the need for any kind of judgment about the relative value of desired objects. For the democrat, "all pleasures are equal and must be valued equally" (561c). The consequence is that the democrat cannot be trusted to use, or even delegate, political power for the good of the community either. For to do so would require making distinctions between better and worse goods that the democrat is unwilling to make. It would also require thinking in terms of justice rather than one's personal pleasures.[23] A democracy such as this is vulnerable to potential tyrants who can learn to manipulate the appetites of the people, turn the wealthy against the rest, and thereby gain power over all (564a–566d).

The key point here is that this argument depends in great part on an assumption that most people will be dominated by *epithumia* and incapable of developing *eros*. Put another way, the *Republic's* critique of democracy is conditional: it is dependent on a belief that only a minority are capable of developing the ability first to distinguish between the value of different kinds of desires and then to act accordingly. What if we do not accept this belief? Imagine, for a moment, a city of people like Socrates.[24] Though the example is an extreme one, surely Plato would accept that with such a citizenry, a democracy would not devolve into anarchy and potential tyranny. Indeed, with a citizenry of people capable of governing their own desires and pursuing the good, no other form of government but democracy would be justified, for the argument for a more hierarchical political order was based on the assumption that people could not maintain order within their own souls. But if it is *eros* that affords the possibility for a just democracy—a democracy in which political power is used for the good of the community—then one key condition for a just democracy is the education of citizens' desires.

Diverging from Plato's Theory of Passion

It remains to emphasize that, while I believe there are valuable lessons to learn from Plato's dialogues, I am in no way arguing for adopting his philosophy wholesale. It is important to move beyond two aspects of Plato's theory of passion in particular: his identification of *eros* as the desire for the one, true good and his association of *eros* with a disembodied masculinity.

As I discussed in Chapter 2, the concept of passion that I argue for does not assume, as Plato's concept of *eros* does, that there is only one true passion, a passion for the objective and universal good. Rather, my concept assumes that there are myriad passions for and commitments to envisioned goods, the value of which are open for debate. What I take from Plato's argument is that there is a meaningful difference between passions: some are short-sighted and others take the long view; some are generous and others are self-serving; some are for largely personal ends and others are for broader, more political ends. A passion for justice is profoundly

68 • The Trouble With Passion

different from a passion for wealth. Clearly this argument presumes that there *is* such a thing as justice—at least as an ideal for which it is worth striving. To say this, however, is not to say, as Plato would, that justice is an objective, unchanging, universal reality that exists independently of human creation. On the contrary, I would argue that justice is a humanly constructed ideal that can only be (imperfectly) approached through the human activity of politics.

There is, of course, a notorious issue here: how is it possible to judge without absolute standards? If justice is a humanly constructed ideal, then it will vary across time, place, culture, and even person, and if that is the case, what makes any one vision of justice better than another? How can there be a meaningful difference between passions if there are no fixed criteria (*eide*) by which to evaluate their objects? Age-old as it is, this issue is hardly one that I can resolve. I can, however, indicate the perspective I take on it. My perspective is that an absence of absolute standards removes neither the need to make judgments, nor the possibility of doing so. We can only debate what would be just—but we *can* debate and we *must* debate. Human judgments need not be arbitrary for being human; they can be responsible to those involved, empathetic, informed about the issues at stake, well considered, attentive to the context, and so forth. Judgments such as these can and should provide guidance in evaluating the objects of passions.

The second main problem with Plato's theory of passion concerns his gendered associations of *eros* with masculinity and *epithumia* with femininity. In Plato's dialogues, *eros* is exhibited solely by men or, at most, women who are like men. As many critics have pointed out, despite the limited radicalism of Book V, women are allowed into the *Republic*'s guardian class only at the expense of any characteristics that Plato would consider womanly (aside from the physical act of bearing children).[25] Much the same point can be made about Diotima in the *Symposium*: although Socrates cites her as an authority on *eros*, she is arguably not very representative of womanhood for Plato.[26] Moreover, Diotima echoes the claims of Aristophanes and Pausanias before her (191d–192b, 181b–c) that the highest form of love is between men, contrasting men who turn to women to beget "mortal children" with men who turn to other men to beget the "fairer and more immortal" creations of the soul (208e–209c). Finally, women are entirely absent from the investigation of *eros* in the *Phaedrus*. Thus is *eros* strongly associated with men and masculinity.

At the same time, women and femininity are explicitly associated with *epithumia*—as well as with the body, appetites, emotions, sexuality, and worldly existence. In a reciprocal process, women are disparaged as mired in bodily appetites and emotions, while all those who are considered mired

"The Madness of Eros Is the Greatest of Heaven's Blessings" • **69**

in bodily appetites and emotions (whether male or female) are disparaged as womanly and effeminate. In discussing the role of poetry and drama in education, for example, Socrates repeatedly argues that men should never imitate women:

> Then we won't allow those for whom we profess to care, and who must grow into good men, to imitate either a young woman or an older one, or one abusing her husband, quarreling with the gods, or bragging because she thinks herself happy, or one suffering misfortune and possessed by sorrows and lamentations, and even less one who is ill, in love, or in labor (395d–e).

As this passage illustrates, Plato depicts women as *characteristically* tied to some emotion or bodily function, clearly a degrading condition that men must do their best to avoid. Again, the guardian women are not portrayed in this way, but that is precisely the sign of their praiseworthy transcendence of any conventionally feminine characteristics. The crucial point is that, although the majority of men in Plato's dialogues are also described as having immoderate desires and unworthy emotions, these characteristics are not incorporated into Plato's understanding of what makes men "manly" as they are incorporated into his understanding of what makes women "womanly."

As already suggested, Plato's disparagement of femininity is connected to his disparagement of the body. There is no doubt that the body is largely disdained in Plato's dialogues.[27] Even in the *Symposium* and the *Phaedrus*, both of which place more value on the emotional aspects of life than other dialogues, detachment from the body is counseled. At the extreme, the body is presented as a "prison" for the soul (*Phaedo*). What Plato ultimately values in *eros*, then, cannot be any of its bodily manifestations. For him, *eros* ideally transcends both sexuality and biological reproduction; it is not oriented towards bodies (or perhaps even people at all) but rather toward the *eide*, and its products are not mortal children but ideas, wisdom, and virtue.[28] Not surprisingly, this view leads to an argument for transcending the body—along with all material things that grow and change and decay—as much as possible. The final result of this argument is a rejection of worldly existence. If the body is a prison for the soul, then the ultimate goal is to transcend the body completely—that is, to die. As Socrates argues in the *Phaedo*, philosophy is actually preparation for death, for "We are in fact convinced that if we are ever to have pure knowledge of anything, we must get rid of the body and contemplate things by themselves with the soul by itself" (66d–e). Thus, Plato's highest form of

70 • The Trouble With Passion

desire is arguably not so much a desire for life as a desire to escape the limitations of life.

What does this mean for Plato's theory of passion? As we have seen, in the *Symposium* and the *Phaedrus* Plato explicitly defines *eros* in opposition to *epithumia*. By ultimately excluding womanliness and bodies and sexuality from (true) *eros*, Plato has also effectively defined *eros* in opposition to these things. One could argue, then (as several feminist and political theorists explicitly do), that Plato's concept of *eros* is in fact disembodied, antiseptic, masculinist, and even death-oriented. Needless to say, I am not interested in conceiving of passion in this way. I am interested in a concept of passion that can embrace multiplicity, change, embodiment, and the needs and pleasures of concrete existence. In my view, passion is about life, not death. It is in part as a counter to this aspect of Plato's thinking that I discuss a number of feminist concepts of *eros* as "life-loving energy" in Chapter 6.

Conclusion

Clearly, I depart from Plato's theory of passion in some significant ways. Nevertheless, the complex picture of passion that his dialogues present is useful as an illustration of how political theorists might take passion seriously, explore its relationship to reason, and consider the ways in which these human capacities combine to play inescapable and potentially valuable roles in politics. Passion can be a blessing as well as a curse; the same holds true for reason. Both can be employed in the service of justice or injustice. Consequently, one of Plato's main messages is that nothing is more important than to encourage the development of just forms of passion and reason—even, and perhaps especially, in a democracy. While this message has its limitations for modern liberal nation-states, I believe it also has some merit, which I shall return to in the concluding chapter. In the next chapter, I turn to Rousseau for an argument that differs from Plato's and yet concurs on the importance of the education of passion.

CHAPTER **5**

"A Man Who Had No Passions Would Be a Very Bad Citizen": Rousseau's Passion for Community

On the topic of the political value of passion, few thinkers offer the kind of help that Rousseau would seem to promise. A theorist of modernity who shares at least some of the values of liberal theory (such as freedom, equality, and popular sovereignty), Rousseau nevertheless offers serious criticisms of liberalism's faith in reason and suspicion of passion. These criticisms are perhaps most evident in his *Discourse on the Origin of Inequality*, an essay that ruthlessly denounces most of the supposed accomplishments of which the "Age of Reason" was so proud, while at the same time paying frequent homage to the dictates of the heart. Indeed, the *Second Discourse* goes so far as to challenge the notion that reason is the source of morality.

But what place does Rousseau in fact make for passion in politics? The answer to this question is not immediately obvious, for much of his specific writing about passion is not explicitly linked to his discussions of politics. Moreover, the question is especially vexing when we consider the *Social Contract*. As many have noted, it is a strange text in the context of Rousseau's other writings.[1] To my mind, the strangest thing about it is its dryness, the unusually detached and dispassionate tone of its voice. Yet the *Social Contract* can hardly be dismissed: it is Rousseau's central political text. My purpose in this chapter is thus to explore Rousseau's argument

71

72 • The Trouble With Passion

about the role of passion and sentiment in politics, with special attention to the case of the *Social Contract*. I argue that, despite the *Social Contract*'s apparent turn toward the kind of dispassionate rationalism criticized in the *Second Discourse*, Rousseau does maintain, in this work as well as others, that certain kinds of passion are crucially important to a healthy political society. I also argue, however, that the *Social Contract*'s comparative silence on the subject of passion does point us to specific shortcomings in its theorization of passion, shortcomings that are instructive for those interested in considering the positive roles that passion might play in politics.

The chapter begins with a discussion of terminology. Next I compare Rousseau's treatment of passion and reason in the *Second Discourse* with that in the *Social Contract*, in order to establish the questions the former might raise about the latter. For it is especially in the context of this earlier essay that one may wonder what has happened in the *Social Contract* to Rousseau's appreciation for the value of passion. After this initial comparison, I explore two interpretations of Rousseau's thought that would seem to indicate that he has indeed largely given up on passion in the *Social Contract*. Both arguments, I argue, are misleading, as attention to some of Rousseau's other explicitly political work shows. Finally, I return for a closer, and at this point I trust clearer, look at the fate of passion in the *Social Contract*. I conclude with some criticisms of Rousseau's theory of passion.

Rousseau's Terminology of Passion and Reason

To speak of "reason" and "passion" in discussing Rousseau's writing is in some ways to reduce and oversimplify his language. He does write about *raison*, but he also writes about, among other things, *l'entendement* (understanding), *refléxion, intellegence*, and *lumiéres* (enlightenment). And while he frequently refers to *passions*, he also refers to *sentiment* (sentiment, feeling), *amour* (love), *pitié, désir, appétit*, and *inclination*. Certainly these terms have at least somewhat differing senses and may be used for different reasons. Failing to acknowledge the distinctions among them risks missing the specifics of Rousseau's arguments. Yet generalizations have their purpose as well: without them we cannot see the proverbial forest for the trees. In Rousseau's case I think it is fair to say that reason and passion are umbrella categories, broad terms that more or less encompass the rest. For one thing, *raison* and *passion* are the terms Rousseau uses most often. Moreover, Rousseau specifically designates *amour, pitié, désir,* and *appétit* as forms of passion or sentiment.[2] Finally, *raison* and *passion* are each freely interchanged with various of the words listed above. In the

Second Discourse, for example, Rousseau writes that "human *understanding* owes much to the passions.... It is by their activity that our *reason* is perfected." Two sentences later, he writes: "For one can *desire* or fear things only by virtue of the ideas one can have of them, or from the simple impulse of nature; and savage man, deprived of every sort of *enlightenment*, feels only the *passion* of the latter sort" (1987, 45–46, my emphasis). Elsewhere, in his discussion of love, he begins by distinguishing between "the moral and the physical aspects of the *sentiment* of *love*," and then asserts that "it is incontestable that *love* itself, like all other *passions*, had acquired only in society that impetuous ardor which so often makes it lethal to men" (56, my emphasis). Given Rousseau's routine alternations between reason, understanding, and enlightenment on the one hand, and desire, sentiment, and passion on the other, considering "reason" and "passion" to be general categories seems justified.

The primary objection to this position, set forth in Amélie Rorty's article "Rousseau's Therapeutic Experiments," is that there is actually an important distinction between passion and sentiment in Rousseau's writing. Rorty bases her argument in part on Rousseau's different entries for *passions* and *sentiments* in *L'Encyclopédie des Sciences et des Arts*, in part on a passage distinguishing the two in the Preface to *Julie*, and in part on her overall reading of Rousseau's corpus. Considering all of these sources, Rorty argues that passions for Rousseau are typically intense, "impulsively motivating," exclusive, uncritical emotions centered around self-preservation and sexuality. Sentiments, on the other hand, are gentler, "less dominating on attention and on action," more inclusive and generalizable emotions that are "implicitly forms of evaluative judgment" (1991, 425). Rorty acknowledges that the categories overlap, that in some cases Rousseau may describe an emotion as both a passion and a sentiment. But she believes the difference is still significant, that sentiments require "principled" "universalizing" reflection and critical examination (thus rendering them "stable" and "benevolent") while passions rely only on a "narrowly prudential calculation" (420).

Rorty's argument is analytically useful insofar as it characterizes the sorts of emotions Rousseau praises versus the sorts he deplores. It also makes the excellent point that reason and passion are less opposed than intertwined in Rousseau's thought, a point that will be discussed in more detail below. But I do not think Rorty's use of the terms *passion* and *sentiment* to differentiate between the two kinds of emotions described above is borne out in Rousseau's writing. The problem is not only that the terms overlap in some cases. The problem is that Rousseau often uses the term *passion* to refer to precisely those emotions that Rorty describes as characteristically sentiments. In both *The Government of Poland* and the

74 • The Trouble With Passion

Discourse on Political Economy, each of which discusses the development of generalized, civic emotions, the primary term Rousseau uses is passion.[3] Likewise, Rousseau frequently uses the term *sentiment* to refer to precisely those emotions Rorty describes as passions, as in the following passage:

> We must not confuse egocentricism (*l'amour propre*) with love of oneself (*l'amour de soi*), two *passions* very different by virtue of both their nature and their effect. Love of oneself is a natural *sentiment* which moves every animal to be vigilant in its own preservation and which, directed in man by reason and modified by pity, produces humanity and virtue. Egocentrism is merely a *sentiment* that is relative, artificial and born in society, which moves each individual to value himself more than anyone else, which inspires in men all the evils they cause one another, and which is the true source of honor (1987, 106, my emphasis).

In short, while Rousseau may distinguish between passion and sentiment in *L'Encyclopédie*, he does not adhere to the distinction in his own writing with any consistency. Following him, I do not distinguish between them in this chapter either.[4]

Pity and Self-love versus a Sublime Reason

Evidence that Rousseau criticizes rationalism and celebrates at least some forms of passion can be found in most of his writings, but I focus here on the *Second Discourse*. The importance of passion is emphasized throughout the *Discourse*, Rousseau's imaginary history of humanity.[5] Early on he identifies the "first and most simple operations of the soul" as *amour de soi* and *pitié* (35). Rousseau argues that these tendencies, which precede the development of reason in human beings, are crucial elements in ensuring that human interactions will be as peaceful as possible. Indeed, Rousseau says that *pitié* "takes the place of laws, mores, and virtue" in the state of nature and thereby helps to preserve the species (55). Now, it is also true that the *Second Discourse* includes numerous references to passions as immoderate and destructive.[6] As we have already seen, the passion of *amour propre* in particular is singled out as that which "inspires in men all the evil they cause one another." In all of his writings Rousseau consistently praises limited and sincere passions and is deeply concerned about the effect of immoderate or inauthentic passions. But the point is that only passions that are excessive in this way are presented as problematic in the *Second Discourse*. Rousseau's praise of simple passions is still a striking— and pivotal—feature of this text.

"A Man Who Had No Passions Would Be a Very Bad Citizen" • **75**

Perhaps the main reason the *Second Discourse*'s defense of simple passions is so striking is because it is accompanied by a radical perspective on the damage caused by reason. In sharp contrast to the *philosophes* of his time, Rousseau presents the "progress" that accompanies the development of reason as in many ways a regress. One of the key ways emerging reason "deteriorat[es] the species" is by stifling natural compassion (59). Reason, says Rousseau, "turns man in upon himself. Reason is what separates him from all that troubles him and afflicts him." The consequence is that the philosopher "has merely to place his hands over his ears and argue with himself a little" to ignore the cries of his fellow man, while "for lack of wisdom and reason [savage man] is always seen thoughtlessly giving in to the first sentiment of humanity" (54–55). Challenging the rationalist argument that moral behavior depends primarily on the use of reason, Rousseau contends that "with all their mores, men would never have been anything but monsters if nature had not given them pity to aid their reason" (54).[7]

It is important to note that despite these criticisms, Rousseau has not made a wholesale argument against reason in the *Second Discourse*. As Jean Starobinski puts it, the essay gives an "ambiguous" role to reflection (1988, 205). The capacity for reason is in large part responsible for human separation from the natural world, and thus has many disastrous consequences, but it also has the potential for important positive consequences as well. Seeing a "greater destination" for the human species than that of those species ruled by instinct, Rousseau makes it quite clear that he would not advocate abandoning reason and social existence even if it were possible to do so (94–95). Of course, he does not believe it *is* possible to avoid or retreat from reason, in part because of human passions, which drive its development: "It is by [the passions'] activity that our reason is perfected. We seek to know only because we desire to have enjoyment; and it is impossible to conceive why someone who had neither desires nor fears would go to the bother of reasoning." Conversely, the development of reason drives the development of passions: "The passions in turn take their origin from our needs, and their progress from our knowledge. For one can desire or fear things only by virtue of the ideas one can have of them" (46). Ultimately, then, Rousseau argues in the *Second Discourse* that there is a complex and inseparable relationship between reason and passion. He also suggests that both capacities have the potential for beneficial and harmful effects, depending on the form they take.[8] Although he does not make much of the point here, Rousseau has set the ground for the argument (made most fully in *Émile*) that one must develop the best forms of each. The notion that both reason and *pitié* are necessary for morality suggests such an argument.

76 • The Trouble With Passion

Based on these positions, one would expect Rousseau to advocate turning to passion as well as reason in political matters. I argue below that indeed he does. But such a conclusion is not easily reached, for the first place one looks for his model of politics, the *Social Contract*, appears to embrace the kind of abstract rationalism he criticizes elsewhere. To argue that Rousseau treats politics as a passionate enterprise thus requires coming to terms with this text. Let me begin with the issue of its tone. I suggested above that the *Social Contract* is the driest, least fervent of all Rousseau's writings. For the purposes of contrast, consider once again the *Second Discourse*. In this essay, the tone is anything but neutral: from the effusive (if perhaps ironic) dedication to Geneva as a model city to the final pages condemning the current state of society, this essay champions the cause of freedom, laments the development of inequality and injustice, and bitterly denounces insincerity and callousness. To support his stands, Rousseau does not call only—or perhaps even primarily—on reason and logic. Rather, he appeals to the imagination and empathy of his readers, asking them to identify with the admittedly fictional characters he presents in his version of humanity's "history" and in this way attempting to get his readers to *care* about the problems he describes. Following the precept later articulated through the tutor in *Émile*, the *Second Discourse* "makes the language of the mind pass through the heart" (1979, 323).

When we proceed to the *Social Contract*, however, we find this passionate language is gone. In its place is a highly abstract, detached, analytical discussion of the way a legitimate political society should be ordered. Speaking explicitly of the tone of the work in his *Confessions*, Rousseau himself describes it as derived from "an enterprise in which I meant to employ solely the power of reason, without any vestige of venom or prejudice" (1953, 378).[9] The particular concern Rousseau expresses here was that the work not bear any marks of Diderot's "satirical" and "caustic" influence on him, but the point is that although his political positions are hardly neutral in this text either, here he deliberately sought to express them in a much more objective-sounding manner. In contrast to the *Second Discourse*'s vivid depictions of individual thoughts and emotions, the *Social Contract* proceeds almost exclusively at the level of general principles. In addition, in this text Rousseau often calls on logic and definition, and even mathematics, to make his arguments. His case against a "right" of slavery, for example, rests heavily on the contention that such a right would be "inconceivable," "absurd," and "contradictory"[10]; what it does *not* rest upon is an evocative depiction of the misery of slavery. At times Rousseau puts so much weight on the definition of terms that his arguments appear as tricks of logic. For example, he argues that a sovereign cannot commit itself to anything that goes against the original act of association,

"A Man Who Had No Passions Would Be a Very Bad Citizen" • **77**

because "to violate the act by which it exists would be to destroy itself, and whatever is nothing produces nothing" (1994, 140). And despite his disclaimer that "geometrical precision does not exist in moral quantities," Rousseau repeatedly attempts in the *Social Contract* to explain the optimum relationships between the sovereign, the government, the citizens, and the subjects in terms of ratios and proportions (167–173). These rhetorical strategies depart significantly from the emotional appeals of the *Second Discourse*.

Furthermore, there is little talk of passions in the *Social Contract*, and what talk there is generally presents them as a problem. True, Rousseau pays some attention here to the role of affect in political unity and behavior. He argues that large states are not good because they diminish the "affection" citizens have for their leaders, their fatherland, and each other; he describes a well-run city as one in which citizens care more about public affairs than private affairs and everyone "rushes" to assemblies (159); and he concludes the book with his famous argument for a civil religion, whose "sentiments of sociability" (192) are necessary to make citizens "love [their] duties" (222).[11] But these references virtually exhaust the explicitly positive remarks about passion in the *Social Contract*, and they are overshadowed by the much more dominant theme of the need to rise above or rule passions, appetites, and inclinations. Shifting perspective from the *Second Discourse*, in the *Social Contract* Rousseau praises the development from the state of nature into an *ideal* civil society in which justice replaces instinct, duty replaces physical impulse, and right replaces appetite. With this development, "man, who until that time only considered himself, find[s] himself forced to act upon other principles and to consult his reason before heeding his inclinations" (141). Here, then, reason would seem to be presented as the solution to the problem of passions. The stated goal is for reason to rule instinct and inclination, replacing them as the guide to behavior. There is, significantly, no mention of *pitié*. Here, too, genuine freedom is conceived as freedom from the rule of passions: "To the foregoing acquisitions of the civil state could be added moral freedom, which alone makes man truly the master of himself. For the impulse of appetite alone is slavery, and obedience to the law one has prescribed for oneself is freedom" (142). Further confirmation of this argument that reason ought to guide and rule passion is provided by Rousseau's discussion of the legislator. The legislator, who guides the people in establishing the rules of society, is himself guided by a "sublime reason" (156). His qualifications include his ability to "[see] all of men's passions yet [experience] none of them" (154). In the argument of the *Social Contract*, then, the founding of a good political society requires transcending "men's passions."

78 • The Trouble With Passion

At this point we might ask: what has happened in the *Social Contract* to the idea of passion as a foundation of humanity and virtue? Indeed, what has happened to the critique of reason? In the *Second Discourse* Rousseau argued that too much reliance on reason leads us astray, encouraging indifference and stifling compassion; in the *Social Contract* he seems to reiterate the familiar refrain that passions lead us astray, and so we must rely on reason to control them. This apparent reversal leads to a further question: what has happened to the argument that reason and passion are inseparable? For while the *Second Discourse* emphasizes the complex relationship between the two, the *Social Contract* demonstrates little acknowledgment of this relationship. In general, the heavy emphasis on *amour de soi* and *pitié* as beneficial sentiments shifts to an equally heavy emphasis on the saving grace of sublime reason. At the same time, the *Second Discourse*'s emotional appeals are replaced by the *Social Contract*'s detached invocation of logic. We are left with a political realm that seems very rational but not very passionate.

The State of Nature versus Modern Society

One might contend that there is an obvious explanation for the difference between the *Second Discourse* and the *Social Contract* in that the texts presume two different contexts: in the first case, the state of nature as contrasted with existing society; in the second case, political society as it might be, if established properly. From this perspective, the shift from passion to reason could be considered to reflect a process of development. While passions in the state of nature are limited to the beneficial sentiments of *amour de soi* and *pitié*, which need not be constrained, passions in society have become excessive and harmful, and therefore must be constrained. Likewise, while reason is originally unnecessary, and may even block access to beneficial passions, once we have left the state of nature it becomes our best resource for controlling harmful passions. Outside the state of nature, in political society, we can no longer count on passion to lead us well and must turn to reason. There is some evidence for this thesis, particularly in the *Second Discourse*. The narrative strategy of this essay sets up a chronological development, centrally marked by changes in both the nature of the passions and the need for reason. The framework encourages the perspective that passion is appropriate in the state of nature and reason is appropriate in society: "In instinct alone, man had everything he needed in order to live in the state of nature; in a cultivated reason, he has only what he needs to live in society" (52). Moreover, Rousseau explicitly suggests that when passions become problematic, reason must come to the rescue. Once the passions have become complex and

"A Man Who Had No Passions Would Be a Very Bad Citizen" • **79**

inflamed, "the unbridled passions of all, stifling natural pity and the still weak voice of justice, made men greedy, ambitious, and wicked" (68). It is under these circumstances that reason must "reestablish on other foundations" (those of justice) the principles of right that were first established by *amour de soi* and *pitié* (35). This construction of the problem would seem to lead directly into the argument of the *Social Contract*.

But although it has persuasive elements, this explanation for the *Social Contract*'s difference from the *Second Discourse* is insufficient. For despite Rousseau's ubiquitous strategy of contraposing "nature" and society, he himself has made it clear that we cannot effectively separate what is natural in human beings from what is social. As he explains in the *Second Discourse*, the task is akin to discerning the true shape of the statue of Glaucus, which has been weathered to the point of being nearly unrecognizable (33). It is for this reason that Rousseau admits from the start that his history of humanity is conjectural. Indeed, he goes so far as to suggest that the state of nature "perhaps never existed" (34). That Rousseau proceeds to offer an account of the state of nature, having said as much, suggests that accurately isolating nature from culture is not his purpose.[12] Rather, his purpose is to make a set of points about the *relationship* between nature and culture. By providing an alternative to the dominant depiction of "the state of nature" as a state of war, Rousseau attempts to unsettle existing assumptions about human nature, assumptions that ignore the profound effects of social and environmental factors on character. The philosophers, he says, have all "transferred to the state of nature the ideas they acquired in society. They spoke about savage man and it was civil man they depicted" (38). In other words, they have ignored the way in which human beings change, behaving differently under different circumstances. What Rousseau's story illustrates, even though the specifics are fictional, is a thesis about the remarkable malleability of human beings. This point is emphasized by his theoretical account of human nature, which crucially includes within that nature the qualities (reason and perfectibility) that will inevitably lead human beings out of the state of nature. Rousseau thus argues, in effect, that it is the nature of human beings to be "unnatural." Put another way, we cannot effectively separate what is natural in human beings from what is social because, other than in some mythical state of nature (and even then, eventually), "human nature" inherently both creates and is created by society.

If this is the case, then there is a serious problem with the framework that views Rousseau's shift in emphasis from passion to reason in terms of the shift from the state of nature to developed society. The problem is that the story of the state of nature cannot be taken literally. The state of nature "no longer exists…perhaps never existed…[and] probably never will exist" (34).

80 • The Trouble With Passion

It will not do, then, to conclude that passions are beneficial in the state of nature but harmful in society. Nature and society are intertwined. Whatever problems and possibilities the passions hold, they exist within this intertwined context. Indeed, if there were no hope that passions could be beneficial in society, there would be no point in Rousseau's ever praising them. The story he tells in the *Second Discourse* is not meant to mourn the irretrievable loss of purely natural passions, but rather to persuade his readers that passions are changeable, that their current harmful forms are not their only possible forms. Following this argument, one of the central projects he takes up in both *Émile* and *Julie* is precisely how to mold passions to be simple and beneficial *in society*, to develop, for example, the *social* virtues of generosity and benevolence that the *Second Discourse* identifies as stemming from *pitié* (54). As it turns out, this is by no means a simple task, but it is a task that Rousseau strongly advocates. The same argument holds for the case of reason: both the possibilities and the problems of reason exist in a natural/social context. There is no tidy division between a time when reason was unnecessary and harmful and a time when it is the only source of salvation. In the natural/social context, reason is always necessary and it is also always a mixed blessing.[13] One of Rousseau's main criticisms of reason, that it blocks access to beneficial passions, is in fact a criticism of how reason is used *in society*—even though he has also argued that reason is a key resource for solving the problems of a developed society. Thus, the nature versus society thesis does not explain why the *Social Contract* differs from the *Second Discourse* in emphasizing reason so much more than passion.

Private Passion versus Public Reason

How else are we to come to terms with the *Social Contract*'s treatment of passion? Perhaps its departure from the *Second Discourse* stems not so much from a different context as from a different purpose. Specifically, one might argue that it is the normative political project of the *Social Contract* that dictates a particularly rational approach and emphasis. Focusing on the issue of rhetorical style, one might contend that the *Second Discourse*'s critique of society is well served by a certain dramatic presentation, but that a more rational mode is required to set out the political principles of the *Social Contract*.[14] While this distinction also has some persuasive power, though, I think it begs the question. For why should a discussion of political principles require a dispassionate tone? As we have seen, Rousseau himself says he wanted the work to "employ solely the power of reason." But he also writes in *Émile* that "One of the

"A Man Who Had No Passions Would Be a Very Bad Citizen" • **81**

errors of our age is to use reason in too unadorned a form, as if men were all mind…. Reason alone is not active. It sometimes restrains, it arouses rarely, and it has never done anything great…. Strong souls have quite another language. It is with this language that one persuades and makes others act" (1979, 321). It seems strange indeed that Rousseau would choose to use language that "persuades and makes others act" in virtually all of his works except the one that presents his model of a legitimate society.[15] But setting this enigma aside, the important point is that the issue of the *Social Contract*'s rational approach cannot be dismissed as simply a matter of "appropriate" style, for Rousseau is consciously critical of such canons.

Perhaps the normative political project of the text dictates its emphasis on reason in a different way, then. Several feminist interpreters have suggested that it is precisely when Rousseau begins to speak of the public realm that he leaves passion behind. These writers draw parallels between Rousseau's exclusion of women from the public sphere and a purported exclusion of passion from the public sphere.[16] Iris Marion Young, for example, contends that for Rousseau "the civic public expresses the universal and impartial point of view of reason, standing opposed to and expelling desire, sentiment, and the particularity of needs and interests." Hence "women must be excluded from the public realm of citizenship because they are the caretakers of affectivity, desire, and the body" (1990, 108–9). For Lynda Lange as well, the general will is "an ideal of reason" in which "ideally, the input of particular bodily or emotional desires is zero." Like Young, Lange notes that Rousseau sees a need for affective ties in the family. But whereas men, in his argument, should "transcend" such affective ties to be good citizens, women should not, primarily because their "moral end" in civil society is "to affirm and maintain particular relations, rather than to strive for generality" (1994, 100, 102, 105).[17] A somewhat different argument for why women must be excluded from public life is put forward by Carole Pateman, who maintains that for Rousseau only men are even capable of being good citizens, because "only men are capable of sublimating their passions and thus capable of the justice that civil life demands" (1989, 22). Despite some variations, each of these interpretations advances a similar thesis, effectively encapsulated in Julia Simon-Ingram's statement that the *Social Contract* "divides the public from the private, and hence men from women and reason from affectivity" (1991, 148).[18]

It is crucial to note that these theorists generally use the terms "desire," sentiment, affectivity, and passion to refer to emotions that have particular and personal (and sometimes even bodily or sexual) objects. When Pateman speaks of passion, for instance, she seems to mean specifically

82 • The Trouble With Passion

sexual passion or, at most, romantic and familial love. Thus, it would be a misrepresentation to say that she explicitly argues that justice requires the sublimation of *all* passions. Moreover, since Rousseau does confine women to the private sphere at least in part because he believes they induce sexual passion in men, it seems indisputable that sexual passion (*passion amoureuse*) is one passion he believes must be excluded from the public sphere. But by conflating passions in general with sexual/romantic passion in particular, Pateman effectively presents Rousseau as excluding all passion from the public sphere. The same is true of the other authors. By discussing only particular and private passions, and discussing them as if they were the only kind of passion, many feminist interpreters of Rousseau have excluded by fiat the possibility of passions that might be appropriate to the public sphere. They have tended to focus on the opposition between (private) passion and (public) reason in his work, but in so doing they have overlooked the opposition between *private* passion and *public* passion in his work.[19] It is the latter distinction, I argue, that is actually the key to Rousseau's argument about passion and politics.

Private Passion versus Public Passion

Given the opposition that Rousseau sets up between the rule of appetite and inclination on the one hand and that of reason and laws on the other, it is not difficult to come to the conclusion that the general will is an achievement of reason that requires the transcendence of citizens' passions. But a look at some of Rousseau's less well-known political work should help to dispel this thesis. In *The Government of Poland*, for example, Rousseau counsels the Poles to "make love of country their governing passion" (1985, 16). Many of his recommendations in this essay are geared to establishing institutions, habits, and rituals that will tie the citizens to each other and to "the fatherland." Alongside these recommendations, Rousseau cautions against the "passions of narrow self-interest" that present obstacles to making the love of country supreme (5). He contends that the paths to satisfying such private desires, especially those for wealth, should be closed down so that desires can be channeled toward the more public goals of attaining merit and virtue. The benefit of shaping desires in this way cannot be overestimated. "Give a different bent to the passions of the Poles," he says, and "You will give the Poles a spiritual vigor that will…cause them to do by inclination and passionate choice the things that men motivated by duty or interest never do quite well enough." In particular, what the citizens will be inclined to do is obey the laws, because the laws "will enjoy the inward assent of their own wills."

Rousseau concludes this segment of his argument with the precept that "Where love of fatherland prevails, even a bad legislation would produce good citizens. And nothing except good citizens will ever make the state powerful and prosperous" (12). In other words, passions make the citizens, and the citizens make the state.

The *Discourse on Political Economy* confirms these points in clear terms. In this essay Rousseau argues that to govern men effectively, one must make them love the laws. And in order to do this, one must "form" them. As he puts it, "It is not enough to say to citizens, be good. It is necessary to teach them to be so" (1992, 150–51). What one must form, in particular, are the citizens' passions. The crucial point, made explicit only in this essay, is that eliminating citizens' passions would *not* be preferable. Rather, the best outcome results from directing their passions toward the right object:

> Now forming citizens is not accomplished in a day, and to have them as men they must be taught as children. Someone may tell me that anyone who has men to govern should not seek, outside of their nature, a perfection of which they are not capable; that he should not want to destroy their passions, and that the execution of such a project would not be any more desirable than it is possible. I will agree the more strongly with all this because *a man who had no passions would be a very bad citizen*. But it must also be agreed that although men cannot be taught to love nothing, it is not impossible to teach them to love one object rather than another, and what is truly beautiful rather than what is deformed. If, for example, they are trained early enough never to consider their persons except as related to the body of the State, and not to perceive their own existence, so to speak, except as part of the state's, they will eventually come to identify themselves in some way with this larger whole; to feel themselves to be members of the fatherland; to love it with that delicate feeling that any isolated man feels only for himself; to elevate their soul perpetually toward this great object; and *thereby to transform into a sublime virtue this dangerous disposition from which all our vices arise* (154–55, my emphasis).

This passage leaves no room for ambiguity. Not only does Rousseau argue that passion is necessary in the political realm, he goes so far as to suggest that the proper politicization of passions is their salvation. For him, a man who had no passions would be a very bad citizen, and a man whose passions were solely private would likely be a very bad man.

84 • The Trouble With Passion

Finally, one can find some examples of properly politicized passions in the discussion of justice in *Émile*. At one point the Tutor explains that even *pitié* will become a weakness unless it is extended to all. The more one generalizes particular interest, however, the more equitable it becomes, so that when one has *pitié* for the whole species then this sentiment accords with justice (1979, 252–53). Indeed, an earlier passage contends that justice itself is "only an ordered development of our primitive affections," a "true affection of the soul enlightened by reason" (235). Here Rousseau returns to the *Second Discourse*'s argument that morality is not based on reason alone, but rather requires an emotional identification with others that extends to them the desire for well-being that one feels for oneself. As he argues in a note, even the idea of the Golden Rule cannot be grounded solely in reason, for there is no reason to treat others as we wish to be treated if we do not expect to be in a similar situation and/or cannot be assured that others will return the favor. "But when the strength of an expansive soul makes me identify myself with my fellow, and I feel that I am, so to speak, in him, it is in order not to suffer that I do not want him to suffer. I am interested in him for love of myself." Rousseau concludes that "love of men derived from love of self is the principle of human justice" (235). In other words, *amour de soi*, properly extended, produces the political virtue of justice.[20]

Rousseau's arguments in *The Government of Poland*, *The Discourse on Political Economy*, and *Émile* thus refute the possibility that he generally believes passion should be confined to the private realm, leaving reason to rule the public realm.[21] With these works in mind we can return to the question of the position of reason and passion in the *Social Contract*. Recall that the *Social Contract* does argue, if briefly, that citizens need to feel connected to each other and to "love their duty." Since these references are so few, however, the key question would seem to revolve around the issue of the general will. As was argued above, one might well interpret the general will as an achievement of reason that requires the transcendence of citizens' passions. In fact there is some support for the first part of this interpretation in the *Discourse on Political Economy*, which describes law as "public reason" (1992, 146). However, while it is true that Rousseau repeatedly discusses the need for citizens to transcend their "appetites" and personal "inclinations," the fact that the general will requires leaving *these* passions behind does not mean that it requires leaving *all* passions behind. It is only the "passions of narrow self-interest" that the general will excludes; passions of the public interest in a sense actually constitute the general will, for the general will *is* the public desire for the public good. Put another way, what is crucial in attaining the general will is not so much to move from passion to reason, from "I desire"

"A Man Who Had No Passions Would Be a Very Bad Citizen" • **85**

to "I think," but rather to move from private passion to public passion, from "I desire" to "we desire." This is not to say that reason plays no part in this process; it is only to say that passion is decidedly not left behind. It is precisely this kind of transformation from private to public passion that Rousseau advocates in *The Government of Poland* and the *Discourse on Political Economy.*

Furthermore, the *Social Contract* also appears to concur with the argument in the *Discourse on Political Economy* that the proper politicization of passions is their salvation. While Rousseau offers many criticisms of citizens' private desires, he has none to offer of the general will, the expression of the citizens' public desires. The general will, he contends, is "always right and always tends toward the public utility." The only problem is that the citizens do not always discern the public good, and "only then does it appear to want what is bad" (1994, 147). Elaborating on this argument a few pages later, Rousseau contrasts private desire with public desire: "Private individuals see the good they reject; the public wants the good it does not see" (154). In other words, whereas individuals may purposely hold on to desires for bad things, the public only desires such things out of ignorance. Rousseau concludes this argument by asserting the need for a legislator who will enlighten the public, but the point here is the distinction he has drawn between private and public passion. Apparently, in the move from "I desire" to "we desire," desire itself is redeemed from any harmful intentions. The "dangerous disposition from which all our vices arise" is "transform[ed] into a sublime virtue." Although one might argue that Rousseau does not fully explain why the general will is by definition virtuous, it is clear that the key to its virtue is its generality, its link to the common interest. The private will, he says, "tends by its nature toward preferences, and the general will toward equality" (145). The general will is also, of course, the guarantee of the citizens' freedom. Since equality and freedom are among the supreme virtues in Rousseau's thought, we can begin to see why he praises the citizens' public passion.

Educating Passions

The disparity between the *Second Discourse* and the *Social Contract* thus turns out to be misleading in this respect: despite appearances, Rousseau has not in fact abandoned passion in favor of reason in the *Social Contract.* What Rousseau argues, in the *Social Contract* as elsewhere, is that passion *in the right form* is a beneficial component of social and political life. Passionate love of "the fatherland" and one's fellow citizens is essential to political unity. The public desire for the public good constitutes the

86 • The Trouble With Passion

general will, which is the foundation of the polity. Finally, *amour de soi* modified by *pitié* is the source of justice. Rousseau believes that a legitimate civil society absolutely depends upon these kinds of passions. For only with such sentiments can citizens live together in a social context without turning it into a state of war; only with such sentiments can equality and freedom be maintained.

While the impression that the *Social Contract* abandons passion may be misleading, though, there is still an important difference in the way the *Social Contract* handles the issue of passion. We have seen that in all of his work Rousseau argues that some forms of passion are beneficial and some are harmful. But in the context of society beneficial passions do not develop reliably on their own. Without proper guidance (and/or under improper influences), people are more likely to end up ruled by harmful passions such as *amour propre*, greed, envy, and so forth. Thus, Rousseau argues that the basic propensity for passion needs to be shaped in the right direction. In support of this argument, the education of passion is a crucial theme in many of his works. The *Discourse on Political Economy* contends that citizens must be taught as children "to love...what is truly beautiful rather than what is deformed." *The Government of Poland* dedicates a chapter to the "important topic" of education, which Rousseau contends must shape the "likes and dislikes" of the citizens (1985, 19). The whole purpose of *Émile*, of course, is to illustrate how children might be properly educated, and the (different) shaping of Émile's and Sophie's passions occupies a central part of their respective educations. The *Second Discourse* shows us the mirror image of *Émile*: that is, how passions develop when they develop improperly. One could even interpret the *Letter to D'Alembert* as emphasizing this theme, insofar as one of Rousseau's main criticisms of the theater is that it does not educate passions, but only embellishes them (1960, 18–21).

The *Social Contract*, however, does not emphasize the education of passions. Two kinds of passions are discussed in this text, private and public, and it is clear that the former is a threat to the polity and the latter crucial to its success. The question of how the citizens will get from one kind to the other is thus essential. But there is virtually no discussion of this process in the *Social Contract*. Now, one might expect the legislator to serve the role of educator, as indeed many interpreters have suggested is the case.[22] And it is true that Rousseau says the legislator should "feel that he is capable of changing human nature" (155), and that he will "attend in secret" to the morals, customs, and opinions of the people (165). But the actual development of this idea is scant at best.

In the first place, far more attention is paid to mechanistic solutions of arranging the institutional framework such that citizens "can do nothing, except with all the others" than is paid to the painstaking process of shaping the citizens' psyches (155). Moreover, close examination of the passage that introduces the need for the legislator shows that he does not in fact *educate* desires or wills: "Private individuals see the good they reject; the public wants the good it does not see. All are equally in need of guides. The former must be obligated to make their wills conform to their reason. The latter must be taught to know what it wants" (154). According to this formulation, individual wills or desires are not educated but rather subordinated, while public desires are also not truly educated but rather simply brought to light. The picture is of a static dichotomy between harmful, private desires that must be ruled by reason and beneficial, public desires that somehow already exist independently, and need only be recognized. It is not a description of how citizens *learn* to want what is best for the polity as a whole. Indeed, since the legislator will likely need to resort, as have those in the past, to putting his decisions "in the mouth of the immortals in order to win over by divine authority those who cannot be moved by prudence" (156–57), it seems clear that deception rather than education is the key to the legislator's effectiveness.[23]

This is the real difference of the *Social Contract*: not that passion is missing, but that the education of passion is missing. It should be clear by now that the political society Rousseau presents in this text relies on certain forms of passion as well as reason. But because the theory effectively takes the existence of these passions for granted, it is easy to miss the importance of the role that they play. The lack of attention to how these passions must develop is in sharp contrast to most of Rousseau's other texts, which as a result appear to grant passion more significance. But though passion *is* significant to the argument of the *Social Contract*, the inattention to the question of its education creates another problem. As is often noted, the polity that Rousseau envisions here depends heavily on a certain psychology among its members.[24] While some of Rousseau's other works provide us with clues as to how this psychology will be achieved, the text that provides by far the most complete treatment of the education of passion, *Émile*, is an inappropriate guide because it describes the process of making a man, not a citizen.[25] As a consequence, Rousseau's most theoretical model of political society is left without the kind of psychological foundation it requires.

There are important lessons here for those who would question the rationalism present in so much of political theory. One lesson is that, far from simply constituting a threat to political life, passion is crucial to it. Insofar as a commitment to justice depends on citizens' passions as well as their reason, a just, democratic polity requires passionate citizens. The liberal goal of constraining passions with law or reason is thus misdirected.

88 • The Trouble With Passion

Yet another lesson, however, is that an argument about the benefits of passion in politics must include a theory of the political education of passion.

Diverging from Rousseau's Theory of Passion

While I believe there are valuable lessons to learn from Rousseau, as with Plato I am not arguing for adopting his philosophy in its entirety. Two elements of Rousseau's thinking about passion are particularly important to challenge: his claim that the general will (the expression of the citizens' public desires) is always good and his claim that women must be excluded from citizenship because of the threat posed by *passion amoureuse*.

To argue, as Rousseau does in the *Discourse on Political Economy*, that men should be "trained early enough never to consider their persons except as related to the body of the State, and not [to] perceive their own existence, so to speak, except as part of the state's" is nothing short of liberalism's worst nightmare, and for good reason. According to Rousseau, as long as passion is properly channeled toward the state, it will be beneficial. But it is not at all clear that the state is a "truly beautiful" object of passion rather than a "deformed" one, and even if it were clear, such automatic identification of citizens with the state would likely preclude the critical thought that is necessary for any political community to aspire towards justice. While I agree with Rousseau that it is important for citizens to develop a capacity to think and feel (some of the time) in terms of a political community, I do not agree that the general will is by definition always right. There are plenty of historical and contemporary examples of polities in which citizens have *agreed* to pursue goals that are harmful to noncitizens, minority populations, future generations, animals, and the environment. In other words, passions must still be questioned, even if they are widely shared.

The problems created by an automatic acceptance of the general will are joined by the problems created by Rousseau's concept of *passion amoureuse*. Rousseau argues that the public sphere can be strong and virtuous only by confining women to the private sphere (and confining their behavior even within this sphere). If women are not constrained in this way, Rousseau believes that they will tyrannize men, corrupt their morals, ruin the institution of the family, and thereby threaten the polity. Why is this so? At the foundation of Rousseau's argument about women's proper role in the polity is his interpretation of the nature and consequences of (hetero)sexual passion. He believes that men are limited in their ability to engage in sexual intercourse, whereas women are not. Furthermore, men are limited in their ability to be certain that a child is theirs, whereas

"A Man Who Had No Passions Would Be a Very Bad Citizen" • **89**

women are not. As a result of these limitations, he argues, men are effectively at women's mercy. "An invariable law of nature…gives woman more facility to excite the desires than man to satisfy them. This causes the latter, whether he likes it or not, to depend on the former's wish and constrains him to seek to please her in turn, so that she will consent to let him be the stronger" (1979, 360).

If women were to behave as men do, that is, if they were to move about freely amongst nonrelated men in the public sphere, the power that they have over men would turn into domination. Not only would they distract men sexually, but, "unable to make themselves into men, the women [would] make us into women" (1960, 100). They would encourage men to devote themselves to petty and private values, corrupting their devotion to the polity. Moreover, if women were to move about freely in the public sphere, they would be unable to preserve their reputations as chaste maidens or sexually faithful wives. Discredited by a reputation for promiscuity, *regardless of its truthfulness*, single women would be unable to attract good men for husbands and married women would be abandoned by their husbands when the husbands lost confidence that the children they were supporting were their own progeny. In these ways, allowing women to venture into the public sphere would undermine both men's morals and the institution of the family, and, in so doing, subvert the polity. For the state needs strong families to serve as "small fatherlands" that attach citizens to the large one (1979, 363) and to provide for the polity's production, reproduction, and education. And a republic, in particular, needs virtuous masculine citizens who will fight to defend it: "Whether a monarch governs men or women ought to be rather indifferent to him, provided that he be obeyed; but in a republic, men are needed" (1960, 100-1).

In order to preserve the state, then, women must behave appropriately: they must stay out of the public sphere of men in order to be sexually faithful, modest, and domestic. "[T]here are no good morals for women outside of a withdrawn and domestic life…the peaceful care of the family and home are their lot" (1960, 82). In preparation for this "withdrawn and domestic" life, women must be educated to be submissive. Whereas boys should be given the freedom to develop according to their own nature, girls should be "exercised in constraint" so that they will be able to accept it throughout their lives (1979, 369). In an oft-cited passage from *Émile*, Rousseau explains that

> the whole education of women ought to relate to men. To please
> men, to be useful to them, to raise them when young, to care for

90 • The Trouble With Passion

> them when grown, to counsel them, to console them, to make their lives agreeable and sweet—these are the duties of women at all times, and they ought to be taught from childhood. So long as one does not return to this principle, one will deviate from the goal, and all the precepts taught women will be of no use for their happiness or ours (365).

Perhaps most importantly, girls must not be overly educated in reason, for too much reasoning teaches a woman to disdain her duties and devalue public opinion, which is the "throne" of her virtue (364). At the same time, a woman must have just enough reason to survive in a male-dominated and potentially corrupt world, else she will be "too easy to seduce" (383).

Throughout his discussions about women's proper education, position, and behavior, Rousseau frequently cites nature to justify his arguments. These defenses are striking in light of the *Second Discourse*'s radical claim that there are virtually no differences between men and women in the state of nature. But the contradiction is only apparent. The fact that women must be educated to be what Rousseau nevertheless calls "natural" betrays his belief that women are *not* in fact naturally more submissive or less capable of reason than men. Rather, they must be shaped to be so. His argument that "Everything that characterizes the fair sex ought to be respected as established by nature" (1979, 363) is patently strategic: he does not say that nature *has* established everything that characterizes the fair sex, only that these characteristics ought to be respected as *(if)* established by nature. He wants an ideology of nature to compensate for what nature has not in fact done. The asserted claims of natural requirements are actually normative prescriptions to be fulfilled through a rigorous socialization, a socialization obscured and bolstered by the ideology of nature.

The justification for this rigorous socialization is functional. As I argued above, women must behave appropriately in order to preserve the state (and not, it should be noted, simply in order to benefit men). In the *Letter to D'Alembert*, for example, after pages of rhetoric that women are naturally chaste, Rousseau ends by switching tactics and asserting: "If the timidity, chasteness, and modesty which are proper to [women] are social inventions, it is in society's interest that women acquire these qualities" (87). To take another example, the question "Are women capable of solid reasoning?" in *Émile* is immediately followed by the question "Is it important that they cultivate it?" And the concern "Will they succeed in cultivating it?" is immediately followed by "Is its cultivation useful for the functions which are imposed on them?" (382). As Penny Weiss has argued, "Rousseau can be most clearly understood as saying that the sexes are not relevantly differentiated by nature, but that sex differences can and should be created, encouraged, and enforced because of what he considers to be their necessary and beneficial consequences" (1993, 83).

But a functional argument must be judged by its results, and in the case of Rousseau's argument about women, even Rousseau himself does not have much faith that his desired results can be achieved. Both of his "model" female characters, Julie and Sophie, die unhappy and untimely deaths. Julie can never overcome her passion for Saint-Preux, despite being surrounded by a devoted husband, friends, and family. She sees death as the only way to preserve her virtue. In the unfinished sequel to *Émile*, Sophie, who has had the ideal education for a woman, nevertheless ends up succumbing to exactly what she was so carefully raised to resist: adultery. Because she is despondent over her parents' deaths, Émile takes her to Paris, where he soon loses interest in her. Feeling rejected, Sophie bears a child to another man. Émile is thus "forced" to leave her, and she can do nothing but die. Some critics have taken Sophie's and Julie's fates as evidence that Rousseau has failed at his own task. But Mira Morgenstern persuasively argues that, on the contrary, Rousseau is deliberately illustrating the weaknesses of the supposedly ideal solutions put forward in these novels. "We must conclude," she says, "that the fate of Rousseau's heroines points not to Rousseau's misogyny but rather to Rousseau's realization that the traditional ways of looking at and treating women are inconsistent with the larger claims for freedom presented in Rousseau's own theory" (1996, 8).

Whether or not Rousseau did realize these problems, they are certainly problems from my perspective. A vision of political community that depends on the exclusion of women is obviously not acceptable. Yet Rousseau's own arguments about the cultural production of "human nature" can be used to criticize this vision. As mentioned above, the roots of the argument that women must be excluded from the public sphere lie in claims that Rousseau makes about men's and women's different sexual needs and abilities. But in claiming that "An invariable law of nature... gives woman more facility to excite the desires than man to satisfy them," Rousseau has made the same mistake that he accuses other social contract theorists of making: he "spoke about savage man [and woman] and it was civil man [and woman he] depicted." Whereas in many other areas of human life he is keenly aware of social influences, here Rousseau is unable to recognize (or acknowledge) those influences. Employing his own methods to investigate the cultural production of men's and women's sexual identities, desires, and expectations allows us to challenge Rousseau's argument for women's privatization.

Conclusion

Once again, while I depart from Rousseau's theory of passion in some ways, I contend that his arguments are useful as another illustration of how political theorists might take passion seriously. Like Plato, Rousseau presents a complex (if somewhat different) picture of the ways in which passion and reason are intertwined. Also like Plato, Rousseau thinks these human capacities combine to play inescapable and potentially valuable roles in politics—especially, according to Rousseau, as an agent of political community. Finally, Rousseau as well as Plato illustrates the need to educate passion toward good ends, even though in the case of the *Social Contract* the illustration is primarily through the consequences of omission. In the next chapter, I turn to contemporary feminist theorists for an argument about the political value of passion that differs from both Plato's and Rousseau's and yet still bears some interesting resemblances.

CHAPTER **6**

"Our Erotic Knowledge Empowers Us": Passion and Action in Contemporary Feminist Theory

In 1978, Audre Lorde presented a seven-page paper entitled "Uses of the Erotic: The Erotic as Power" at the Fourth Berkshire Conference on the History of Women. The paper was subsequently published not only in *Sister Outsider*, a collection of Lorde's essays and speeches, but also as a stand-alone pamphlet, available for 50 cents in women's bookstores. More than 25 years after it was presented, it continues to be read in Women's Studies courses across the United States. Clearly, "Uses of the Erotic" has had an enduring resonance for feminist activists, scholars, and students. Its ongoing appeal is undoubtedly a testament to the evocative power and economy of Lorde's writing, but I think it is also a testament to the essay's meaningful but relatively uncommon subject matter. For while there has been a great deal of feminist discussion about such subjects as sexuality, desire, emotion, and care, the capacity that Lorde refers to as eros is not sufficiently articulated in any of these discussions. Thus, Lorde's tribute to eros continues to strike a chord.

I mean to pick up on that chord in this chapter. Here I examine Lorde's essay as well as the work of a handful of other feminists who have joined her in writing about eros (Goodison 1983; Hartsock 1983; Heyward 1984, 1989; Lorde 1984B; Trask 1986; Schott 1988; Dimen 1989; Brock 1991). These authors work within several different disciplines and have influences

94 • The Trouble With Passion

as diverse as classical Greek literature, analytic philosophy, Marxist theory, Freudian and Marcusian thought, and Christian theology (as well as, in all cases, the literature and political practice of 20th-century Western feminism). Accordingly, they vary somewhat in their approach to eros, and even, to a certain extent, on the term's definition. Nevertheless, a remarkably similar thesis about the "promise" or potential "use" of eros runs throughout their works. My initial purpose in this chapter is to draw out the structure of that thesis.[1] Challenging the perspective that eros is debilitating, these theorists argue that, on the contrary, it is empowering. In particular, they emphasize that eros is crucial in struggles against oppression. Because they theorize a concept of passion that does not exclude femininity or sensuality, feminist theorists of eros offer an important corrective to the masculinism and asceticism of Plato and Rousseau's theories. At the same time, they exhibit a significant tendency to idealize eros, paying scant attention to the question of how to handle passions for harmful things. My final purpose in the chapter is thus to use this example to illustrate the importance of thinking about methods to educate passion.

The chapter begins with an exploration of how eros is conceptualized in this literature. The next two sections analyze the theorists' central argument that conventional conceptions of eros lead to a cultural imperative to deny and repress this capacity, which in turn leads to violence and alienation. The fourth section identifies the significance of the intersection of eros and power in these authors' thinking and examines what they consider to be the positive "uses" of the erotic. The chapter concludes with my criticisms of the feminist literature on eros.

Feminist Conceptions of Eros

What do feminist theorists of eros mean by "eros"? As noted above, there is some variation in the way they use the term, but there is also considerable overlap. Moreover, there is as much variation within texts as there is between them. Considering all of the texts together thus reveals several clusters of meaning, each of which runs more or less throughout the literature. In all of these clusters, eros is conceived as a kind of link that joins us to something important.

In the first and most basic cluster of meaning, eros refers to our link to our own core self. Audre Lorde provides several examples of this definition when she speaks of eros as "the *yes* within ourselves, our deepest cravings," "depth of feeling," "[the] capacity for joy," and "an internal sense of satisfaction" (1984B, 54–57). In the second cluster, a link to other people is added. Again Lorde provides an example, describing eros as "what is deepest and

"Our Erotic Knowledge Empowers Us" • **95**

strongest and richest within each of us, being shared: the passions of love in its deepest meanings." Echoing this aspect of eros, Carter Heyward describes it as "our drive toward one another; our movement in love; our expression of our sense of being bonded together in life and death" (1984, 86) and Rita Nakashima Brock calls it "the power of our primal interrelatedness" (1991, 26).[2]

In a third cluster of meaning, eros is our link to the sensuous world and our participation in its (and our own) becoming. Nancy Hartsock lists "the pleasure in the effortful achievement of purpose" as one aspect of eros.[3] She explains that eros may include "intellectual creativity in philosophy and art, physical work on the substances of nature, or the generation of children through sexual relations" (1983, 166, 67). Lorde, too, emphasizes this sense of eros when she calls it "creative energy empowered" (1984B, 55). For both Lorde and Hartsock, work is (or can be) erotic. On the other hand, Brock speaks of eros as "play," the free-flowing and adventurous interaction between the self and the world (1991, 35–39, 45–47). Through play, she argues, the self creates itself and reality anew. Thus, eros is "the divine yearning for playful becoming" (47). Either way, eros is identified as creativity, generativity, productive activity.

Fourth, eros is conceived as our link to life itself. Following Freud and Marcuse, several authors define eros as "the life force." Lorde says "When I speak of the erotic, then, I speak of it as an assertion of the lifeforce of women" (1984B, 55). Haunani-Kay Trask interprets this concept of the life force as "the instinct to encourage and protect life" (1986, 61). She calls on Mary Daly's concept of "life-loving energy" and argues that "The feminist Eros is a conscious, informed love of the body and the life which it enables" (110, 143). Brock goes even further, defining eros as "the fundamental power of life" (1991, 25).

Finally, for many of the authors, eros is our link to the good, or a set of values about the right way to live. Trask's concept of the "feminist Eros" explicitly involves consciousness as well as instinct. She describes it as a perspective or vision, drawn from women's experience of relational caretaking, about how best to live.[4] She delineates this vision through a reading of several prominent feminist writers, including Mary Daly, Jill Johnston, Audre Lorde, Cherríe Moraga, Robin Morgan, and Adrienne Rich.[5] In the work of these writers, she says, "the feminist Eros encompasses the 'life force,' the unique human energy which springs from the desire for existence with meaning, for a consciousness informed by feeling, for experience that integrates the sensual and the rational, the spiritual and the political. In the feminist vision, Eros is both love *and* power" (1986, 92–93). She adds that the feminist Eros "unleashes a desire—for creative expression, especially in the areas of sexuality and work; for balance

96 • The Trouble With Passion

among needs, particularly those of autonomy and nurturance; for sharing and interdependence without bondage" (94).

In a similar vein, Brock claims, "Feminist Eros is grounded in the relational lives of women and in critical, self-aware consciousness that unites the psychological and political spheres of life, binding love with power.... Eros is a sensuous, transformative whole-making wisdom that emerges with the subjective engagement of the whole heart in relationships" (1991, 26). The notion that eros is a form of wisdom is echoed by Lorde, who argues that "The erotic is the nurturer or nursemaid of all our deepest knowledge" (1984B, 56). Finally, Heyward's concept of eros is also deeply imbued with ethical content. For her, the erotic is "our most fully embodied experience of the love of God." Love of God, in her view, is a commitment to justice, or right relation; hence, "The erotic is the divine spirit's yearning, through our bodyselves, toward mutually empowering relation" (1989, 99). Put another way, eros is what moves us to make connections, and therefore leads to the common good: it is "the power, the yearning, the hunger, the drive, the YES to the breaking down of the walls that separate person from person, creature from creature, creature from creator; and to the making of the connections between and among us in which we find our common good" (1984, 130).[6]

Clearly, feminist theorists of eros include many things under the category: passion, desire, love, pleasure, energy, and more. This range is much broader than the sense of passion I have emphasized. Moreover, as I discuss at length at the end of this chapter, I do not accept the notion that eros or passion is inherently for the good. Nevertheless, there are a number of core similarities between these writers' concept(s) of eros and my concept of passion. Like my concept of passion, their concept of eros conveys an enthusiastic appreciation of and commitment to something valued. And like my concept of passion, their concept of eros may be directed not only towards people but also towards objects, activities, and ideas. Finally, like my concept of passion, their concept of eros indicates intensity of feeling but is not opposed to reason, self-possession, or agency. Given these similarities, I find the feminist literature on eros particularly relevant to explore.

The Conventional Conception of Eros

As with all feminist thought, the roots of feminist thought about eros lie in a critique of existing social and political conditions. In particular, this literature highlights two primary sets of problems in the United States today: first, the all-too-frequent presence of violence, oppression, and inequality (especially, but by no means exclusively, as related to gender); and second,

"Our Erotic Knowledge Empowers Us" • **97**

the all-too-frequent absence of genuine intimacy and love and community; of joy and a sense of meaning in life; and of the energy to resist oppression and fight for change.[7] For convenience, I will refer to the first set as problems of violence and the second set as problems of alienation.[8] Now, critiques of violence and alienation underlie the projects of many, if not most, feminists. What is distinctive about the group of writers I am concerned with is their particular diagnosis of these problems, for, in their view, both sets have something to do with eros. It follows that the solution to these problems also has something to do with eros. And indeed, feminist theorists of eros argue that if we could change the way we approach this capacity, we might have the key to nothing less than a more peaceful, just, loving, and joyful existence.

The first step in this argument is an analysis of how eros is generally understood in Western cultures, and especially in the United States. Specifically, feminist theorists of eros argue that eros has been "reduced" to sexuality, limited to the private sphere, perceived as irrational and debilitating, and associated with femininity. As we shall see, each of these conceptual moves builds upon and reinforces the others, for sexuality, privacy, irrationality, weakness, and femininity are themselves all linked in Western conceptual frameworks.

Let us begin, then, with the issue of eros' scope. In her essay, Lorde lists "dancing, building a bookcase, writing a poem, [and] examining an idea" as examples of erotically satisfying experiences (1984B, 56–57). Likewise, Heyward says that eros is expressed "not only between lovers in personal relationship, but also in the work of an artist who loves her painting or her poetry, a father who loves his children, a revolutionary who loves her people" (1984, 86). Yet, in Brock's words, "In our male-dominant society Eros is often equivalent to lust or sexuality" (1991, 26). Thus, eros as these authors would like to define it is not even an intelligible concept in contemporary U.S. society. Because sex preoccupies our imagination, they argue, we tend to see passion and pleasure, and at times even love, in terms of sex, or not at all. Moreover, this perspective is culturally enforced: "we are taught to separate the erotic demand from most vital areas of our lives other than sex"; the erotic is "relegated to the bedroom alone, when it is recognized at all" (Lorde 1984B, 55, 57).

Having made this point that eros has been conceptually "reduced" to sexuality, though, feminist theorists of eros go on to describe the approach taken to the broader range of feelings that they would include under the category. They point out, first of all, that passion, desire, emotion, and love are all seen as properly private. In part this follows from the association of these feelings with sex: when the erotic is relegated to the bedroom, according to Lorde, it is separated from both work and politics (1984B,

98 • The Trouble With Passion

55–56).[9] But sex is not the only thing seen as private. As many feminists have argued, Western masculinist thought systems have long distinguished between public and private spheres and associated different qualities with the different spheres.[10] Along these same lines, then, Trask argues that the modern industrialized and bureaucratized state dichotomizes love and power, nurturance and autonomy, sensuality and rationality, and spirituality and politics, associating the former with the private sphere and the latter with the public. Other authors would agree that the qualities they include under the rubric of eros are all currently placed in the private sphere by Western thought systems.

Another significant element in Western conceptions of eros is that eros is seen as irrational. Like the opposition between public and private, and running parallel to it, the opposition between reason and emotion (of any kind) has a long history in Western thought: 2500 years after the *Republic*, the two capacities are still commonly seen as mutually exclusive and in contest for influence within the person. One can either be rational, or one can be emotional—never both at the same time. The result of this dichotomy, Robin Schott argues, is that emotion, desire, and sexuality have been perceived as a threat to rational control (1988, viii).

This conception of eros as irrational leads directly to the conception of eros as debilitating. Feminist theorists of eros point out that Western masculinist cultures generally identify rationality as the source of people's ability to "take charge" of themselves, and therefore others. From this point of view, "giving in" to the irrationality of eros is weakening because it means losing this ability to control oneself and others. Accordingly, these authors argue, we have been taught that we must suppress eros in order to be strong (Lorde 1984B, 53). We have even been taught that pleasure makes us soft, and that the ability to suffer impassively is a sign of strength (Heyward 1984, 129).

Lastly, feminist theorists of eros argue that eros is popularly associated with women or "the feminine." Feelings, desire, pleasure, passion, and love—all of these qualities are generally considered to be more feminine than masculine. In other words, eros plays a key role in the dominant ideology of what it means to be a "real woman" or a "real man." Insofar as a woman appears to lack emotionality or a focus on love, she is seen as lacking in femininity; insofar as a man expresses emotions (other than anger) or appears to prioritize connections with others rather than independence, he is seen as lacking in masculinity.[11] As these writers would admit, it is true that in one respect—that of being a sexual *actor*—eros tends to be associated with men more than with women. In many periods of Western history, lust and sexual initiation have been seen as the purview of men and not women (or at least not "good" women). But the crux of the argument is that even if men are supposed to desire and initiate sexual activity, they are not defined in terms of sex the way that women are. Sexuality is seen as only one part of men's lives, whereas it is seen as a (or even *the*) defining feature of women's lives.[12] Thus, the mapping of eros onto women is concordant with all of the previous conceptualizations of eros, for women are also associated with sexuality, with the private sphere, with irrationality, and with weakness in ways that men are not.

Consequences of the Conventional Conception of Eros: Repression and Oppression

Feminist theorists of eros argue that these interpretations constitute a denigration of eros within our cultural value systems. This situation is most obvious in the case of eros' purported irrationality and weakening effect. In a culture that indisputably values rationality and power, such a conception of eros clearly constitutes a negative view. The devaluation involved in associating eros with femininity is only slightly less obvious in a culture that sometimes rewards women for being more like men but almost never rewards men for being more like women. Only the final associations of eros with sexuality and privacy may be difficult to see as devaluations, since both sexuality and privacy would seem to be much desired in contemporary Western culture. But part of the point here is that to refuse to acknowledge any but the most private, sexual forms of eros is effectively to depreciate a great part of its nature. Moreover, feminist theorists of eros contend that sexuality is not in fact valued highly in this culture, in spite of our obsession with it (more on this in just a moment), and that the private sphere still holds less status than the public.[13]

The practical outcome of a negative conception of eros is a cultural imperative to deny and repress it. As Lorde argues, "We have been taught to suspect this resource [of the erotic], vilified, abused, and devalued within western society" (1984B, 53).[14] Now, again this argument may seem surprising given the inordinate amount of attention paid to sexuality, especially in contemporary times. But it is important to remember, first, that according to these writers sexuality is only one aspect of eros, and, second, that preoccupation is not the same as acceptance. For example, Nancy Hartsock argues that the cultural obsession with pornography in fact betrays a deep discomfort with sexuality and the body. In her view, the excitement of pornography relies on the experience of the body as shameful. The thrill comes from seeing what is supposed to be hidden away. "Transgression is important here: Forbidden practices are being engaged in" (1983, 172–74). Thus, the existence of a taboo is proven by the

100 • The Trouble With Passion

excitement generated in violating it, and the apparent celebration of bodies and sex is in fact a manifestation of the reverse.

This denial and control of sexuality and the body follows from the perception of them as frighteningly irrational, debilitating, messy, and wild. Carter Heyward, who writes from a critical position within the Christian tradition, argues that Christianity has played a powerful role in this view of sex: "As a chaotic and passionate resource, sex must be controlled by whatever means necessary: such has been a dominant christian motif" (1989, 89).[15] But sex is only one of the aspects of eros that we attempt to control. In the interests of feeling in charge of ourselves and appearing invulnerable, these authors argue, we also attempt to control our emotions. In the interests of not needing things from others, which we believe would threaten our independence and power, we attempt to control our desires. In the interests of keeping our wits about us and preserving a dignified appearance, we attempt to limit experiences (or at least the display) of pleasure. And in the interests of attaining or preserving autonomy, we attempt to maintain distance in our relations with others, limiting our connectedness. In general, as Lorde puts it, "We have been raised to fear the *yes* within ourselves, our deepest cravings" (1984B, 57). Because of the dominant conception of eros, we suspect it, and learn to stifle it in ourselves.

Although these imperatives apply to everyone in the culture, they are not gender neutral. Feminist theorists of eros argue that the requirement to control and repress eros takes on greater urgency for men than for women.[16] This situation is the consequence of the role that eros plays in the dominant ideology of masculinity and femininity. Eros is associated not only with weakness but with femininity; thus, men can little afford to express it. Indeed, controlling emotions, passions, and desires—things that women are perceived to be less able to control—lies at the heart of what it means to be a "real man" in the dominant Western culture. According to Hartsock, "in the community structured by a masculine eros,[17] bodies and their appetites and desires are treated as loathsome, even inhuman, things that must be overcome if a man is to remain powerful and free. To meet the cultural standards of masculinity, individuals must separate themselves from and conquer the feelings and desires of the body" (Hartsock 1983, 177–78). According to Schott, male philosophers (such as Kant) who have a special commitment to the Western conception of rationality have often struggled long and hard to "purify" thought of sensuality and emotion. The result of all of this, in Heyward's words, is that "Men…have undervalued, even denied, the power of body, their own juices, their own neediness, their own yearnings to touch and be touched" (1984, 197).

"Our Erotic Knowledge Empowers Us" • **101**

Implicit in these gender differences, according to this argument, is a further outcome of the Western conception of eros: the perpetuation of the oppression of women. For while it may be deemed more important for men than for women to control eros, women are nevertheless castigated for their supposed greater acquiescence to eros. In other words, if eros is associated with women and eros must be suppressed, then women must be suppressed as well. Feminist theorists of eros discuss several ways in which this mechanism can operate. First, by projecting a *negative* trait onto women, men can justify viewing women as inferior (and women can come to see themselves as inferior as well). "On the one hand, the superficially erotic has been encouraged as a sign of female inferiority; on the other hand, women have been made to suffer and to feel both contemptible and suspect by virtue of its existence" (Lorde 1984B, 53). Second, by projecting a supposedly *dangerous* trait onto women, men can justify controlling women. As with the feminine within men, the feminine without must be kept in its place in order to keep eros from taking over. "Because she is [held to be] the ever-desired reality of man's lower and more dangerous because more gratifying nature, woman is continually subordinated to man as nature is subordinated to culture" (Trask 1986, 11).[18] Finally, by *projecting* a negative and dangerous trait onto women, men can benefit from this trait without having to feel either tainted or threatened by it. By encouraging women to perform the "emotional labor" of feeling and caring for others without participating in it themselves, these authors argue, men appropriate women's labor (Lorde 1984B, 53–54; Trask 1986, 61). The result of all of these strategies is a reciprocal process in which controlling eros entails controlling women and controlling women entails controlling eros. "The repression of Eros emerges with misogyny, hate of the female as symbol of Eros, the displacement of Eros onto women, and the denial of Eros through aggression against women and alienation from intimacy" (Brock 1991, summarizing Trask 1986, 25–26).

Consequences of the Denial and Repression of Eros: Violence and Alienation

So the denigration of eros leads to the cultural imperative to deny and/or repress it. The next step in the argument is the claim that denying and repressing eros in turn leads to violence and alienation. What happens when people suppress or become detached from eros? One possibility, feminist theorists of eros argue, is that eros may be "distorted" or "perverted"—"turned completely around from itself"—and thus transformed into violence. The second possibility is that eros may simply be lost, and with it the zest for life. In this case, the consequence is alienation. Most of

102 • The Trouble With Passion

the authors include both possibilities in some fashion, without necessarily classifying and dividing them as such. For the purposes of analysis, I first discuss each outcome separately, and then discuss the connections between the two.

There are at least two different, although not necessarily mutually exclusive, lines of argument about how eros can become distorted into violence. One argument focuses on the psychological health of those who suppress or deny feelings, desires, and connections to others. According to Brock, intimate, supportive relationships with others are necessary for the development of a confident, flexible, self-accepting self. Without such relationships the self may become fearful, defensive, and rigid. To protect itself from the perceived threats of the outside world, it may develop a need to assert control over others (1991, 27, 33). Thus, the denial of eros (here in the sense of intimacy) results in dominating behavior: "Erotic power denied and crushed produces dominance and control" (36). Likewise, Trask argues that those who do not develop emotional capacities (for example, men who rely on women's emotional labor instead of learning to deal with their own feelings) often end up turning to violence in the face of relational strain (1986, 61). Heyward supports this argument with her claim that people who live up to the cultural model of invulnerability to others are actually the ones most likely to hurt others:

> Strong, vulnerable people do not rape, batter, beat, and destroy one another. Rape is an act of violence, indeed of sexual perversion, as are all acts of violence. (Perverted: turned completely around from itself.) Invulnerable, impassive persons...who boast of "strength" are those best equipped and most likely to assault humanity on the streets, on the battlefield, or behind the button (1984, 131).

Another line of argument emphasizes the way in which the repression and denial of eros creates the split between mind and body (with feelings and desires identified with the body). Mind and body are not, according to this view, inherently opposed; they only become so through the refusal to accept eros as part of the self. The body is thus objectified, posited as something separate from the "real" person. And this objectification allows for domination of the body—whether one's own or another's. As Heyward argues,

> By lopping off the body from real power, value, creativity, and spirit, and by projecting the body in its enigmatic mystery and neediness onto women, and by equating body with woman/

"Our Erotic Knowledge Empowers Us" • **103**

feelings/lust/out-of-controlness/scary places/evil/death, men have split themselves in two. On the one hand, there is the rational, creative, reasonable, constructive, and spiritual self. On the other, there is the irrational, emotional, chaotic, needy body—which, like a woman, can be hung on the meat rack, admired, and fucked, without affecting in any way the daily life, work, and character of the rational, spiritual, hard-working, all American man whose sense of himself bears no relation to his sense of his body (1984, 197).

That is, suppression of eros results in an objectified body that can be "fucked."

Schott echoes this argument in her analysis of masculinist philosophy. Her claim is that the suppression of sensuality results in a "distortion of the erotic interests of human beings" (1988, xi). Attempts to eliminate eros are inevitably counterproductive, for eros does not disappear: it is merely diverted in another direction (171–72). For example, Schott argues that the obsessive concern with objectivity in philosophy is in fact a displacement of forbidden eroticism (172–73). The concern with objectivity is not neutral but rather a reaction to the forces of sensuality that male philosophers are trying to control, and a passionate reaction at that. Moreover, it is a problematic reaction because it creates the mind/body split:

[P]hilosophy's claim to have escaped erotic life is suspect. Rather than providing a liberation from the body, the philosophical paradigm has made normative a deformation of erotic interest, an objectification of our sentient being. The philosophical imperative to eliminate sensuality from one's apprehension of oneself, of other persons, and of objects creates a split between an embodied and a reflective self. Rational consciousness becomes detached from feelings or desires, indicating a fundamental alienation within the subject, which is manifested in the relation to the body inscribed in philosophy. The body becomes reduced to its status as a mere physical object...[and] when pleasures and desires are recognized by consciousness they appear as a dehumanizing force, a natural contamination that is opposed to the qualities of personhood. Although the ascetic demand to distance reflection from embodied existence seeks to maintain rational control over physical desires and passions, it has not resulted in the control of pure rationality over the polluted body. Instead, these ascetic commitments have resulted in an inherent objectifying dynamic within philosophical thought (183).

104 • The Trouble With Passion

Erotic interest is displaced from subjects to objects. Again, this process enables domination of those (such as women) who become identified as objects. Furthermore, the suppression of eros, as Schott describes it, is a self-perpetuating dynamic. She argues that in creating the split between rational consciousness and feelings or desires, the attempt to escape eros only reinforces the view of eros as a "natural contamination opposed to the qualities of personhood." Denigration and fear of eros leads to eros' suppression, which leads to its distortion, which leads to more denigration and fear of eros.

Lorde continues the focus on objectification as an outcome of the repression of eros. In her view, refusing to acknowledge the erotic in our lives, "misnaming" our need for sharing deep feelings and "looking away" from our interactions with others, gives rise to "that distortion which results in pornography and obscenity—the abuse of feeling" (1984B, 59). This is because when we do not recognize the experiences we share with others, we treat other people as objects: we use their feelings rather than sharing them.

> When we look away from the importance of the erotic in the development and sustenance of our power, or when we look away from ourselves as we satisfy our erotic needs in concert with others, we use each other as objects of satisfaction rather than share our joy in the satisfying, rather than make connection with our similarities and our differences. To refuse to be conscious of what we are feeling at any time, however comfortable that might seem, is to deny a large part of the experience, and to allow ourselves to be reduced to the pornographic, the abused, and the absurd (1984B, 59).

Again, denying eros produces objectification produces domination (abuse).

Thus, feminist theorists of eros argue that violence often has its roots in the denigration, denial, and suppression of eros. The alternative outcome of this cultural relationship to eros, they contend, is the complex situation I have termed alienation: that is, lack of genuine intimacy and love and community; lack of joy and a sense of meaning in life; lack of respect for the value of life; and lack of the commitment and energy to resist oppression and fight for change. In explaining this general problem of alienation, these authors tend to speak less of the repression of eros, such that it becomes distorted into something violent, and more of an estrangement from eros that leaves people without crucial resources and qualities they need for a good life. In their arguments, it is as if eros comes back to haunt

"Our Erotic Knowledge Empowers Us" • **105**

those who attempt to eliminate it, but simply abandons those who do not or cannot actively embrace and value it.

Alienation in general is linked to an estrangement from eros because to be estranged from eros is to be estranged from oneself, from others, from creative expression, and from the life force. Obviously, this argument follows from these authors' particular understanding of eros; as previously noted, for them eros *is* our link to these things. To be cut off from eros thus has devastating implications: we become isolated, apathetic, self-negating. We lose any sense of joy in living. Many of the authors stress that we have no self-knowledge, or knowledge of others, without access to the erotic. Specifically, they mean that we do not have a sense of what we need and want, of what we care about and what matters to us in the world, or of how other people are important to us. We are left without direction, and, as a result, without control of our own destinies: "When we live outside ourselves, and by that I mean on external directives only rather than from our internal knowledge and needs, when we live away from those erotic guides from within ourselves, then our lives are limited by external and alien forms, and we conform to the needs of a structure that is not based on human need, let alone an individual's" (Lorde 1984B, 58).

Moreover, these authors argue, when we are alienated from eros we have no motivation and energy to fight back and take control of our lives. Alienation from eros engenders depression, despair, resignation, numbness, and hopelessness (Lorde 1984B, 58). And such states of disaffection induce docility and obedience to those with power over us. We end up colluding in our own oppression. In Lorde's words, "The fear of our desires keeps them suspect and indiscriminately powerful, for to suppress any truth is to give it strength beyond endurance. The fear that we cannot grow beyond whatever distortions we may find within ourselves keeps us docile and loyal and obedient, externally defined, and leads us to accept many facets of our oppression as women" (1984B, 57–58). Or as Muriel Dimen puts it, the constraint of desire "leads directly to self-betrayal and social bad faith. We suffer not from too much desire but from too little. Our failures to rebel, our incomplete revolutions, are rooted in the repression of desire that, essential to sexual oppression, truncates hope" (1989, 48–49).[19]

The Heart of the Issue: The Power of Eros

According to this argument, then, both violence and alienation are the consequence of the Western cultural relationship to eros—a relationship of denigration and thus denial and repression. One might wonder at this point what determines which of the two problems, violence or alienation,

106 • The Trouble With Passion

will result from this negative relationship to eros. A provisional answer to the question would return us to the element of gender, for in the feminist literature on eros, the problem of violence is almost always seen as a problem exhibited by men, and the problem of alienation most importantly (though not exclusively) a problem exhibited by women. Recall that there is some difference in the way these writers describe the problematic relationship to eros: in one case, eros is actively repressed and becomes distorted; in the other case, a person becomes (somewhat more passively) alienated from eros. The implication would seem to be that men repress eros while women become estranged from it, with the result that men become violent while women become depressed and self-negating.

But why should men and women have such different relationships to eros? The answer lies with the original perceptions of eros, perceptions that are deeply gendered. Eros is associated with the feminine; therefore it is especially important for men to repress it. Indeed, the man who actively conquers the erotic in himself is valorized. At the same time, although women are identified with eros, they are punished for this association, particularly when they appear to indulge in the erotic for their own purposes or enjoyment. The consequence is that women learn to use eros only in the service of men and children. One might say they lose ownership of eros: they are associated with it, but it does not "belong" to them. This is the nature of alienation. Moreover, Lorde makes a representative point in arguing that the form of the erotic that is associated with women is actually a shallow and reductionist one: "the *superficially* erotic has been encouraged as a sign of female inferiority" (1984B, 53, my emphasis). Eros in the fuller sense may well remain out of reach. Thus, women are alienated from eros while men repress it. The problems associated with eros are gendered because the negative relationships to eros are gendered because eros itself is gendered.

Ultimately, though, the question of why a negative relationship to eros leads to violence or to alienation is actually a side issue. The important point is that these problems are in fact deeply related. I have been discussing them separately, but for feminist theorists of eros violence and alienation are actually part of the same dynamic: a dynamic of power. It is easy to see the connection to power in the case of violence. The theorists' crucial claim is that alienation is also about power. It is, in effect, the absence of power. Consider the consequences of alienation: self-denial, loss of control, resignation, docility. These are conditions of powerlessness. Thus, the two problems of violence and alienation are in fact obverse sides of a single dynamic of domination and powerlessness.

As we have seen, these theorists argue that the denial and suppression of eros is implicated in both sides of this dynamic. As Brock puts it, "both

"Our Erotic Knowledge Empowers Us" • **107**

male domination and female dependency require the suppression of the self's own feelings" (1991, 32). People who do not establish intimacy with the world

> seek to assert control over the world or to give in as victims of it.... In this narrowing of freedom, gender identity and power fall into polarized sides of self-deceptive, fused relationships: in masculine identity by the attempt to shape the world according to the isolated self; in feminine identity by the surrender of self to the external world. Both result from control.... Erotic power denied and crushed produces dominance and control (1991, 36).

Put another way, the repression of eros produces a situation in which violence takes over, whether one is the perpetrator or the victim of such violence. Heyward uses the term "sadomasochism" to describe this situation (1989, 105). By sadomasochism she does not mean only or even especially sexual sadomasochism, but rather the impulse toward and acceptance of "power-over" and "power-under" in all kinds of circumstances. Here, alienation is interpreted as violence turned inward, that is, masochism. It is the swallowing of violence that others project outwards. Heyward argues that when feelings and desires are denied or repressed, relationships become abusive. People lash out at others or they allow themselves to be dominated. In either case, they are being "jerked off" by domination:

> To deny the sacred power of our embodied yearnings is to be pulled away from one another and hence from ourselves. To have our bodyselves trivialized and demeaned is to be snatched out of our senses and alienated from our erotic desires. This process of alienation from our sacred power produces antierotic (or pornographic) psyches and lives, in which our bodies and feelings are jerked off by abusive power dynamics: domination, coercion, and violence (1989, 95).

At this level, it does not matter (nor does Heyward specify) whether one is a sadist or a masochist; what matters is that both exist in a dynamic caused by the denial of eros.[20]

In this way, feminist theorists of eros argue, our relationship to eros shapes our structures of power. Although it should be clear by now *how* this occurs, it may not yet be clear *why*. The answer to this question is apparent from the argument that alienation is a condition of powerlessness. If alienation in general implies powerlessness, and the specific source of alienation is an estrangement from eros, what does this tell us about

108 • The Trouble With Passion

eros? It tells us that it is a source of power. In the quotation above, Heyward equates "alienation from our erotic desires" with "alienation from our sacred power." Although not all of the theorists use the language of sanctity, all formulate a similar equation. Likewise, recall that most of the theorists view domination as the result of a perversion of eros. Here again eros is a source of power: one that can be corrupted into something other than its originally pure state.[21] Thus, our relationship to eros shapes our structures of power because eros itself is power. When this power is repressed, denied, and perverted, a sadomasochistic form of eros/power is the consequence. As Hartsock puts it, "eros and power are deeply connected, and when eros takes negative, masculine forms that point toward death rather than life, the community as a whole will be structured by those dynamics" (1983, 202).

The argument advanced by feminist theorists of eros turns on the contention that alternatives to sadomasochism exist. If our structures of power are shaped by our relationship to eros, then a different relationship to eros would produce a different structure of power. But, they argue, at present we are trapped in a dynamic of domination and powerlessness because of the way in which we see (and do not see) eros. Specifically, the fact that we see eros as something that weakens us not only helps to create this dynamic but is also the reason we can see no way out of it. For the conception of eros as debilitating conceals precisely the possibility that these theorists want to emphasize: that eros is power—and a different kind of power at that.

So what is the power of eros? Trask summarizes it as "the courage of self-assertion, the struggle for an alternative, and the strength to live one's passion" (1986, 152). The argument is effectively compressed in Lorde's claim that "our erotic knowledge empowers us" (1984B, 57). This claim has two parts. The first part is that eros, if we are attuned to it, provides us with knowledge: knowledge of what we need and want in the world, knowledge of what matters to us and gives our lives richness and meaning. Building on this point, the second part of the claim is that such knowledge provides power. In Lorde's words,

> once we begin to feel deeply all the aspects of our lives, we begin to demand from ourselves and from our life-pursuits that they feel in accordance with that joy which we know ourselves to be capable of. Our erotic knowledge empowers us, becomes a lens through which we scrutinize all aspects of our existence, forcing us to evaluate those aspects honestly in terms of their relative meaning within our lives. And this is a grave responsibility, projected within

"Our Erotic Knowledge Empowers Us" • **109**

each of us, not to settle for the convenient, the shoddy, the conventionally expected, nor the merely safe (1984B, 57).

Knowledge of what gives our lives joy and meaning is empowering, then, because it establishes a standard that we can use to evaluate our endeavors. It thus helps *guide* us in making good choices in our lives, choices that will be in accordance with our values. Beyond this, knowledge of what gives our lives joy and meaning is empowering because it *inspires* us to live more meaningfully. It is not easy, Lorde acknowledges, to live up to the responsibility not to "settle," to "demand the most from ourselves, from our lives, from our work"—but, she argues, the erotic experience of satisfaction when we do reminds us that the effort is worthwhile (1984B, 54). The more in touch we are both with what we value and with the satisfaction that living up to it brings, the greater our ability and our motivation to "demand the most" will be. Thus, eros provides great power because it guides and inspires people to take charge of their lives.

Such power is especially important for those who are oppressed, those who do not start out in charge of their own lives and who have certainly been expected to settle. Anyone in this situation must *fight* for a more meaningful and joyful existence, and yet many in this situation end up passive out of alienation and hopelessness. For feminist theorists of eros, eros' greatest power is that it gives us the motivation to do this. Because it means knowing what we want and what our values are, because it means wanting to live life to the fullest, eros impels us to resist oppression and to work for a better world where human needs are a priority and we can all live fully. In short, when we are in touch with the erotic we are no longer hopeless and resigned; therefore we are no longer docile and obedient:

> [W]hen we begin to live from within outward, in touch with the power of the erotic within ourselves, and allowing that power to inform and illuminate our actions upon the world around us, then we begin to be responsible to ourselves in the deepest sense. For as we begin to recognize our deepest feelings, we begin to give up, of necessity, being satisfied with suffering and self-negation, and with the numbness which so often seems like their only alternative in our society. Our acts against oppression become integral with self, motivated and empowered from within (Lorde 1984B, 58).[22]

It is important to emphasize that accessing this power depends on reconceiving eros as something that can infuse a broad range of experiences. This argument is especially explicit in an essay by Lucy Goodison

110 • The Trouble With Passion

entitled "Really Being in Love Means Wanting to Live in a Different World." Goodison acknowledges that erotic feelings have been experienced as problematic (especially by women) because they can make us feel helpless, passive, and dependent, "the very feelings we are struggling to leave behind" (1983, 48). But, she argues, the experience can be entirely the opposite if we can learn how better to choose and direct the excitement and passion entailed in falling in love. As she puts it, "Perhaps the question is not why we have these 'incorrect' and humiliating experiences and how we can stop having them, but rather why that intensity and vitality of contact is confined to such a localized area; and how we can gain more access to experiencing and directing that vitality in other areas of our lives" (63). She contends that this is entirely possible, for

> We hear of non-sexual relationships between women which carry passion, fascination, delight and a peculiar resonance for the two friends involved. Mothers describe being "in love" with their babies, intimately bonded by a magic line as strong as an umbilical cord. And it does not stop with people. A teenager may claim to be "in love" with a horse. And what about moments of work which we can suddenly connect to, or the love-affair with a particular career or activity which may last stormily over many years? Or the times when ideas seize us and obsess us? Or the feeling of uplift on a mass demonstration when we feel intensely towards every other human being there? We can "fall in love" with ourselves, or with a country, or with a movement. Perhaps recognizing and nurturing those experiences can be one way of diffusing the passionate intimacy and contact of "falling in love" into wider areas of our life. Enormous power and vitality is involved: imagine what we could do with it (65).

Thus, whereas the narrow experience of eros in a sexual/romantic relationship may not be empowering, a broader experience of eros is. "[T]ransforming our love from a bewildering passion for one person to a deep-rooted lust for all of life" is the key (66).

Lorde makes a remarkably similar argument in her essay. At one point in the essay she proposes an unusual metaphor for what she means by the erotic. She recalls how during World War II margarine was sold in packets with a tiny pellet of yellow coloring that had to be pinched and spread throughout the bag. She says, "I find the erotic such a kernel within myself. When released from its intense and constrained pellet, it flows through and colors my life with a kind of energy that heightens and sensitizes and strengthens all my experience" (1984B, 57). This passage illustrates Lorde's point that the erotic has been constrained into one area of life (sexuality), but need not be. We can release it from this constraint and allow it to infuse the rest of our life. When we do, we find that it provides the energy to "color," "heighten," "sensitize," and "strengthen" experience. Thus, recognizing the expansive range of eros is the way to make use of its power to bring color (meaning) into our lives, which in turn can "give us the energy to pursue genuine change within our world, rather than merely settling for a shift of characters in the same weary drama" (1984B, 59).

This possibility of genuine change is why eros is so important to these theorists. Given that we live in a social world plagued by both violence and alienation, change is both imperative and difficult. As Dimen puts it, "The intransigence of the patriarchal state is the reason that we must maintain a utopian vision of a society in which desire is empowering, not weakening, in which all parts of the self can come out of the closet—passion and need, will and empathy, the anger that, through a paradoxical love, can make our society realize its ideals of democracy and decency even while hell-bent on betraying them" (1989, 48). The feminist theorists I have been discussing turn to eros to explain both the difficulty and the solution. They argue that our problems are in great part caused by our conceptions of and approaches to eros. Because we are convinced that eros is a threat to rationality and power, we disdain and suppress it. The result is that we are trapped in sadomasochistic structures of domination and powerlessness. Yet if we could only understand that eros is in fact a key source of power, we would have exactly what we needed to get out of this trap. A positive view of eros would allow us to accept it and integrate it into our lives. Doing so would both eliminate the violence that results from the repression of eros and replace the powerlessness of alienation with meaning, energy, motivation, and connections: a beneficent form of power that would help us to fight oppression and create a better world.

Diverging from Feminist Theories of Eros

As I have been arguing throughout this book, eros or passion does need to be reconceived and revalued. It is an important part of life, yet it is not adequately recognized as such. While it could certainly be said that the culture of late-modern industrial capitalist societies profoundly privileges the pursuit of individual desire, this pursuit is often conceived in highly rationalist terms: the object is to maximize "interests" and material acquisition, not to honor passions. Indeed, the acknowledgment and expression of passions and desires may be seen as a hindrance to the goal of maximizing one's interest, insofar as it is seen to jeopardize one's power and control. By and large, the dominant culture in the United States celebrates and

112 • The Trouble With Passion

rewards the cool, controlled power broker, tough, independent, ambitious, and virile.[23] Of course, there are exceptions to this celebration. In particular, those who do not belong to the dominant culture or gender are not expected to exhibit these qualities, and indeed may be punished when they do. Nonetheless, this is the cultural ideal that is most valued. Those who do not live up to this ideal, *even when they are not supposed to*, are not viewed with as much respect nor given as much authority as those who do. It seems fair to say that on the whole eros is not valued highly in mainstream U.S. culture.

The feminist literature on eros adds a valuable piece to this argument in illustrating the role that conventional conceptions of and approaches to passion play in bolstering oppressive relationships and structures. It also helps to challenge these relationships and structures by spelling out the richness and vitality that passion can bring to life. At the same time, the literature has two primary weaknesses. First, some of the authors continue to associate eros with women. Second, and even more importantly, almost all of the authors idealize eros. The result is that these theories ultimately merely reverse the hierarchies of reason and eros rather than truly dismantling them.

The only conventional quality of eros that is not challenged by all of the theorists is the association of eros with women or the feminine. All of them object, of course, to the reciprocal dynamic in which women are devalued by association with eros and eros is devalued by association with women. They disagree, however, about the most effective strategy for change. Some argue that only when the link between eros and gender is broken—only when eros is as much a quality of men as of women—will the devaluation of both be broken. Others argue that women and eros can be revalued simultaneously, that their association can be affirmed as a positive thing. For example, in Heyward's view, "Linking ourselves as women with body and nature and darkness and moisture and dirt and sex can illuminate the sacred: She can be for us, in this predominantly white western male historical moment, a resource of woman power that is passionate, dark, and intelligent" (1989, 103). And in Lorde's view, when we recognize the power of the erotic, "we do that which is female and self-affirming in the face of a racist, patriarchal, and anti-erotic society" (1984B, 59).

It is certainly crucial to challenge the devaluation of both eros and women. But endorsing a link between the two jeopardizes this goal. Associating eros with women reinforces both the opposition of masculinity to eros and the opposition of masculinity to femininity. It perpetuates the notion that eros is not a quality of men, thus contributing to the likelihood that men will feel the need to distance themselves from it. It also contributes to the distinction of a category of people called men from a category

"Our Erotic Knowledge Empowers Us" • **113**

of people called women. Finally, in a gendered society where men still have structural power over women, insisting on associating eros with women (and not men) ensures that eros will continue to be devalued, for unless and until a quality is associated with those in power, it will not be valued as highly as those qualities that are. To continue to claim that eros is a distinctively feminine trait thus endangers the theorists' own goals.

There is a further point. As I argue below, despite claims to the contrary, some of the authors also perpetuate the opposition between reason and eros. The coalescence of these two sets of oppositions—that between masculinity and femininity and that between reason and eros—is a particularly pernicious dynamic because it entails the associations of men with reason and women with passion. These associations in turn further perpetuate the oppositions between men (who are defined as rational) and women (who are defined as emotional) and between reason (which is defined as a masculine quality) and eros (which is defined as a feminine quality). The oppositions and associations thus mutually reinforce each other. For this reason, I argue that the associations as well as the oppositions must be dismantled.

Turning now to the second and most fundamental problem with feminist theories of eros, one might begin by noticing that the central argument is somewhat overstated. While it may be true, for example, that eros is often denied and repressed in the dominant culture, there are significant exceptions. What about the emotional fervor and dedication inspired by spectator sports? Or the enthusiasm frequently displayed when the country goes to war? Or the powerful desire for success? In none of these cases does the claim that eros is denied seem valid.[24] Indeed, because such instances of eros are not especially associated with weakness or femininity, the absence of a cultural imperative to control them is entirely consistent with the authors' own argument as to why eros is repressed. Another overstatement is the claim that the repression of eros necessarily leads to violence or alienation.[25] If the instances of eros just mentioned—the passion for money or war or organized sports—were repressed (or at least if their expression were not nurtured and encouraged), there might very well be less violence rather than more. Nor would such an approach necessarily result in depression, resignation, hopelessness, and despair. Loss of these particular passions is not equivalent to the loss of all passion, or even arguably to the loss of passions that are crucial to the sustenance of a rich and full life. The point is that whether or not the repression of eros leads to violence and/or alienation depends on what *kind* of eros it is.

What these problems of overstatement actually reflect is that eros has been idealized in this literature. Consider the claim that the repression of eros always leads to violence or alienation. Such a claim assumes that eros

114 • The Trouble With Passion

itself is inherently good, else why would its denial necessarily have bad consequences? Consider as well the lack of recognition of forms of eros that are not repressed. This oversight occurs, I would argue, because these forms of eros are not especially positive ones (at least from a feminist viewpoint), and therefore not what the authors have in mind when they think about eros. In many ways, then, the oversimplifications of the argument can be traced to an idealized conception of eros.

To say that the authors idealize eros is to say that they assume that our desires and passions are inherently for the best. They have argued that we should respect "the yes within ourselves, our deepest cravings," that we should embrace "those physical, emotional, and psychic expressions of what is deepest and strongest and richest within each of us" (Lorde 1984B, 57, 56). But what happens if we desire or enjoy something that isn't good for us, or someone else? What if our "deepest cravings" are for murder? What if hate, or envy, or shame is what's "strongest" within each of us? In these cases, one might doubt that it would be best to embrace the erotic, especially as a guide for action. Yet these kinds of possibilities are not raised much in the feminist literature on eros. This lacuna illustrates the extent of the authors' assumptions: the argument that embracing eros will have a positive influence is based on the assumption that eros is good.

The notion that eros is inherently good is particularly evident in the work of the theological writers, Carter Heyward and Rita Nakashima Brock. According to both Brock and Heyward, eros is in fact divine. Brock calls it "the incarnation of divine love" (1991, 45–46); Heyward calls it "the divine spirit's yearning," and "our most fully embodied experience of God as love" (1989, 99). Heyward also consistently speaks of the "sacred" power of the erotic. Since God is nothing if not good, to call eros divine is clearly to assert its intrinsic goodness. While the other writers do not explicitly assert the sanctity of eros, a similar tone of reverence is often present in their work as well. Certainly the overall picture of eros in this literature is as a benevolent force.[26]

Now, one might contend that the picture is not exclusively benevolent because most of the theorists have some concept of a distorted or perverted or deformed eros. Trask is more or less representative in her claim that, in patriarchal society, "Eros (love-life, symbolized by sex) is perverted by Thanatos (aggression-death, symbolized by war)" (1986, 35). This concept of perversion or distortion is intended to explain such things as sexual violence and the abuse of treating people as objects. Often "distorted eros" is specifically identified as "pornography." For example, Lorde argues that "looking away" from our experience of the erotic gives rise to "that distortion which results in pornography and obscenity—the abuse of feeling" (1984B, 59). Thus, one could argue that these authors do not ignore

"Our Erotic Knowledge Empowers Us" • **115**

potentially destructive or harmful instances of eros. But the language of distortion and perversion only confirms the point that eros itself has been idealized. To speak of something as having been perverted builds into the statement the premise that the thing itself is good or true or morally right. Likewise, to speak of something as having been distorted implies that there is a natural or normal or original condition of the thing. Taken together, the language of distortion and perversion in these texts reveals the core assumption of an original, pure, good eros.

How is it that these authors end up idealizing eros in this way? I think that they are led to do so through the combination of two implicit theoretical maneuvers. First, they assume that human nature is essentially good, and second, they conflate notions of eros as a natural phenomenon with notions of eros as an ethical ideal. Each maneuver reinforces the other, making it more difficult to see that either one has taken place. To begin with the assumption about human nature, notice that the argument that access to the erotic will guide and inspire us in beneficial ways assumes both that we have a true or authentic self and that this self is good. Deep down, we care about the right things, because deep down, we are good-natured people. Brock, for example, distinguishes between a "true self" and a "false self"—the difference between the two being precisely that the true self can express all its feelings, while the false self represses them (1991, 10–12).[27] She then goes on to assert that self-acceptance means "reclaiming" our "truest human character," and that this character is what gives us the strength to love the world and fight for right (24). Lorde displays a similar essentialism when she argues that resignation, despair, self-effacement, depression, and self-denial are states of being that are not "native" to her (or, presumably, us) (1984B, 58). And Heyward appears to rely on an inherent goodness accessible in human nature when she suggests that "If we learn to trust our senses, our capacities to touch, taste, smell, hear, see, and thereby know, they can teach us what is good and what is bad, what is real and what is false" (1989, 93). In each of these cases, authenticity and morality are linked: our true human nature is good.[28] If human nature is good, then it follows that any human capacity that is natural will also be good.

The concept of a true self brings up the question of the ways in which people are shaped by the contexts in which they live. Feminist theorists of eros are not unaware of social influences on the self. Indeed, their awareness of such influences is proven by their belief that changes in social relations and cultural ideologies can change how people view themselves and act in the world (as well as vice versa). On the specific issue of passion and desire, the authors would not dispute that what we want and care about is at least partly affected by the world in which we live. But even when they

116 • The Trouble With Passion

depict the influence of the environment on passion and desire, most present it as an outside layer that can be peeled away. The idea that eros gets distorted in patriarchal society perfectly exemplifies this approach.

So, while it is rarely explicitly identified as such, eros is frequently treated as a sort of force of nature in this literature. But at the same time, the term eros is also effectively used to stand for a set of positive values. Recall that for many of the authors eros functions as an ethic, a vision of the right way to live. This move is most evident in Trask's work, where what she calls "the feminist Eros" is explicitly identified as a form of consciousness that affirms the need for certain things. As Trask puts it, the feminist Eros "unleashes a desire—for creative expression, especially in the areas of sexuality and work; for balance among needs, particularly those of autonomy and nurturance; for sharing and interdependence without bondage" (1986, 94). Heyward makes similar moves: the extent to which eros actually functions as an ethic for her is evident in her insistence that "love *is* justice" (1984, 85, my emphasis).[29] The erotic is thus a "yearning" for "mutually empowering relation" (1989, 99). In these cases, eros is not just any desire but rather a very specific desire for things that these authors consider deeply valuable.

The final source of the problem is that there is a conflation between these two approaches, between treating eros as a natural impulse and treating eros as a conscious vision about how best to live. This conflation is facilitated by the assumption that our natural tendencies are for the best.[30] Whether or not they are in accordance, natural impulses and conscious principles are not the same thing. Yet the authors tend to move back and forth between understandings of eros as one or the other without distinguishing them. As a result, desire in general becomes identified with desire for such things as sharing and interdependence and relationships that are mutually empowering. It is precisely this conflation that elides any vision of the possibility that we may desire things that are not good.

The assumption that our passions and desires are naturally for the best is not warranted. Surely there are innumerable cases where people have wanted and cared about things that were not good for them and/or others. One might take the position, as several of the theorists do, that such desires are the product of an unfortunate cultural influence that distorts human instinct, but how could one know if this were true? Along with many others, I would argue that in the complex realm of human consciousness and behavior it is extremely difficult if not impossible to separate what is natural from what is cultural.[31] Does this mean that the opposite and more familiar assumption—that our passions and desires are naturally for the worst—is better? Such an assumption cannot be proven any more reliably than the first one can. The best assumption, then, is that our passions and desires, whether inherent, or socially constructed, or some combination of the two, may be either beneficial or destructive to our greater well-being.[32] This assumption is the best because it allows for the widest range of human possibility and is the least reliant on a simple and fixed picture of human nature. Moreover, it has the advantage of according with our common experience of the complexity of our emotional lives.

In part because it is an assumption that is not warranted, the notion that eros is inherently good has detrimental consequences for the project of calling on eros to motivate genuine social change. As has been argued above, we cannot assume that our passions and desires will necessarily be beneficial to our (and/or others') well-being. We need to consider that feelings may be of hate or envy or shame, that cravings may be for murder, and so forth. Most importantly, we need to think about *how* to approach or treat such potentially harmful instances of eros. What, if anything, are we to *do* with them? The most serious problem with the feminist theories of eros is that they lack an effective response to this question.

Now, this is not to say that the theorists are blind to the problem. As already noted, most of them do acknowledge that some passions and desires are less than ideal when they talk about those that are distorted or perverted. The question is, how do they address these kinds of passions and desires? By and large, it seems that their strategy is simply to classify them *as* distorted and to imply that, once they are identified as such, the need to change them will be self-evident and the ability forthcoming. For example, Heyward acknowledges that, given the alienated and unjust world in which we live, we all have "sadomasochistic sensibilities." She argues that we cannot simply deny these sensibilities, yet the obvious goal is to move beyond them. The only suggestion she offers for how to do this is to encourage "struggle" and practice at "mutuality." "Mutuality," she says, "is a relational process of moving through sadomasochism, in which the energy for domination/submission is transformed erotically into power for sharing" (1989, 106). This is a rather mysterious-sounding process; it is not at all clear *how* the energy is to be transformed. Moreover, there is a curiously automatic quality to it, in part due to the absence of an active subject in the sentence (who or what will do the transforming?). What this passage reveals, I think, is that Heyward is relying on a pure form of eros to transfigure any distorted forms. (Recall that she has defined eros as "the divine spirit's yearning toward mutually empowering relation.") In other words, she implicitly argues that the way to deal with distorted desires is to get in touch with our truest feelings, which will eventually (although not without some struggle) lead us away from our distorted desires.

118 • The Trouble With Passion

Lorde has a similar approach to desires that may be harmful. She acknowledges our fear of our own desires, "the fear that we cannot grow beyond whatever distortions we may find within ourselves" (1984B, 58). But she does not share the fear; on the contrary, her concern is that this fear holds us back from making use of the power of the erotic, thereby keeping us "docile and loyal and obedient." The reason she does not think we should be afraid of distorted desires and cravings is because she believes that "once recognized, those which do not enhance our future lose their power and can be altered" (57). Again, there is a strangely automatic or passive quality to the process of overcoming distorted desires. *How* do they lose their power? Apparently, it is enough for us to recognize them as distorted and they will wither away.[33] Thus, for Lorde, potentially harmful desires do not pose much of a threat because they will disappear as a matter of course.

The problem with this treatment of negative desires is most evident in Lorde's response. The question of distorted desires is uncomplicated for her because she does not address the most important questions: What *constitutes* a distorted desire? How do we recognize it *as* distorted? And *how* do we grow beyond it? To reply that a distorted desire is one that does not enhance our future, and that we can grow beyond it by just realizing this, is to beg the question. We still do not know what constitutes an enhancement of our future (not to mention who "we" are), how we can know this, and *how* it is that such knowledge leads to emotional growth. Such a response greatly oversimplifies the problem. Because it relies on an essentialized and idealized vision of human nature, the pure/distorted framework closes out crucial questions: it assumes precisely what should be up for debate. In addition, because it relies on our supposedly natural good feelings to lead the way, it automates the process of dealing with potentially harmful instances of eros instead of suggesting possible ways we might think about and approach them. In short, there is in this literature no method for responding to the enormous variety of human desires and passions.

This absence of method points to the absence of a role for reflection and judgment in the theory. If our passions and desires may be either beneficial or destructive, then somehow we need to make judgments about which of them to act on and which not, which to nourish and which to attempt to transform. But the authors who write about eros depend not on a capacity for judgment but on feeling alone for this kind of guidance. They do not specify how reason may be involved in the process.[34] In neglecting to do so, they undermine what I believe is one of the most important components of their own argument: the criticism of the opposition between reason and eros. Although they dispute the supposed irrationality of eros, in the end most of the authors do not effectively challenge the dichotomy between reason and eros. For instead of providing models of an integration of the two, they appear to believe that eros alone is sufficient to guide our actions. And although they challenge the hierarchy that values reason over eros, they do not challenge the hierarchical system itself; rather, they tend to reverse it and claim that eros is more valuable than reason.

A passage from another essay by Audre Lorde, entitled "Poetry Is Not a Luxury," provides an example of this outcome. As with several of the other authors, Lorde first argues that the opposition between reason and eros should be deconstructed, and then fails to follow through with this deconstruction. In this essay she writes:

> When we view living in the european mode only as a problem to be solved, we rely solely upon our ideas to make us free, for these were what the white fathers told us were precious.
>
> But as we come more into touch with our own ancient, non-european consciousness of living as a situation to be experienced and interacted with, we learn more and more to cherish our feelings, and to respect those hidden sources of our power from where true knowledge and, therefore, lasting action comes.
>
> At this point in time, I believe that women carry within ourselves the possibility for fusion of these two approaches so necessary for survival, and we come closest to this combination in our poetry (Lorde 1984A, 37).[35]

Setting aside essentialisms of gender and race in the passage, Lorde's call for a fusion of ideas and feelings is important. But she undermines the point later in the essay when she proclaims: "The white fathers told us: I think, therefore I am. The Black mother within each of us—the poet—whispers in our dreams: I feel, therefore I can be free" (1984A, 38). This is not a fusion; it is a reversal. It does nothing to help us see how thinking and feeling can work together. The argument ends up reinforcing the opposition between eros and reason that it originally criticized. In this way, it does not achieve a full revaluation of eros.

Conclusion

Ultimately, the combination of the idealization of eros and the exclusion of reason prevent the theory from working in the way it is intended. The idea is that we can use eros to empower ourselves to resist oppression and to create more meaningful lives for ourselves. Our passions and desires are a

120 • The Trouble With Passion

resource available to be tapped; if only we can learn to "listen" to them, they will guide and inspire us in beneficial ways. But as we have seen, this argument depends on an unwarranted assumption that our desires are naturally for the best. Because of this assumption, scant attention is paid to how to deal with problematic passions and desires. As a result, the argument cannot ensure that embracing eros will have a beneficially empowering effect, that it will help us to make *good* choices and encourage us to bring about *positive* social change. Another way to put this is to say that eros cannot serve as a means when it is already identified with the end one is trying to achieve. If eros simply comes to stand for "the good," then it has in fact left the realm of ordinary, complex human desire behind. The consequence is that we lose a sense of how ordinary passion can move us toward "the good."

But the promise that passion can function as a positive source of personal and political empowerment remains. What is necessary is to acknowledge the power of passion without relying on an idealized picture of it. A theory of passion should not assume that passion is inherently good any more than it should assume that passion is inherently bad. Most importantly, a theory of passion should pay attention to the question of how to handle passions that may not be constructive and liberating. Doing so requires thinking about the education of passion, a topic I address in the next and final chapter.

CHAPTER 7

Passion, Politics, and Democratic Education

Troubling Passion

What is the trouble with passion in politics? For many political theorists, passion is disturbing because it raises the specter of violent behavior. It is a (if not *the*) source of intolerance, belligerence, and persecution, and for that reason deeply troubling. I have argued that the trouble with passion is more complicated. For one thing, violence is not the product of passion alone but rather of reason and passion working together. So the specter that haunts us is rather different from the one that is commonly depicted. For another thing, while passion can contribute to violence, it can also contribute to cooperation and justice. Indeed, cooperation and justice cannot exist without passion. The trouble with passion, then—and the trouble with reason, too—is that they are both, together, as necessary for good as they are for evil. For this reason, attempts to demarcate reason and passion, to foster the former and discourage the latter in hopes of creating a just polity, are fundamentally misguided. The challenge, rather, is how to foster more generous forms of reason-passion.

This challenge is especially pressing for polities that aspire to be democracies. Democracy, as I envision it, is a set of institutions and practices through which the citizens of a polity explore the issues involved in living together (whatever "together" might mean), make choices about how to handle those issues, and act on their choices (i.e., engage in politics).

122 • The Trouble With Passion

Clearly this model is one in which citizen participation is key. Without delving into much-debated questions about what kind and how much participation there can and should be, I think it is still possible to say that if there is no meaningful citizen participation in the political process, there is no democracy. Participation in itself, however, is not sufficient, for certain kinds of political activity can unjustly privilege the voices of some citizens at the expense of others. For political participation to be democratic, then, the equal possibility for all citizens to participate in the political process must be ongoing. *Democratically* to explore issues, make choices, and act requires that citizens work to take account of each others' perspectives in their understanding of what problems the community faces and what responses to those problems might be most viable and just. It requires that citizens create and pursue ways of living together that will neither sacrifice individuals to the community nor sacrifice the community to individuals. Finally, it requires that citizens learn to deal with difference and conflict respectfully—appreciatively, even—since both differences and conflicts will remain. These sorts of political practices, even more so than less democratic ones, depend on citizens' abilities to cultivate generous forms of reason-passion.

In Chapter 3 I argued that liberal political rationalism fails to address key components of political life adequately because it fails to consider passion as well as reason as an important political resource. In this chapter I make use of my discussions in subsequent chapters to think beyond liberal political rationalism. My first purpose here is thus to consider some ways of thinking about the political value of the capacity for passion. Drawing on my readings of Plato, Rousseau, and feminist theorists of eros, I argue that passion is crucial for making political choices, creating political community, and motivating political action. Since reading these theories has also illustrated the critical importance of educating passion alongside reason, the second purpose of this chapter is to consider some ways of thinking about how passion can be educated for democracy. I discuss in particular two aspects of such an education: learning to work with one's passions (rather than seeing oneself as a passive victim of them) and developing a passion for democracy itself.[1]

Passion in Politics: Political Ideals, Political Community, and Political Action

In contrast to those who see passion as opposed to reason, power, and justice, as well as those who barely see passion at all, Plato, Rousseau, and feminist theorists of eros all suggest a different view. In their arguments, passion is in fact linked, or at least potentially so, to reason, power, and justice. None of these theories is without its limitations, whether it be a tendency to idealize, disembody, homogenize, or gender passion. But we need not accept the theories wholesale in order to benefit from their thinking about passion and politics.

One of the primary themes that emerges from reading Plato's dialogues is the link between passion and ideals or values. In Plato's terms, *eros* is the desire for the good. I have recast this understanding in broader terms: passion is the enthusiasm for and commitment to an envisioned good. Although in some cases this "good" involves only an individual or a small circle of people, in other cases it involves a larger community. Envisioned goods of this sort constitute political ideals or values, and in this way passion is a key component of political ideals. In turn, political ideals and values (hence passion) influence the choices that make up a great deal of the activity of politics. As an example, consider the debates that ensue whenever a nominally democratic state such as the United States is faced with the question of whether to use its military forces abroad. Some discussions, of course, center around what might be considered technical questions, such as "What are the opposing forces the military is likely to encounter?" and "Can the use of military force effectively accomplish the goals set for it?" Such questions surely call for answers based on as much factual information and rational calculation as possible. But connected to these discussions are deeper disputes about the different passions that people hold for different ideals: passions to be preeminent among nations, or to protect the lives of one's own citizens above all, or to support the cause of justice by any means necessary, or to uphold an ideal of nonviolence, and so forth. Consistent with the understanding of passion I have emphasized, these are all devotions to values and activities perceived to be good. The crucial point, to reiterate, is that such passions are not just personal emotions that are out of place in the public realm. On the contrary, they are an important part of a political debate about the values that should guide the polity's actions.

In making this argument, I do not mean to imply that every political choice involves an equal measure of passion. When, for example, professional politicians and bureaucrats make decisions, the level of passion involved may well be lower than when citizens do.[2] I think it is telling, though, that it is precisely those politicians perceived to be devoid of passion who are often most disliked by citizens. Former Vice President Al Gore is a prime example: throughout his 2000 campaign for the presidency he was continually plagued by the perception that he was "wooden" and "robotic." This perception created problems for him partly because it left him unable to inspire voters. But even more importantly, Gore's apparent lack of passion led to a belief that he was "up for

124 • The Trouble With Passion

sale," willing to change position on issues and even to modify aspects of his personality in order to get elected. In other words, his lack of passion was perceived as a lack of integrity. Why might passion be used as a barometer of integrity? Because integrity, like passion, entails caring about and being committed to something (in this case, one's principles). To put the point another way, citizens are more trusting of leaders who are guided by something above and beyond instrumental reason, for much the same reasons that Socrates argues for the true lover over the nonlover in the *Phaedrus*. The nonlover is guided only by "worldly prudence"—that is, a narrow interest for self-preservation. In order to protect this interest, he will coolly do whatever he has calculated is necessary. Anyone who appears devoid of passion may be perceived as similarly calculating and amoral. Of course, people may feel passion without showing it, and they may feign passion they do not feel. Ultimately our perceptions of others may not be accurate. But we can only judge as best we can, and insofar as the presence or absence of passion is genuine, it can be a good indication of commitment to principle. Furthermore, while the issue of trust may be somewhat more pressing in the case of elected representatives, the integrity of any political actor is nonetheless relevant to the political process.

Whereas reading Plato draws attention to the point that political *ideals* involve passion, reading Rousseau draws attention to the point that political *community* requires passion. Recall that in *The Government of Poland*, Rousseau counsels the Poles to "make love of country their governing passion." Rousseau argues that passions neither can nor should be eliminated from the political realm; on the contrary, "a man who had no passions would be a very bad citizen." The reason is that a man without passions would be unable to feel himself *as* a citizen, that is, "to identify [himself] in some way with this larger whole; to feel [himself] to be a member of the fatherland; to love it with that delicate feeling that any isolated man feels only for himself" (1992, 154–55). Lacking a sense of connection to the polity, a person will lack the motivation to think in terms of a general will or common good, to move beyond "I desire" to "we desire." She will also lack the motivation to obey the laws as (if they were) her own precepts, or, as Rousseau puts it, "do by inclination and passionate choice the things that men motivated by duty or interest never do quite well enough" (1985, 12). A community of any kind, however close or loose-knit, requires some threshold of emotional commitment amongst the people who constitute its members.[3]

What is the nature of this commitment? Surely it will take different shapes in different cases; still, I would like to point out that in any community of considerable size, the emotional commitment will not be to individual members of the group—most of whom will be strangers—but rather to the community as a whole and the values for which the community stands. To the extent that citizens may have an affinity for other members of the polity, the affinity is for the values they symbolize, not the people themselves. In this way, the link between passion and ideals/values also figures into the role that passion plays in creating community. And because of this connection, community is possible even when citizens do not identify with, or perhaps even care for, other members of the polity.[4]

Thinking of passions that connect people to an existing or desired polity most commonly calls to mind patriotism or nationalism. I argue below that these are not the only kinds of passion that can form the basis of a political community. Here, however, I want to address the concerns that immediately surface with the thought of these passions. There are some good reasons why political theorists have often worried about them: patriotic and nationalist fervor have not infrequently fueled repression, war, and even genocide. But, once again, these acts are not the consequence of passion alone: reason, too, is involved in their conception, self-justification, and execution. As I argued in Chapter 3, liberal theorists generally miss this unavoidable involvement of reason, and so focus mistakenly on trying to eliminate passion from politics in an effort to minimize the prospect of violence and intolerance.[5] Unless the goal is to eliminate the polity itself (and probably even then), this strategy is ineffective. For without passion, there can be no political community, and without some measure of community, a polity cannot exist for long.

If Plato points out that political ideals and choices require passion, and Rousseau points out that political community requires passion, contemporary feminists point out that political *action* requires passion. As Audre Lorde argues, "our erotic knowledge empowers us" (1984B, 57). Knowledge of what gives people joy and meaning provides power because it helps guide and inspire them to pursue the things they value in life. The critical point is that passion motivates and empowers people to act not only in their private lives, but in their public lives as well. Political apathy among citizens is a commonly noted problem, especially in the United States. But apathy is nothing other than lack of passion. As feminist theorists of eros argue, without passion people lack the energy and commitment to take political action, because they lack the sense that their actions will have any meaning or effect. Alienation from desire engenders despair, hopelessness, and resignation (Lorde 1984B, 58). In order to become politically involved, then, people must *care* about an issue, they must have some *vision* of how things ought to be done, and they must have *hope* that at least some progress can be made toward realizing this vision. But this caring, this vision, and this hope are precisely the work of passion. It is

126 • The Trouble With Passion

passion that motivates people to engage with the world around them and to try to make a difference in their lives.

Passion is a particularly important force in political movements working for change. Resignation and disaffection keep people docile and obedient to the dominant political order. Indeed, apathy may support the status quo better than any repressive institution. The motivating power of a desire for a better world is thus crucial to the ability to challenge existing political arrangements and policies. Passion, the enthusiasm for an envisioned good, works against the alienation and hopelessness of those who have not had equal power to determine the circumstances of their lives. It encourages them to fight for what they want, to try to bring their dreams into being. As such, it is the foundation of any grassroots political movement. In Michael Walzer's words,

> no political party or movement that sets itself against the established hierarchies of power and wealth will ever succeed unless it arouses the affiliative and combative passions of the people at the lower end of the hierarchies. The passions that it arouses are certain to include envy, resentment, and hatred, since these are the common consequences of hierarchical domination.... But anger at injustice and the sense of solidarity are also among the passions aroused by any anti-hierarchical politics, which means that we also have good reasons not to surrender too quickly to the anxieties [that such passions inspire]. Maybe things will not fall apart; maybe the center can hold; maybe a new center will form. Meanwhile, there is no way to join the parties and movements that are struggling for social change, and to support the "good" passions and convictions against the "bad" ones, except to do so—passionately (2002, 631–32).

Educating Passion and Reason for Democracy

I have argued that passion is a necessary component of political life. Cultivating democracy thus requires, among other things, cultivating passions that will promote democracy. To be sure, this suggestion flies in the face of common beliefs that passions either cannot or should not be educated. Yet people's passions, their enthusiasms for and commitments to various envisioned goods, will inevitably be shaped by the cultures in which they live. The question, then, is not *whether* to educate passions, but *how*. If, as many liberals argue, passionate politics makes for dangerous politics, it is because passion (*and* reason) have been cultivated in ways that encourage fear of and intolerance towards difference, individualism at the

Passion, Politics, and Democratic Education • 127

expense of a common good, and the pleasures of domination instead of the pleasures of justice. Protecting against these dangers does not require eliminating passion from politics, which is not possible in any case, but rather helping citizens to develop forms of passion and reason that will sustain democracy.

What is entailed in such an education? While a comprehensive answer to this question is beyond the scope of this book, I would like to discuss here two aspects that seem especially important: learning to work with one's passions and developing a passion for democracy itself. I will discuss the first aspect in greater detail, since its meaning and relevance to democracy are less immediately obvious.

What, then, do I mean by "working with" one's passions? The phrase is rather nebulous, but the endeavor is not one that is easily specified: it will take a multitude of different forms, depending on the person and circumstance. What I find useful about the phrase is that it conveys both engagement (*working* with one's passions) and collaboration (working *with* one's passions). Learning to engage actively and constructively with one's passions requires, more than anything, learning that such a process is even possible. We are not limited to controlling our passions or being controlled by them; on the contrary, we can experience, explore, challenge, and change our passions in a myriad number of ways. As Robert Solomon argues, speaking of emotions in general, understanding emotions *as* something we choose is key to their *being* something we choose:

> We cannot simply have an emotion or stop having an emotion, but we can open ourselves to argument, persuasion, and evidence. We can force ourselves to be self-reflective, to make just those judgments regarding the causes and purposes of our emotions, and also to make the judgment that we are all the while *choosing* our emotions, which will "defuse" our emotions. This is not to opt for a life without emotions: it is to argue for a conception of emotions which will make clear that emotions are our choice. In a sense, our thesis here is self-confirming: to think of our emotions as chosen is to *make* them our choices. Emotional control is not learning to employ rational techniques to force into submission a brutal "it" which has victimized us but rather the willingness to become self-aware, to search out, and challenge the normative judgments embedded in every emotional response. To come to believe that one has this power *is* to have this power (1984, 270–71).

In keeping with my argument that the connection between passion and reason goes both ways, I would add that it is just as important to understand

128 • The Trouble With Passion

that our beliefs and judgments are infused with passion as it is to understand that our passions are infused with beliefs and judgments. Because passion and reason are deeply tied, working with one's passions *is* working with one's reasons, and vice versa. Doing this work thus involves both *thinking* about the judgments implicit in what we call our passions and *feeling* the care implicit in what we call our reasons.

What is the point of doing more thinking and feeling in this way? The point, to begin with, is to increase self-awareness of one's various reason-passions: that is, to become more conscious of their existence, to clarify their true objects, to understand better the goods they envision, and to become more cognizant of the beliefs and judgments entailed in those visions. Such awareness in turn enables one to explore the value of these beliefs and judgments, and the emotional commitments they involve, in the context of one's life. Are these the judgments and commitments one thought one had? Are they judgments and commitments one wishes to maintain? Are they consonant with one's best understanding of the overall good for oneself and others?[6] We all have experiences of internal confusion and struggle, times when it's hard to figure out what we're really feeling and why we're doing what we're doing, times when we're torn between courses of action or have feelings that seem contradictory. I am not suggesting that such experiences can or should be eliminated. It is neither possible nor desirable to achieve perfect clarity or harmony—among other reasons, because that would entail perfect stasis. At the same time, living with significant internal confusion and/or discord can be quite debilitating. We end up doing things we regret, or not doing things we actually think are important, or just feeling paralyzed. Particularly if the situation goes on indefinitely, it can be frustrating, draining, and damaging. The question, then, is not whether one can prevent experiences of confusion and discord, but whether one can work through them. To what extent can one reach *greater* (not perfect) clarity in one's own thought-feelings? To what extent can one find ways to mediate significant conflicts in belief systems and priorities without simply rejecting and repressing one aspect of oneself? The greater one's ability to engage in these kinds of processes, the more empowered one will feel on an individual level.

Because it is so easy to fall back into a model that dichotomizes reason and passion, I want to emphasize one more time that working with one's passions is not just another version of reason controlling passion. The conventional Western paradigm of maturity is a person who is eminently reasonable, a person who has brought "his" unruly passions under the control of his reason and so acts with unified and judicious purpose. A more complex paradigm might depict a person who can bring her reason into accordance with her passions as well as vice versa, but even this picture is too dichotomized. For although it is not always easy to see, whenever there is internal conflict, there is reason and passion on both sides. As a result, mediating such conflict is actually a matter of negotiating between one nexus of reason and passion and another nexus. For example, I might say that I feel torn because I think I should spend my vacation catching up on work but I want to travel instead. Notice that this description of my struggle already casts it as a contest between reason (what I think) and passion (what I want). Yet if my belief that it is important to catch up on work is a genuine belief and not just a hollow precept, it will be intertwined with a vision of why doing my work is good and an emotional commitment to that vision. Likewise, if my passion to travel is a genuine passion and not just an arbitrary choice of activity, it will be accompanied by a set of reasons for why traveling is a desirable pursuit. It may well be that my enthusiasm for work is weaker than my enthusiasm for traveling, but if I have *no* emotional commitment to catching up on work, then either I will experience no conflict, or it will turn out that the conflict is not internal but rather between my employer and me. Internal conflict is not between reason and passion; it is between competing sets of reason-passion. Mediating such conflict is thus not a matter of using reason to control passion but rather a matter of determining how to balance the competing sets through thinking and feeling more about the beliefs, judgments, visions, and emotional commitments incorporated in each of them.

My discussion so far has focused on the need for individuals to develop the ability to work with their own passions. One might fairly ask how this quite personal activity contributes to democracy. My answer is that it contributes by helping people to become both more rooted and more receptive, two qualities that citizens must be able to combine if they are to create a vigorous democracy. By "rooted" I mean connected to one's sense of oneself, conscious of one's current thought-feelings about the world. Such self-awareness is an important touchstone for the conversation of democracy. To put the point simply, good conversations require participants who have something meaningful to say about their perspectives. And having something meaningful to say requires doing the work of thinking and feeling that I have been talking about.

Yet good conversations also require participants who have some receptivity, some openness to each others' perspectives. Working with one's passions contributes to receptivity by illustrating that engagement and collaboration carry potential that domination does not. I suggested above that empowerment is achieved through finding ways to respond to internal confusion and conflict without simply repressing one part of oneself. Implicit in this argument is the contention that attempting to *force* one part (or aspect, or tendency) of oneself to comply with another part is

130 • The Trouble With Passion

ultimately not very effective. Sooner or later, that which is ignored, silenced, rejected, or repressed will return. In contrast, acknowledging the dissonance, exploring it, and learning as much as possible from the different voices provides more chance of genuinely moving to a new position. My argument is that this experience of dealing with internal conflict can serve as inspiration for the possibilities of dealing with external conflict.[7] Now, unlike Socrates, I do not want to claim a direct analogy between the individual and the polity. The differences *between* people may be entirely different from the differences *within* people. Nevertheless, I think there is a principle that applies in both cases: that in the long run, it does not pay to silence dissent. Whatever hope there is of making lasting progress in the face of disagreement (by which I mean coming to terms, whatever those terms may be) lies in being open to the different voices. And if people can observe this principle in action within themselves, they can better understand its importance within community (and vice versa). In summary, then, citizens who can work with their passions will be better able to develop their own perspectives as well as be more receptive to the perspectives of others. Helping citizens to cultivate this ability thus helps prepare them to participate well in democracy.

I turn now to the second aspect of educating passions for democracy: developing a passion for democracy itself. As I said in the beginning of the chapter, I envision democracy as a set of institutions and practices through which citizens work to take account of each others' perspectives in their understanding of what problems the community faces and what responses to those problems might be most viable and just. In my view, this process of "taking account" is the core of democracy. The more citizens can understand and incorporate each others' perspectives in thinking about what should be done, the more the polity will be genuinely of, by, and for *all* of its citizens (and not just the majority).[8] From my perspective, then, developing a passion for democracy means coming to value this process, becoming *committed* to this process.

The emphasis on process is important. In the best-case scenario, working to take account of each others' perspectives would be a synergistic enterprise, generating possibilities individuals could not have imagined on their own. But even in such cases, the goal would not be perfect harmony. Real conflicts between perspectives exist, and are rarely, if ever, amenable to complete resolution. All resolutions leave something (and/or someone) out. Thus, the aim should not be to eliminate differences and conflict but rather to deal with them respectfully.[9] Democracy is not an end-state to be achieved; it is an ongoing practice to be followed. A passion for democracy is a commitment to continue working together—engaging, collaborating, and refusing to resort to force—even when challenged by disagreement.

Both of the aspects of educating passion that I have discussed are necessary (and probably more, as well). The ability to work with one's passions is a skill that *enables* citizens to participate well in a democracy. But skills for working with whatever passions one might have are not sufficient. Citizens also need *motivation* to participate in a democracy, else it cease to be democratic. Thus, citizens must develop a passion for democracy itself.

Unavoidable Consequences of Educating Passions

While political theorists generally believe that it is in a democracy's interests to develop its citizens' capacities to use their reason, they do not tend to believe that—or even discuss whether—it is in a democracy's interests to develop its citizens' capacities to use their passion. I have already explored a number of reasons for political theorists' inattention to passion. Here I want to address specific concerns about the prospect of educating passion. I want to argue that, although these concerns may be overstated, some of them are valid; nevertheless, there is no better alternative for a democracy than educating citizens' passions in and toward democratic skills and values.

There are at least two ways in which the project of educating passions may be troubling. The first way should be familiar by now: it is a concern with the *content* of such an education. Specifically, the concern is that encouraging citizens' passions for democracy would be encouraging a nationalist passion that is likely to be harmful, especially to all of those who are perceived as foreigners (whether resident or not). I think this worry is misplaced. While I have argued that political community requires some level of passion, this passion need not take the form of patriotism or nationalism. What I am arguing for is a passion for democracy, above and beyond any particular nation-state. I believe such a passion can provide a foundation for community that is not based on chauvinism against outsiders or repression of difference but rather on the reality and value of interdependence. A shared passion for democratic ideals can be the value through which citizens who are strangers come to feel that they have something in common with each other. Moreover, citizens with a passion for democracy would be *more* rather than *less* likely to question and criticize their country's priorities and actions, especially insofar as they appeared to violate democratic norms. Despite some of the violent causes for which the United States has used "democracy" as a justification, the real practice of democracy—listening to the perspectives of others, developing and pursuing common ends, learning to deal with difference and conflict respectfully—in fact operates against xenophobia, colonialist oppression, and jingoistic loyalty.

132 • The Trouble With Passion

The second concern with the project of educating passions is with the *practice* of such an education, specifically a concern that it would be a matter of the state "controlling" citizens' passions and/or "instilling" passions into them, which hardly seems consistent with a democracy. Does educating citizens in how to work with their own passions and how to work passionately with others imply telling them what and how to feel, forbidding some passions and inculcating others? If so, isn't this a process of subjection? I do not think this worry is entirely misplaced. Education of any kind is an exercise of power. It is, at the very least, an attempt to influence. But influence cannot be avoided. As I have argued, our passions are inevitably shaped by the people we interact with and the cultures in which we live, whether through formal processes of education or informal processes of socialization. All values, and thus passions, are externally introduced to some extent. Once again, then, the question is not whether to educate passions, but how.

Since subjection cannot be avoided, education should be judged on the extent to which it increases the potential for individual and collective self-determination and justice. I believe an education that emphasized democratic values and fostered democratic practices by helping people increase their self-awareness and their abilities to listen to others, create common goals, and respect differences would indeed increase the potential for self-determination and justice. Although it would discourage, if not forbid, some passions (such as the passion for dominance) and encourage, if not inculcate, others (such as the passion for democracy), it would by the same token help people to work actively with their own passions and reason and to contribute actively to a democratic polity. In this way, such an education would not result in the passive, obedient, uncritical citizenry that some might fear from an education of passion. Educating passions may seem like "programming" if passions (in contrast to reasons) are perceived as unchangeable once they have developed in a particular way. But this is a familiar misconception. In spite of external influences, people are not simply passive victims of their own passions. They help to construct them, and though it is not always easy, they can change them. This agency is why it is possible to talk about educating passions in the first place.

Conclusion

Good citizenship involves a willingness and ability to think *and* feel, at least to some extent, in terms of the community. It also involves a commitment to take responsibility for evaluating and working with one's *own* passions. When citizens have difficulty doing these things, then democracy will be less just as a result. Indeed, when citizens have difficulty

Passion, Politics, and Democratic Education • **133**

thinking and feeling in terms of the community, then democracy will be weaker—less democratic—as well. For under such circumstances, citizens may be unwilling to devote their time and energy to participating actively in politics. Indeed, under such circumstances, those who *are* concerned for the community may well discourage popular participation in politics. Worried that citizens' passions will be partial and selfish, they may attempt to banish passion in general from the public sphere. In doing so, however, they will effectively cultivate apathy. A vigorous democracy is a *spirited* democracy. Developing such a democracy, then, requires preparing citizens to participate actively in politics by educating their passion along with their reason.

My purpose in this book has been to identify the attempt to marginalize passion in liberal political theory, to argue that this attempt is neither feasible nor desirable, and to explore the work of Plato, Rousseau, and contemporary feminists for inspiration in developing an argument for the importance of passion to politics. As the desire for an envisioned good, passion is, and should be, a key component of a just political community. Rather than questioning whether and how politics can be "purified" of passion, or perhaps ignoring it altogether, political theorists need to focus their attention on questions of how better to understand and develop constructive forms of the human capacity for passion. These are projects that at the beginning of Western political theory were considered crucial. I believe that taking them up again would be a fruitful move—most of all for those who are interested in political change.

Notes

Chapter 1

1. Here my argument differs significantly from Nancy Rosenblum's argument in *Another Liberalism: Romanticism and the Reconstruction of Liberal Thought* (1987).

2. See, for example, George Marcus' provocative argument for the political value of anxiety in *The Sentimental Citizen: Emotion in Democratic Politics* (2002).

3. On the privileging of reason over authority, tradition, custom, and practice, see, for example, Edmund Burke and Michael Oakeshott. On the privileging of reason over qualitative (nontechnical) forms of knowledge, see members of the Frankfurt School. On the privileging of reason over the will to power, see, of course, Nietzsche. On the privileging of reason over the unconscious, see any number of psychoanalytic and postmodern thinkers.

4. Works include Calhoun (1984), Cooper (1999), de Sousa (1987), James (1997), Nussbaum and Glover (1995), Rorty (1980), Singer (1984), and Solomon (1993). Robert Solomon's *A Passion for Justice* (1995) and Martha Nussbaum's more recent writing on the political significance of compassion (e.g., Nussbaum 2001) are exceptions.

    Feminist philosophers (see especially Lloyd 1984; Harvey and Okruhlik 1992; Antony and Witt 1993; Ferguson 1993) who have addressed the gendered political implications of the association of reason with masculinity and passion with femininity are another notable exception. But their work does not provide a framework for thinking about the role of passion in politics more generally. And although some feminist political theorists and philosophers (such as Elshtain, 1981; Flax, 1993; and Young, 1990) have paid more explicit attention to general issues of politics, arguing that reason is associated not only with masculinity but with the public sphere, their discussions of these issues have been brief and/or limited to critique.

    As a political philosopher, Allan Bloom is a special case. In *Love and Friendship* Bloom is concerned with the "fall of eros" in contemporary Western (liberal) civilization, a fall that he believes damages both our personal and our political lives. Nevertheless, as he works to "recover the power, the danger, and the beauty of eros" (1993, 13) through 550 pages of readings of Plato, Rousseau, Shakespeare, and various novelists, Bloom mentions politics but rarely. Moreover, his most frequent point about politics is that it is *unerotic* (409), in tension with both the erotic family and the erotic endeavor of philosophy. Despite some outward similarities with Bloom's project, my argument differs starkly from his because my understandings of passion, politics, Plato, Rousseau, and contemporary feminist theory all differ starkly from his.

136 • Notes

Chapter 2

1. Two words that communicate a very similar kind of emotional orientation are love and desire. Passion, love, and desire all refer to a feeling that an object is valuable and therefore worthy of pursuit and/or care and support. Despite this close relationship, however, there are some key differences between these terms. Although love, if taken in its broadest sense, can apply to objects, activities, and concepts (for example, we might speak of "loving justice"), it is far more commonly used to describe a feeling that one person has for another living being. Indeed, I would argue that one of love's distinctive characteristics is that it develops in the context of a relationship. Love implies the possibility of being loved in return. Passion, on the other hand, need not. I think this special character of love is worth preserving. Since justice cannot return our "love" of it, I prefer to speak of having a passion for justice.

   I also think a passion for justice is not quite the same as a desire for justice. For one thing, a desire can be casual or passing, whereas a passion is more often a devotion that persists over time. For another, desire is all-too-frequently conceived in terms of a desire for personal possession, while passion is less bound to this association. If I say that I desire justice, the primary implication is that I desire justice for myself. If I say that I have a passion for justice, the implication is much broader. Because I am interested in this broader view, I focus on passion rather than desire.

   I thank Barbara Koziak for encouraging me to clarify how my understanding of passion stands in relationship to my understanding of love, desire, and emotion.

2. This historical tracing comes from *The New Shorter Oxford English Dictionary*. Additional definitions come from *Webster's New Collegiate Dictionary*. These two references are the source of all further definitions in this chapter.

3. As I argue below, the word enthusiasm cannot effectively do the job because it is too anemic. On the other hand, the words ardor and zeal are both too fierce, as well as too exotic.

4. The term "feeling rules" comes from Arlie Hochschild's now-classic study *The Managed Heart: Commercialization of Human Feeling* (1983). Philosopher Ronald de Sousa (1987), anthropologist Catherine Lutz (1988), feminist philosopher Naomi Scheman (1993), and historian David Stearns (1994) are but a few authors who discuss cultural and historical differences in how emotions are expressed and understood.

5. For interesting feminist explorations of how rules about reason have changed over time, see Susan Bordo (1987), Genevieve Lloyd (1984), Linda Nicholson (1999), and Andrea Nye (1990).

6. Unfortunately, it is difficult to convey a sense of passion and reason as fully conjoined while using the very words with which they have long been distinguished. The problem is partly a matter of historical associations, but it is also a matter of language itself: to use two different words is to imply two different things, however closely related. Inventing a new word that melds the two might solve the problem, but, at least for the time being, such a solution risks losing any link to current points of reference. I use the two terms "passion" and "reason," then, with the recognition that doing so perpetuates a distinction between the two, but with the hope of emphasizing interconnections nevertheless.

7. It is important to note that these authors differ to some extent on the issue of how, precisely, emotion is related to cognition and judgment. Nevertheless, all agree that emotion, cognition, and judgment are integrally related.

8. My discussion of passion and appetite in this paragraph owes much to David Halperin's discussion of *eros* and *epithumia* in Plato's dialogues. Distinguishing *eros* from *epithumia*, Halperin writes that "erotic desire incorporates an implicit, positive value-judgment about its object, whereas appetitive desire expresses no such judgment—it merely aims at the gratification of a need" (1985, 171–72).

9. Jowett translates *eros* as "love" in this passage and throughout the *Symposium*. But I am persuaded by several Platonic scholars (see especially Hyland 1968 and Halperin 1985) that "desire" is a better translation than love.

10. I am grateful to several people for encouraging me to articulate my reasons for speaking of passion in the singular, especially Annalise Acorn, Cynthia Burack, and Shane Phelan.

11. One could argue that there is one more problem: that fanatics are not open to any argument about their thoughts/feelings. (Michael Walzer makes such an argument in "Passion and Politics," 2002.) Fanatics might thus be described as rational but not reasonable. But

even if this is the case, I would point out that the problem is still not attributable to passion alone, for it involves a cognitive as well as emotional orientation towards alternative perspectives.

Chapter 3

1. This is not to suggest that passion is reason's only foe in liberal theories. Theorists have also argued for reason as a corrective for pure will, power, authority, tradition, religion, nature, and ignorance. Still, the concern with passion is a major theme that runs throughout such arguments.
2. This quotation serves as the epigram and inspiration for the title for Holmes (1995, 1).
3. Hobbes does include some passions (fear of death and desire of ease) in his argument for why people are *motivated* to move out of—or cease acting as if they were still in—the state of nature. Still, the correct use of reason is what *enables* them to transcend their other passions and understand the value of making—or acknowledging—the social contract (1994, passim).
4. Of course Hobbes' status as a liberal is a subject of debate. Nonetheless, on the issue of passion as the source of divisiveness, I think he can fairly be considered, at minimum, a proto-liberal.
5. The subtitle of Hirschman's book is *Political Arguments for Capitalism Before Its Triumph*. However, the arguments for capitalism were largely arguments for liberalism as well.
6. As an indication of this silence, one might consider that contemporary liberal texts rarely include index entries for the terms "passion," "emotion," "sentiment," or even "desire."
7. One significant exception to this is the fairly recent liberal literature on nationalism and patriotism. See, for example, Rorty (1998), Tamir (1993), and Miller (1995).
8. Spragens contends that contemporary liberal theorists have in fact "abandoned rationalist political norms altogether, looking for morally sound 'habits of the heart' to suffice in the stead of apparently perverse reasons of the head" (1990, 1). His aim is thus to "recall liberalism to its initial faith in the salutary power of reason in public life" (9). It is not entirely clear to whom Spragens is referring in this criticism, aside from Robert Bellah, who is not a liberal theorist. It is clear, however, that Spragens considers arguments for the instrumentalist use of reason to satisfy subjective desires as "irrationalist" rather than rationalist. Even so, I would argue that, contrary to his charge, both instrumentalist and other "reasons of the head" remain in strong favor among contemporary liberal theorists.
9. It should be noted that for Spragens, reason does include eros, although eros is here defined as not much more than the motivation toward rational cognition (1990, 18).
10. Again, debates about nationalism are a notable exception.
11. Rosenblum focuses her discussion (and criticisms) on "Romantic" arguments that include arguments for the value of passion. Unlike these writers, I do not advocate Romanticism. Rosenblum, in turn, does not argue against all passions, and acknowledges some political and ethical value in concepts of passion that are similar to mine (1987, 47–49). Thus, there is some overlap in our arguments. At the same time, she does not pursue the challenges these less romantic concepts of passion pose to liberalism, and her persistent focus on "arrant emotionalism" tends to obscure consideration of emotions that are not "arrant" and do not require the denial of principles and institutions. It is precisely these sorts of emotions that I wish to consider.
12. I am indebted to an anonymous reviewer for the phrasing of this objection.
13. Michael Walzer makes some similar points in his essay "Passion and Politics." In discussing the assumption that passion is to be blamed for territorial aggression, he notes, "But our hostility to aggression is just as passionate as aggression itself.... Passionate intensity is evident in the aims and actions of both sides. And so is rational conviction, for the aggressors probably believe—at least they are likely to tell themselves as well as the rest of us—that they have a legitimate claim to the land they are attacking. And we certainly believe that violent border crossings pose a universal threat. This is how things actually are: there are 'good' and 'bad' combinations of reason and passion, which we distinguish rationally and passionately" (2002, 629).
14. I am indebted to Steve Johnston for helping me to formulate this argument.

138 • Notes

15. The title of Rawls' book, *Political Liberalism*, indicates his acknowledgment that there are other kinds of liberalism. Although this collection of lectures departs from *A Theory of Justice* in some significant ways, none of them bear on my argument; therefore, I do not consider the differences between the two texts in this chapter.
16. The exception is the basic and minimal conception of those goods that are necessary for any other conception of the good (i.e., the "thin theory of the good") (1971, 397).
17. In *Political Liberalism* Rawls calls these desires "principle- and conception-dependent desires" as opposed to "object-dependent desires" (1993, 82–85).
18. Moreover, as Susan Moller Okin shows, the passion for justice is also at the core of the heuristic device of the original position, insofar as the original position requires highly developed capacities for imagination and empathy, as well as reason, in order to work (1989, 244–45). Okin argues that because we actually do know who we are, but must imagine being in the shoes of others who may be very different from us, thinking through the problems of the original position requires knowledge gained from good communication and emotional identification with others—and, I would add, the desire to pursue and take account of such knowledge (246). This desire is but another element of the desire to propose and honor terms of cooperation that would be fair to others as well as to ourselves.
19. For example, Rawls never directly compares or discusses the relationship between the two kinds of desires or sentiments discussed in this section (those involved in conceptions of the good and those involved in the sense of justice). In particular, that one kind of desire is politically important and the other is not goes unremarked.
20. The gendered significance of the association of reason with the public sphere and passion with the private sphere will be explored in more detail in Chapter 6.

Chapter 4

1. Another term that one might investigate is *thumos*. Barbara Koziak offers an extended exploration of *thumos* in her book *Retrieving Political Emotion: Thumos, Aristotle, and Gender* (2000). She notes that, while the word has been variously translated as "spiritedness," "heart," "passion," and "anger" (31), at least in Aristotle's usage *thumos* has an even broader connotation as the general capacity for emotion. In Plato's usage, however, as both Koziak and John Cooper demonstrate, the meaning of *thumos* is narrowed almost exclusively to anger (despite the common translation as spirit). Although this usage may well constitute an impoverishment of the term, my primary focus is not anger, so I do not focus on Plato's treatment of *thumos* here. For more on Plato's concept of *thumos* and its political implications, see Chapter Two of Koziak's book and Chapter Four of John Cooper's book, *Reason and Emotion: Essays on Ancient Moral Psychology and Ethical Theory* (1999).
2. A crucial passage in the *Republic* conveys Plato's argument that the *epithumiai* do not discriminate between objects as to their goodness. In discussing the nature of the desires, Socrates raises the possibility that "no one desires drink, but good drink, nor food but good food; for everyone, after all, desires good things; if then, thirst is a desire, it would be for good drink or for good whatever it is, and similarly with the other desires" (1992, 438a). He rejects this claim, however, on the grounds that a general quality is related only to a general object, not to a particular object, and concludes that "a particular sort of thirst is for a particular kind of drink, but thirst itself is neither for much nor little, good nor bad" (439a). This is the same argument as that which established that there are different parts of the soul. If, as Socrates has argued, "the soul of the man who's thirsty, insofar as it thirsts, wishes *nothing other* than to drink" (439a–b), then whatever may draw the soul back from drinking cannot be the part that thirsts. In other words, if *epithumia* has no discriminating powers within itself, then it cannot in itself be responsible for holding the soul back from pursuing something that is not good. Such an action must be the product of another, different part of the soul. Socrates declares this part to be calculation, and thus reaches his conclusion that the desiring and calculating parts of the soul are different.
3. I discuss the specific ways in which Plato's usage of *eros* departs from the conventional usage in more detail later in the chapter. Here, let me emphasize that it is quite clear that *eros* is not reducible to sexual desire for him, because he uses it in contexts where sex is precisely not the point—as when chastity is counseled in the *Phaedrus* (1953A, 256c)—or even impossible in a literal sense—as in the *Symposium*'s ascent, where desire comes to be directed toward

Notes • **139**

the beauty in institutions, laws, sciences, and the *eide* themselves (1953B, 210). Plato does have some grounds for using *eros* in this way, for it originally meant any longing capable of satisfaction (Halperin 1985, 164–65; Santas 1988, 53), and it "can sometimes be used synonymously with 'desire' in general, as the most characteristic of desires or as representative of the character of desire" (Bloom, Note #43 to Plato's *Republic*, 452–53). I have been aided a great deal in my understanding of the Platonic concepts of *eros* and *epithumia* by Halperin's detailed and extensive study of these concepts in "Platonic *Eros* and What Men Call Love."

4. The conclusion that *eros* is not irrational may seem suspect given that Socrates defends *eros* as a form of madness in the *Phaedrus*. This objection will be addressed below.

5. Despite its frequent translation as "love," or, sometimes, "desire," I am persuaded that *eros* is best understood as "the experience of finding an object endlessly attractive, fascinating, admirable, or valuable in some respect" (Halperin 1985, 179). This is equivalent neither to love, if love is taken to mean primarily feelings of fondness and concern for an individual person, nor to desire, if desire is taken to mean an appetite that can be satisfied by the acquisition or consummation of an object. Although for grammatical reasons I primarily use the word desire in speaking of *eros* in this chapter, I do so with the understanding that in these cases it is quite close to passion. In the interests of accuracy, I leave *eros* untranslated or substitute "desire" for "love" when quoting from Plato's texts.

6. I discuss the exception of the philosopher's *eros* later in the chapter.

7. Plato uses the masculine pronoun in discussing the tyrant (as well as in most other situations). Although it is possible that he could have imagined a female tyrant, he clearly chooses to describe the tyrant in masculine terms (in contrast to his gender inclusive description of the guardian class in Book V). In the interests of accuracy, then, I will use the masculine pronoun as well. It is not meant generically.

8. Interpretation of Plato's dialogues is by no means a simple matter. No one voice in a dialogue—not even that of Socrates—can be taken as wholly and directly expressive of Plato's views. In the case of the *Symposium*, every one of the speeches is important; the dialogue cannot be reduced to Socrates' recounting of what he learned from Diotima. Nevertheless, the interpretation that the earlier speeches serve to put forward elements of the conventional views of *eros* and that Diotima's/Socrates' contribution to the debate most closely represents Plato's argument about *eros* is widely held among scholars of the *Symposium*.

9. There was no need for Agathon to provide an explanation for why *eros* is the desire of beauty because the statement *was* obvious; that is, this definition was the common understanding of the term *eros*. Diotima's substitution of "the good" for "the beautiful" as the object of *eros* is part of Plato's strategy of incorporating and yet challenging this common understanding. The purpose of the substitution is to try to explain the true *aim* of what was generally defined as the desire for beauty (*eros*) (Halperin 1985, 176–77). For although it may seem obvious that one should desire the beautiful, in fact it is not at all clear what one actually "gets" from the possession of beauty. The point of the argument is that, although we may think we want to possess beauty, what we really want to possess is the good. Our desire may be *inspired* or *aroused* by beauty, but it is *for* the good. According to Halperin, the distinction is between the *object* and the *aim* of *eros*. (I should note that Halperin discusses the significance of beauty as the object of *eros* in far more detail than I can do justice to here.) The fact that Plato preserves the connection to beauty in his discussion of *eros* should not be surprising, given his metaphysical position that the good is what is truly beautiful. ("Is not the good also the beautiful?") But in my view, what is most important is that *eros* is the desire of the good; therefore, in this chapter I do not emphasize the connection between *eros* and beauty.

10. In "Reason and *Eros* in the 'Ascent' Passage of the Symposium," J. M. E. Moravcsik gives an extremely detailed description of the "roles and interrelations of reason and *eros*" in the steps of the ascent. Among the interesting results of his analysis is that "neither do we have reason or *eros* dominate the other, nor do we have a simple cycle of mutual dependence... (i.e., a pattern where *eros* and reason consistently alternate with each step)" (1971, 287). In some cases, he argues, *eros* alone is responsible for making the next step, and in some cases reason alone is responsible. It should be noted that the analytical nature of Moravcsik's approach requires (and produces) an emphasis on the distinctness between reason and *eros*. It is quite possible to read the same passage and focus, as many other commentators do, on the way in which reason and *eros* effectively blend in the process.

140 • Notes

11. As Irving Singer puts it, "In Platonism true love and true rationality coincide." For, "As the basis of both knowledge and valuation, the Good is the only object worthy of being loved or capable of giving knowledge about reality" (1984, 82). Samuel Scolnicov makes a similar point in his essay "Reason and Passion in the Platonic Soul." In Scolnicov's words, the doctrine of the *Symposium* is that "there is no essential difference between passion and reason—the summit of intellectual contemplation is also the summit of emotional yearning, and *Eros* encompasses both" (1978, 43).

12. My interpretation of the *Phaedrus* here has been aided by Chapter Seven in Martha Nussbaum's *The Fragility of Goodness: Luck and Ethics in Greek Tragedy and Philosophy* (1986), "'This Story Isn't True': Madness, Reason, and Recantation in the *Phaedrus.*"

13. Ferrari arrives at this conclusion through an extremely close reading of this passage of the *Phaedrus.* In arguing that the bad horse uses "the methods of reason" he means to convey that the bad horse uses verbal skill at persuasion in his attempts to get what he wants. There is no one specific word to characterize the methods of the bad horse in the *Phaedrus*; rather, these methods are illustrated through the story. However, given that the second central concern of the dialogue (after *eros*) is rhetoric, it seems plausible that the bad horse (like Lysias) is meant to illustrate the bad form of this kind of reason. Of course in a technical sense false rhetoric does not count as Platonic reason at all, as Ferrari will eventually argue (1987, 198), but his point here is that it is not entirely lacking in intelligence, either. My use of reason in the following pages will follow Ferrari's looser sense; that is, as a faculty including both prudential calculation and much higher forms of deliberation.

14. As Ferrari points out, even the noble horse is limited in this way: although its own desire happens to be a good one, it cannot deliberate about what desires are good for the whole soul either. This is why it is a horse and not a human being.

    This argument about what is best for the whole soul versus what is satisfying to only a part of the soul echoes the argument Socrates makes against tyranny in the *Republic* (1992, 577–79). In that passage he uses his analogy between the city and the soul to argue that, just as the whole city under a tyranny is not happy even if the tyrant is, so the whole soul under tyrannical desires is not happy even if the desires themselves are satisfied.

15. See Martha Nussbaum (1986, note 21 at 459, note 7 at 465, and note 5 at 470). See also W. K. C. Guthrie, *A History of Greek Philosophy* (1975, 396).

16. "'This Story Isn't True': Madness, Reason, and Recantation in the *Phaedrus*" in *The Fragility of Goodness* (1986). The term "recantation" comes from the *Phaedrus* itself, in which Socrates says he must recant his first speech condemning *eros* before he loses his sight as punishment from the gods he has blasphemed (1953A, 243a–b). Clearly Nussbaum reads Socrates' recantation of his earlier speech on *eros* as Plato's recantation of the position of his earlier dialogues on *eros* (and desire in general).

    It is important to note that in Nussbaum's argument, the *Symposium* is similar to the *Republic* in its condemnation of desire, with the *Phaedrus* thus opposed to both dialogues. In my opinion, this is the least persuasive element of an argument that is otherwise quite powerful. While I agree that there are some significant differences between the *Symposium* and the *Phaedrus*, overall I think these differences are far less significant than the difference between both dialogues and the *Republic.*

17. While I find this to be an interesting *analogy* between *eros* and tyranny, as I shall argue below, I do not accept the interpretation that there is any *causal* connection between "true" *eros* and tyranny in Plato's thought.

18. As Rosen comments, "if the origin of the just city is dependent upon philosophy, and if philosophy is essentially erotic, then despite the public rebuke given to *Eros, the city is erotic in its very origins.* The city is a form of *Eros*, as becomes clear when we think of the brotherly love of its citizens for each other, and of their filial love for the land from which they believe themselves to have been generated. But the city is not the *highest* form of *Eros*, as is symbolized by its origin in a lie, however noble" (1965, 461).

19. I am indebted to George Kateb for this interpretation of the *Republic.*

20. The resemblance between Socrates and the *Symposium*'s figure of *Eros* (both poor and ugly, both wandering barefoot about the streets and sleeping in doorways) has oft been noted.

21. Samuel Scolnicov points out that Plato's theory of education shows his attention to both reason and emotion. Plato knows that real change (that is, moving from opinion to knowledge) requires not only the effort of reason but a shift in emotional commitments as well (1978,

Notes • **141**

44). The reason that knowledge is virtue for Plato is because for him "knowledge of the good is not mere knowledge but…a unified activity of the soul, which includes cognition, desire and creation" (45). Scolnicov argues that Plato "knew full well that there is knowledge of the good that does not cause its possessor to do the good." Such knowledge, however, is purely intellectual, and thus lacks these other elements (46). Hence the emphasis on the integration of the soul in attaining knowledge of the good.

22. This is not, of course, to argue that Plato is a democrat—only to suggest that there are some elements of his arguments that can be used in support of democracy. A number of scholars have recently offered this sort of interpretation of Plato, including J. Peter Euben, "Democracy and Political Theory: A Reading of Plato's *Gorgias*" (1994), S. Sara Monoson, *Plato's Democratic Entanglements: Athenian Politics and the Practice of Philosophy* (2000), and Arlene Saxonhouse, "Democracy, Equality, and *Eide* in Plato's *Republic*" (1992).

23. As Arlene Saxonhouse puts it, "Democracy here is the private regime in which we act as individuals, not as parts of a common enterprise" (1992, 278).

24. Of course this scenario is precisely what Madison imagines in Federalist #55. Madison concludes that every Athenian assembly would still have been a mob, but I do not think Plato would agree.

25. Among the critics who have made versions of this argument are Monique Canto (1986), Jean Bethke Elshtain (1981), Arlene Saxonhouse (1976; 1984), Robin Schott (1988), and Elizabeth Spelman (1988). It should also be noted that, even within Book V, Socrates tends to slip from his suggestion that women are to be full guardians, frequently using such expressions as "our guardians and their women" (454e). (See also 451c, 453d, 457c–d, 458c, and 461e for examples of the possession of women by the [apparently male] guardians.)

26. There has been some debate in both Platonic and feminist scholarship about the significance of Diotima's gender. Many Platonic commentators have suggested that Plato used a woman to voice the wisdom of *eros* simply in order to avoid the problems (such as an apparent endorsement of pederasty) that using a man would have entailed. (See Halperin 1990, 259–61.) Feminist scholars, on the other hand, are divided between those (e.g., Nye 1989, and Saxonhouse) who suggest that there is in fact something typically feminine about the *Symposium*'s philosophy of *eros*, hence that Diotima's gender is no accident, and those (e.g., Hartsock 1983, and Schott) who suggest that the *Symposium*'s philosophy of *eros* is in fact quite masculine, hence that Diotima's gender is effectively neutralized. The most sustained exploration of the possible significance of Diotima's gender that I am aware of can be found in David Halperin's article "Why Is Diotima a Woman? Platonic *Eros* and the Figuration of Gender" (1990). Halperin takes the position that Plato is advocating a new form of *eros* that is, for him, culturally more feminine than the prevailing form, but Halperin makes it quite clear that this does not mean that women are to be included in this *eros*. In his view, Diotima is not a woman but a Woman, a symbol Plato uses to help convey the new (feminine) content he is trying to give to *eros*: "'Diotima,' in short, is a trope for 'Sokrates': 'she' is a figure by means of which Plato represents the reciprocal and (pro)creative erotics of (male) philosophical intercourse" (297). In this vein, I think it is significant that Diotima is never shown in *any* erotic state, while many of the other symposiasts, including Socrates, are.

27. Elizabeth Spelman coined this phenomenon "somatophobia" (1982).

28. Actually, the extent to which *eros* must transcend sexuality and the love of individuals is a point of some debate in Platonic literature. Some critics (among them Halperin, Nussbaum, Nye, and Singer) would argue that although Plato argues that one must go *beyond* sexual relationships, he does not always argue that one need leave them entirely *behind*. Other critics (among them Hartsock, Schott, and Vlastos 1973) contend that in the end Plato's *eros* has nothing to do with what we would recognize as sexual desire. My position is that, at the very least, Plato always values the things of the mind more than the things of the body, and thus it seems fair to say that *eros* is largely, if not wholly, desensualized.

Chapter 5

1. Ernst Cassirer, for example, speaks of the *Social Contract* as a "dramatic turning point which still astonishes his interpreters" (1967, 52). From Cassirer's perspective the text is a dramatic turning point because it proceeds to offer "the code for the very society which he has rejected and castigated as the cause of all the depravity and unhappiness of mankind," a code

142 • Notes

that moreover seems to advocate a virtually omnipotent state. Nevertheless, Cassirer concludes that the *Second Discourse* and the *Social Contract* actually "interlock and complement each other" (65).

2. "It is therefore quite certain that *pity* is a natural *sentiment*" (1987, 55).

3. See the discussion of this issue in the section on "Private passion versus public passion" below. Consider also the following passage, in which sentiment and passion are used interchangeably: "It is certain that the greatest miracles of virtue have been produced by the love of country (*l'amour de la patrie*). In joining together the force of self-love (*amour propre*) and all the beauty of virtue, this sweet and lively *sentiment* takes on an energy that, without disfiguring it, makes it the most heroic of all the *passions*" (1992, 121, my emphasis).

4. My argument that passion and sentiment are not clearly distinguished in Rousseau's writing echoes my argument in Chapter 2 that the distinction between the two is often overdrawn.

5. Rousseau's term is "man" (*l'homme*). In most of Rousseau's writing, it seems clear that "man" refers specifically to male human beings; indeed, in his usage, even "the people" (*le peuple*) refers specifically to male human beings, for Rousseau uses the word to refer to the (male) citizens. However, even though the *Second Discourse* at times seems to presume a male subject ("the only goods [savage man] knows in the universe are nourishment, a female and rest" [46]), Rousseau explicitly says that women and men would have been virtually indistinguishable in the state of nature. Accordingly, I mark the *Second Discourse*'s exceptional inclusion of women by replacing the ambiguous language of "man" with the clearly gender neutral language of "humanity." When referring to his arguments elsewhere, I shall use "man" and "men" to convey that women are no longer included.

6. Rousseau's diagnosis of the probable causes of modern illnesses, which include "immoderate outbursts of every passion," is but one example of this kind of reference (42).

7. The point is presented as an interpretation of Mandeville, whom Rousseau has just quoted. But if this is Mandeville's point, it is clearly Rousseau's own as well.

8. In Rorty's words, "even for the corrupt social subject, the alleged opposition of reason and the passions is more perspicuously construed as a paired set of oppositions: true sentiments and a well-formed principled rationality are allied against the corrupt rationality that is at the service of corrupt passions. Narrowly prudential calculation directed to the satisfaction of subjective interests—interests that rest on a misconception of the true nature of the individual person—can be at odds with genuinely self-critical, universalizing rationality. Similarly, the narrow passions of the prepolitical self are tensed against the socially informed sentiments that serve the citizen-person. In a corrupt polity, what is commonly thought of as the opposition between prudential reason and the passions reflects what Rousseau sees as the deeper divisions between narrowly calculative and generalized, self-critical rationality, between the passions of the social subject and the sentiments of the civic citizen" (1991, 420).

9. The enterprise from which the *Social Contract* is derived is the abandoned *Political Institutions*.

10. "To say that a man gives himself gratuitously is to say something absurd and inconceivable. Such an act is illegitimate and null, if only because he who does so is not in his right mind" (1994, 134). "Thus, from whatever point of view things are considered, the right of slavery is null, not merely because it is illegitimate, but because it is absurd and signifies nothing. The words *slavery* and *right* are contradictory; they are mutually exclusive" (137).

11. I am indebted to Steve Johnston for directing my attention to the passage describing citizens rushing to assemblies.

12. The interpretation of Rousseau's concept and use of "nature" is of course very fraught. One of the difficulties in this case is that Rousseau hedges his claims about the state of nature. He says the statue of Glaucus is *nearly* unrecognizable and that the state of nature *perhaps* never existed. He also says that despite the impossibility of obtaining accurate knowledge of the state of nature, "it is nevertheless necessary to have precise notions [about it] in order to judge our present state correctly" (34). But I would argue that one must take this claim in the context of the question posed by the Academy, which asks about the "origins" of inequality and whether it is authorized by "natural law." Rousseau effectively discredits the terms of this question in the preface to his discourse, where he points out that it is not possible to determine what is authorized by natural law unless and until one can determine the nature of human beings (as well as the definition of "law") (35). If it is not in fact possible to isolate the true nature of human beings, lurking somewhere in prehistory and/or beneath

Notes • **143**

layers of social influence, then by implication the whole strategy of looking to natural law for the "real foundations of human society" (34) becomes suspect. Either we cannot "judge properly our own present state," or we must rethink our standards of judgment and find some other ground than that of nature. I think Rousseau means to offer such an alternative ground in the standard of equality and liberty.

None of this is to deny that Rousseau continually praises "Nature" and often speaks as if access to it would be desirable. It is to say, however, that he employs the *concept* of nature largely as a rhetorical foil to highlight his criticisms of society. Rousseau may share the desire to know what is truly natural, but he is more prescient than others in seeing that he cannot. See David Cameron for a similar argument that Rousseau's "particular employment of the state-of-nature model strains the assumptions of that approach to the breaking point" (1973, 173).

13. That is, reason is always necessary eventually for adult men.

14. I am indebted to Edward Portis for the formulation of this particular perspective. Starobinski suggests a similar account for the difference in language between the two texts: "There are two forms of eloquence: an ideal form, useful for setting forth political principles, and a desperate, polemical form, useful for deploring deviations from those principles and for explaining why such deviations have occurred. In the *Social Contract* he adopts the former. In the two *Discourses* and *Émile* he adopts the latter" (1988, 319). As I argue below, I think this distinction begs the question.

15. Hilail Gildin argues that Rousseau does not use passionate language in the *Social Contract* precisely because he does not want to encourage action: "Rousseau's *Social Contract* is his least eloquent and impassioned work dealing with moral and political matters. The restraint Rousseau exhibits at least in that work is caused by his reluctance to incite men living under illegitimate rulers—that is, most men—to throw off their chains" (1983, 39). According to Gildin, Rousseau does not want to incite men to throw off their chains because the conditions for a just society are so rare that most revolutions would merely bring about utter lawlessness, which would be even worse than an illegitimate regime.

While it is certainly plausible to argue that Rousseau did not wish to inspire revolution when it would not help matters, it is not clear why such reluctance would have affected his use of language in the *Social Contract* but not in his other work. The *Second Discourse* in particular can easily be interpreted as encouraging resistance to illegitimate authority, despite its lack of a positive model. Gildin's argument thus fails to explain the reasons for Rousseau's different approaches in these two works.

16. As I argue in the next paragraph, I do not find this parallel to be persuasive because I do not believe that Rousseau in fact excludes passion from the public sphere. Among other things, the problem here is that these authors have attributed to Rousseau a dichotomy between reason and passion that is sharper than he himself maintains, as well as an identification of passion with women that is more exclusive than he maintains.

Nevertheless, there is no doubt that Rousseau does banish *women* from the public sphere. In this vein, it is interesting to note that, as Linda Zerilli points out, the *Social Contract* is a text that is uncharacteristically silent on the topic of women. While Zerilli grants that it is not surprising that women are absent as citizens, in her words it is still "remarkable" that the word "women" appears but three times in a text that was published at almost the same time as *Émile* (1994, 50). I have suggested that something similar might be said of the words "passion" and "sentiment." Although I do not think that Rousseau is silent about passion simply because he is silent about women (or vice versa), I think there may be a different connection between the two silences. As I argue later in this essay, what the *Social Contract* actually ignores is not so much the importance of passion for politics as the importance of the *education* of passion for politics. For Rousseau, though, the proper education of passion depends a great deal on women (who should, ideally, help influence their children and husbands to care about the right things). Perhaps, then, the omission of women as a subject from the *Social Contract* is at least partially linked to the omission of passion's education (and vice versa).

There is one further point. In a passage from the *Discourse on Political Economy* (quoted in the next section), Rousseau makes clear that the proper education of passion is actually a process of politicization; that is, it is a process of learning to channel passions toward the good of the polity. Since Rousseau believes that women must remain in the private sphere as

144 • Notes

wives and mothers in order to help with this process (see, e.g., Weiss and Harper 1990; Fermon 1997), it appears that, ironically, women must be privatized precisely so that passions may be politicized. Lange's argument that "women must be excluded from the public realm of citizenship because they are the caretakers of affectivity" turns out to be the case, but for the opposite reason than the one she gives: not because affectivity must be private but because it must be public.

It should be clear that although I find value in Rousseau's arguments for a political form of passion, I reject his contention that women must be confined to the private sphere in order to produce such passion. I am indebted to an anonymous reviewer for *Polity* for encouraging me to think more about this issue, and for directing me to Weiss and Harper's essay.

17. Lange also argues that women's presence in the public realm must be prohibited because it would only incite *amour propre* among men, thus obstructing the discovery of the general will (97).

18. To give one last example, Moira Gatens argues that "it is man who has access to both reason in civic life and passion on the private sphere," while women are in effect denied both (Gatens 1991, 18).

19. This is not to say that all feminist interpreters of Rousseau have argued that there is an opposition between passion and reason in his work. Indeed, a number of authors take pains to point out Rousseau's challenge to this opposition. See, for example, Rorty (1991), Lloyd (1983), and Tuana (1992). Still, the consequence for the role of passion in the public sphere is seldom developed.

20. These passages demonstrate the misleading nature of Pateman's argument that "love" and justice are antagonistic virtues for Rousseau (1989, 21). Justice does not require the "sublimation of passions"; rather, justice requires the *generalization* of the particular passion of *amour de soi*.

21. As has already been suggested, one exception to this claim is sexual passion (*passion amoureuse*). Rousseau does argue that women must be confined to the private sphere, in great part because they induce sexual passion in men. Sexual passion is thus one passion that men must leave behind in private in order to be good citizens. Other particular forms of passion that must be left behind will be discussed below.

22. Two examples are Cameron (1973) and Shklar (1969, 174). In Cameron's words, "The wishes of the people are akin to a natural force, blindly searching for the good...the legislator must harness this public desire, shape and define it, direct its flow, and finally transform it from a natural into a political force" (133).

23. I am indebted to Hilail Gildin's work for drawing my attention to this point (1983, 70).

24. As Rorty puts it, "whether this solution [of the *Social Contract*] is more than a verbal tour de force entirely depends on whether the psychology of the subject has...been transformed into the psychology of the citizen" (1991, 422). See also Cassirer, Shklar, and Levine (1976, 169). Cassirer seems to assume that the state not only must, but does in fact, "*create* the sort of subjects to whom it can address its call" (1967, 62–63). My argument here is that, at least in the pages of the *Social Contract*, it must, but does not.

25. "From these necessarily opposed objects [of being a citizen or a man] come two contrary forms of instruction—the one, public and common; the other, individual and domestic.... Public instruction no longer exists and can no longer exist, because where there is no longer fatherland, there can no longer be citizens.... There remains, finally, domestic education or the education of nature" (1979, 40–41). It is to the "education of nature" that Rousseau devotes himself in *Émile*.

Chapter 6

1. It should be noted that, in the process of integrating these works, I impose an analytic framework that is not overtly stated in any of these texts.

2. In this essay, Heyward uses the word sexuality rather than eros. However, in later works she switches to eros to refer to this same phenomenon. Since the two arguments are entirely consistent, I consider the terms justifiably interchangeable.

3. Hartsock takes this phrase from Dorothy Dinnerstein, *The Mermaid and the Minotaur: Sexual Arrangements and Human Malaise* (New York: Harper & Row, 1976).

Notes • 145

4. Trask argues that this vision will most likely come from women since it is primarily women who do the work of caretaking (of children, sick people, older people, men, and other women) in our society. Men who consistently do this kind of work may well have this perspective as well.

5. Most of these authors are, interestingly, primarily poets. With the exception of Moraga, they are generally classified as cultural or radical feminists within taxonomies of feminism, meaning, among other things, that they tend to identify sexuality as a primary locus of women's oppression.

6. Again, although the word used here is sexuality, the term is equivalent to what Heyward eventually comes to call eros.

7. With occasional exceptions, these authors usually do not specify which cultures are the subject of their discussions. Given the references they make, however, I believe they are presuming a Western, and often United States, context, and so I have made this presumption explicit. My choice to restrict the application of the argument to Western and/or U.S. culture is not meant to imply that the authors consistently and explicitly make claims to that effect.

8. By violence I mean physical injury and abuse, but also the violation or transgression of basic human rights (including both freedom and equality). I am thus using the term in both literal and metaphoric senses. By alienation I mean to convey loosely the situation of isolation and detachment described above. I am not using the term in a specifically Marxist sense, although there may be some overlap in what Marx means by alienation and the phenomena these feminist authors are discussing.

9. Lorde also argues that when the erotic is reduced to sex it is separated from spirituality. But in Western cultures spirituality is usually considered to be private rather than public.

10. For just one example, see Jean Bethke Elshtain, *Public Man, Private Woman* (1981).

11. The emphasis on dominant ideology is important here, since what it means to be a "real woman" and a "real man" varies by culture. In the case of men in particular, cultural norms do not always exclude open displays of emotion or the acknowledgment of strong passions. Nevertheless, the most hegemonic cultures in the West do tend to exclude these things from their ideals of masculinity.

12. As Wendy Brown puts it in her article "Where Is the Sex in Political Theory?" sex has been "displaced" onto women. One can speak of men without speaking of sex, but it is difficult to speak of women without speaking of sex. The paradox of the situation is nicely summed up in her question: "How can women simultaneously embody sexuality yet be construed as the passive object of male sexuality?" (1977, 5–6).

13. This point gains some strength if one considers Hannah Arendt's argument in *The Human Condition* that the modern age has seen the development of a new sphere, "the social," which lies between the old senses of public and private. It is this sphere that now takes primacy over the public as the place where "real life" is lived (1958, 38–49). Eros is assigned to the domestic sphere, the most private of all, which remains secondary to the more public social or economic world.

14. The lowercase spelling of Western is Lorde's choice.

15. The lowercase spelling of Christian is Heyward's choice.

16. Except perhaps in the case of sexual desire, which, as noted before, is the one aspect of eros that in some ways is associated with men more than with women.

17. Hartsock uses the term "masculine" eros to describe the conceptions and practices of eros that prevail in a male-dominated society.

18. Again, Heyward argues that Christianity has been a leader in this form of behavior toward women and eros: "For early Church Fathers, evil, woman, and sex were the same passionate phenomenon. 'Evil,' 'woman,' 'sex,' and 'passion' became, in the history of christian experience, different words for the same experience, the same demon, against which holy men believe they must contend for the sake of an antiseptic God, in whose pure image they are created and whose fatherly work they strive to accomplish—to curse passionate bodies and bless dispassionate souls" (1984, 21).

19. Dimen uses the word desire instead of eros, but her arguments about desire are quite parallel to the arguments that other writers make about eros. Therefore I include her in the trend of feminist work on eros.

20. In Trask's formulation, both Eros and Thanatos are "mutilated" by the repression of Eros: "For both Freud and Marcuse, surplus-repression of the sex instincts weakens Eros, altering

146 • Notes

the balance between Life and Death. This weakening mutilates both instincts. Thanatos appears as unlimited aggression (no longer as a desire for peace). Eros appears as alienation—the absence of gratification, the negation of the pleasure principle" (1986, 10).

21. Some of the authors go so far as to argue that eros is the source of all power, whether pure or corrupt: "All power emerges from erotic power either, in life-giving form, from our acknowledgment of it and our ability to live in that understanding or, in destructive form, from the brokenheartedness that refuses to understand it" (Brock 1991, 41).

22. Trask's language echoes Lorde's: "[Feminists'] search has led them to a multilayered, intimate knowledge of the physical and the instinctual, the basis of their return to love through a return to our most basic inner feelings, those acute understandings of what brings joy and meaning. The recognition of these feelings is the beginning of a new knowledge which empowers, which carries us out of alienation, the numbing of our feelings, into courageous living: 'passionate thinking' and passionate living'" (1986, 94).

23. David Stearns provides interesting evidence to support this point in *American Cool: Constructing a Twentieth-Century Emotional Style* (1994).

24. Nancy Hartsock provides a significant exception here. She differs from almost all of the other feminists writing about eros in that she focuses primarily on the negative forms that eros takes in Western patriarchal culture, and at least attempts to avoid viewing these forms as distortions of some original, pure form. She is, for example, quite willing to see an enthusiasm for warfare as a genuine instance of eros. As a result, she does not argue that eros is typically repressed in this culture (although she does think that one aspect of eros—sensuality and bodily pleasure—is repressed). Because of her different approach, much of my criticism in this chapter does not apply as well to Hartsock as it does to the other authors. Nevertheless, despite Hartsock's explicitly constructionist perspective, she too sometimes slips into essentializing and idealizing eros. For example, she says our society "puts eros in the service of violence" (1983, 168), a statement implying that violence was originally alien to eros. As part of her general feminist standpoint theory, she also argues that if eros were structured by women's experience instead of men's, it might take more positive forms (255–59). To the extent that Hartsock takes these kinds of positions, I include her in my criticism.

25. It is also not the case that *all* violence and *all* alienation are caused by the denial and repression of eros. Violence and oppression are at least as much the result of certain political and economic systems as of any individual actions. Likewise, alienation may have various sources, including the scale, mobility, and rapid cultural change of contemporary Western society. The authors are certainly aware of such political, economic, and social factors in the production of violence and alienation, yet the force of their argument would seem to reduce them all to the question of our relationship to eros. The dichotomy of domination and powerlessness is not caused solely by a negative relationship to eros. Another way to say this is to say that eros is not, as Brock contends, the only source of power (1991, 25).

26. Again, the notable exception to this trend is Hartsock.

27. Brock contends that this concept of the true self is not essentialist because the self is an "achievement of relationality." It does not have an essence but is "recreated every moment by relationships and memory." Nonetheless, arguments about our "truest human character" imply that, as a species, human beings have a specific essence.

28. Hartsock and Trask would both disclaim any connection to the idea that we have a true human nature, let alone that it is good. Both purport to take a more constructionist view of human beings. Indeed, both make some version of a standpoint argument, which holds that social practices and relations greatly determine how people see the world and the shape their characters take. But standpoint arguments do presume that some ways of seeing the world (generally from the position of the oppressed) are "epistemologically privileged," that is, better able to see "reality." And they also tend to hold that these ways of seeing the world could lead to a better way of life. Thus, they make their own connection between "truth" and morality. (It should also be noted that Trask is less consistent in her commitment to standpoint theory; she often argues from different and more directly essentialist positions, such as a Marcusian belief in the great battle between the human instincts of Eros and Thanatos.)

29. The theme of love as justice runs throughout Heyward's work. Another example: "Love is active, effective, a matter of making reciprocal and mutually beneficial relation with one's

Notes • **147**

friends and enemies. Love creates righteousness, or justice, here on earth. To make love is to make justice" (1984, 186).

30. It is a telling point that the authors who rely least on essentialist assumptions about human nature (again, Hartsock and sometimes Trask) are the ones most likely to offer some support for their version of the argument that passions and desires are for the best. Their version of the argument is that we can count on certain people's passions and desires (those of women, and perhaps men of oppressed groups) as having liberatory and life-enhancing potential, or at least more so than the passions and desires of those in power. According to these authors, it is both the negative experience of oppression and the positive experience of taking care of the material necessities of life (which work has been delegated to women and lower-class men) that affords these people this privileged view. For example, Trask says, "I have tried to show that it is not biological mothering but the entire sphere of relational obligations which brings women closer to a protective, beneficent form of love and power that seeks to cherish life and life's continuity" (1986, 144). Such arguments are certainly not indisputable, but they are at least arguments and not just assumptions.

31. As Rousseau so eloquently put it in the Preface to his *Second Discourse,* "And how will man manage to see himself as nature formed him, through all the changes that the sequence of time and things must have produced in his original constitution, and to separate what he gets from his own stock from what circumstances and his progress have added to or changed in his primitive state? Like the statue of Glaucus, which time, sea, and storms had so disfigured that it looked less like a god than a wild beast, the human soul, altered in the bosom of society by a thousand continually renewed causes, by the acquisition of a mass of knowledge and errors, by changes that occurred in the constitution of bodies, and by the continual impact of the passions, has, so to speak, changed its appearance to the point of being nearly unrecognizable" (1987, 33).

32. I use the language of benefit, harm, and well-being here because I think that in many ways the question of the "goodness" of eros comes down to a concern with these things. I could just as well say that the best assumption is that our desires may be for either good or bad things. By using the language of benefit and harm I do not at all mean to imply that it is obvious or fixed what is beneficial or harmful, anymore than that it is obvious or fixed what "the good" is; rather, I think this is precisely what must be explored and debated.

33. Lorde's position here is consistent with her argument about how eros gets distorted in the first place: by our "looking away" from it; that is, by our refusal to recognize it. Recognition is thus the key to the purity of the erotic. When the erotic is not recognized, it becomes distorted. And when distorted desires are recognized, they become purified.

34. With the very significant exception of Robin May Schott, who explicitly writes about the relationship between eros and reason (or knowledge) and who is much more successful at providing at least some suggestions as to how reason and eros may involve each other.

35. The lowercase spelling of European is Lorde's choice.

Chapter 7

1. I want to emphasize here what I will discuss in greater detail below: because passion and reason are deeply tied, working with one's passions is also working with one's reason, and vice versa. To stress this point, I have at times used the compound word "reason-passion." Because the word reads awkwardly, however, I refrain from using it regularly.

2. I pursue this example at the risk of overemphasizing "professional" politicians in this discussion. In fact I am more interested in the passions of ordinary citizens, in accordance with my vision of democracy as participatory.

3. In talking about political community, I do not mean to suggest that there will only ever be one community. On the contrary, there will likely be a variety of interlocking and cross-cutting communities (family, ethnic, vocational, etc.). As a result, part of the process of working with passions will be negotiating one's membership in these various communities, emotionally as well as intellectually. However, my focus here is on the largest political unit.

4. I am indebted to Susan Bickford for this point.

5. As I have mentioned in previous chapters, this importance of patriotism has received some acknowledgment in recent years by liberal theorists who have persuasively argued that not

148 • Notes

all forms of patriotism are harmful or dangerous, and that, indeed, some forms are quite necessary. See, for example, Miller (1995) and Tamir (1993).

6. Clearly this argument is influenced by Plato's distinction between *eros* and *epithumia* insofar as it suggests that some passions and rationalizations are relatively unreflective, that others are much more thoughtful about what constitutes a good life, and that growth entails developing and coming to prioritize the latter. However, I hasten to note, once again, that despite the use of this distinction, I do not accept Plato's argument that sensual pleasures necessarily fall into the former category.

7. Likewise, the experience of dealing with external conflict can serve as inspiration for the possibilities of dealing with internal conflict.

8. In the contemporary context, Benjamin Barber (1994) and Jane Mansbridge (1983) were early advocates of this point. They have been followed by an increasing number of theorists of participatory and deliberative democracy.

9. See, for example, Bickford (1996), Mansbridge (1983), and Young (1996) on the dangers of too much emphasis on the "common good."

Bibliography

Anderson, C. W. (1990). *Pragmatic Liberalism*. Chicago: University of Chicago Press.
Antony, L. M. and C. Witt, eds. (1993). *A Mind of One's Own: Feminist Essays on Reason & Objectivity*. Boulder, CO: Westview Press.
Arendt, H. (1958). *The Human Condition*. Chicago: University of Chicago Press.
Barber, B. (1994). *Strong Democracy: Participatory Politics for a New Age*. Berkeley: University of California Press.
Bickford, S. (1996). *The Dissonance of Democracy: Listening, Conflict, and Citizenship*. Ithaca, NY: Cornell University Press.
Bloom, A. (1993). *Love and Friendship*. New York: Simon & Schuster.
Bordo, S. (1987). *The Flight to Objectivity: Essays on Cartesianism & Culture*. Albany: State University of New York Press.
Brock, R. N. (1991). *Journeys by Heart: A Christology of Erotic Power*. New York: Crossroad Publishing Co.
Brown, W. (1977). "Where Is the Sex in Political Theory?" *Women and Politics* 7(1): 3–23.
Calhoun, C. (1984). "Cognitive Emotions." In *What Is an Emotion? Classical Readings in Philosophical Psychology*. C. Calhoun and R. C. Solomon, eds. New York: Oxford University Press.
Calhoun, C. and R. C. Solomon, eds. (1984). "Introduction." In *What Is an Emotion? Classic Readings in Philosophical Psychology*. New York: Oxford University Press.
Cameron, D. (1973). *The Social Thought of Rousseau and Burke: A Comparative Study*. Toronto: University of Toronto Press.
Canto, M. (1986). "The Politics of Women's Bodies: Reflections on Plato." In *The Female Body in Western Culture: Contemporary Perspectives*. S. R. Suleiman, ed. Cambridge: Cambridge University Press.
Carson, A. (1986). *Eros the Bittersweet*. Princeton: Princeton University Press.
Cassirer, E. (1967). "The Question of Jean-Jacques Rousseau." In *Modern Critical Views: Jean-Jacques Rousseau*. H. Bloom, ed. Bloomington: Indiana University Press.
Cooper, J. (1999). *Reason and Emotion: Essays on Ancient Moral Psychology and Ethical Theory*. Princeton: Princeton University Press.
D'Agostino, F. (1996). *Free Public Reason: Making It Up As We Go*. Oxford: Oxford University Press.
Damasio, A. (1994). *Descartes' Error: Emotion, Reason, and the Human Brain*. New York: G. P. Putnam's Sons.
de Sousa, R. (1987). *The Rationality of Emotion*. Cambridge, MA: MIT Press.
Dimen, M. (1989). "Power, Sexuality, and Intimacy." In *Gender/Body/Knowledge*. A. M. Jaggar and S. R. Berdo, eds. New Brunswick: Rutgers University Press.
Elshtain, J. B. (1981). *Public Man, Private Woman: Women in Social and Political Thought*. Princeton: Princeton University Press.

150 • Bibliography

Euben, J. P. (1994). "Democracy and Political Theory: A Reading of Plato's Gorgias." In *Athenian Political Thought and the Reconstruction of American Democracy*. J. P. Euben, J. R. Wallach, and J. Ober, eds. Ithaca, NY: Cornell University Press.

Ferguson, A. (1993). "Does Reason Have a Gender?" In *Radical Philosophy: Tradition, Counter-Tradition, Politics*. R. S. Gottlieb, ed. Philadelphia: Temple University Press.

Fermon, N. (1997). *Domesticating Passions: Rousseau, Woman, and Nation*. Middletown, CT: Wesleyan University Press.

Ferrari, G. R. (1987). *Listening to the Cicadas: A Study of Plato's Phaedrus*. Cambridge: Cambridge University Press.

Flax, J. (1993). *Disputed Subjects: Essays on Psychoanalysis, Politics, and Philosophy*. New York: Routledge.

Gatens, M. (1991). *Feminism and Philosophy*. Bloomington: Indiana University Press.

Gildin, H. (1983). *Rousseau's Social Contract: The Design of the Argument*. Chicago: University of Chicago Press.

Goodison, L. (1983). "Really Being in Love Means Wanting to Live in a Different World." In *Sex and Love: New Thoughts on Old Contradictions*. S. Cartledge and J. Ryan, eds. London: The Women's Press.

Guthrie, W. K. C. (1975). *A History of Greek Philosophy*. Cambridge: Cambridge University Press.

Halperin, D. (1985). "Platonic Eros and What Men Call Love." *American Philosophy* 5: 161–204.

———. (1990). "Why Is Diotima a Woman? Platonic Eros and the Figuration of Gender." In *Before Sexuality: The Construction of Erotic Experience in the Ancient Greek World*. D. Halperin and F. E. Zertlin, eds. Princeton: Princeton University Press.

Hamilton, A., J. Madison, and J. Jay. (1961). *The Federalist Papers*. New York: Mentor Books.

Hartsock, N. C. M. (1983). *Money, Sex, and Power: Toward a Feminist Historical Materialism*. New York and London: Longman Press.

Harvey, E. D. and K. Okruhlik, eds. (1992). *Women and Reason*. Ann Arbor: University of Michigan Press.

Heyward, C. (1984). *Our Passion for Justice: Images of Power, Sexuality, and Liberation*. New York: Pilgrim Press.

———. (1989). *Touching Our Strength: The Erotic as Power and the Love of God*. San Francisco: Harper & Row.

Hirschman, A. O. (1977). *The Passions and the Interests: Political Arguments for Capitalism Before Its Triumph*. Princeton: Princeton University Press.

Hobbes, T. (1994). *Leviathan*. Indianapolis: Hackett Publishing Company.

Hochschild, A. R. (1983). *The Managed Heart: Commercialization of Human Feeling*. Berkeley: University of California Press.

Holmes, S. (1995). *Passions and Constraint: On the Theory of Liberal Democracy*. Chicago: University of Chicago Press.

Hume, D. (1978). *A Treatise of Human Nature*. Oxford: Clarendon Press.

Hyland, P. A. (1968). "Eros, Epithymia, and Philia in Plato." *Phronesis: A Journal for Ancient Philosophy* 13: 32–46.

James, S. (1997). *Passion and Action: The Emotions in Seventeenth-Century Philosophy*. New York: Oxford University Press.

Koziak, B. (2000). *Retrieving Political Emotion: Thumos, Aristotle, and Gender*. University Park: Pennsylvania State University Press.

Lange, L. (1994). "Women and Rousseau's Democratic Theory: Philosopher Monsters and Authoritarian Equality." In *Modern Engendering: Critical Feminist Readings in Modern Western Philosophy*. B.-A. Bar On, ed. Albany: State University of New York Press.

Levine, A. (1976). *The Politics of Autonomy: A Kantian Reading of Rousseau's Social Contract*. Amherst: University of Massachusetts Press.

Lloyd, G. (1983). "Rousseau on Reason, Nature and Women." *Metaphilosophy* 143(4): 308–326.

———. (1984). *The Man of Reason: 'Male' and 'Female' in Western Philosophy*. Minneapolis: University of Minnesota Press.

Locke, J. (1980). *Second Treatise of Government*. Indianapolis: Hackett Publishing Company, Inc.

Lorde, A. (1984A). "Poetry Is Not a Luxury." In *Sister Outsider*. Trumansberg, NY: The Crossing Press.

———. (1984B). "Uses of the Erotic: The Erotic as Power." In *Sister Outsider*. Trumansberg, NY: The Crossing Press.

Bibliography • 151

Lutz, C. A. (1988). *Unnatural Emotions: Everyday Sentiments on a Micronesian Atoll and Their Challenge to Western Theory*. Chicago: University of Chicago Press.

Mansbridge, J. (1983). *Beyond Adversary Democracy*. Chicago: University of Chicago Press.

Marcus, G. E. (2002). *The Sentimental Citizen: Emotion in Democratic Politics*. University Park: Pennsylvania State University Press.

Matthews, R. K. (1995). If Men Were Angels: James Madison and the Heartless Empire of Reason. Lawrence: University Press of Kansas.

Miller, D. (1995). *On Nationality*. Oxford: Clarendon Press.

Monoson, S. S. (2000). *Plato's Democratic Entanglements: Athenian Politics and the Practice of Philosophy*. Princeton: Princeton University Press.

Moravcsik, J. M. E. (1971). "Reason and Eros in the 'Ascent' Passage of the Symposium." In *Essays in Ancient Greek Philosophy*. Anton and Kustas, eds. New York: State University of New York Press.

Morgenstern, M. (1996). *Rousseau and the Politics of Ambiguity: Self, Culture, and Society*. University Park: Pennsylvania State University Press.

Newell, W. R. (2000). *Ruling Passion: The Erotics of Statecraft in Platonic Political Philosophy*. Lanham, MD: Rowman & Littlefield Publishers, Inc.

Nicholson, L. (1999). *The Play of Reason: From the Modern to the Postmodern*. Ithaca, NY: Cornell University Press.

Nussbaum, M. C. (1986). *The Fragility of Goodness: Luck and Ethics in Greek Tragedy and Philosophy*. Cambridge: Cambridge University Press.

———. (1990). *Love's Knowledge: Essays on Philosophy and Literature*. New York: Oxford University Press.

———. (2001). *Upheavals of Thought: The Intelligence of Emotions*. Cambridge: Cambridge University Press.

Nussbaum, M. C. and J. Glover (1995). "Rational Emotions." In *Poetic Justice: The Literary Imagination and Public Life*. Boston: Beacon Press.

Nye, A. (1989). "The Hidden Host: Irigaray and Diotima at Plato's Symposium." *Hypatia* 3(3): 45–61.

———. (1990). *Words of Power: A Feminist Reading of the History of Logic*. New York: Routledge Press.

Okin, S. M. (1989). "Reason and Feeling in Thinking about Justice." *Ethics* 99: 229–29.

Pateman, C. (1989). "The Disorder of Women": Women, Love, and the Sense of Justice. In *The Disorder of Women: Democracy, Feminism and Political Theory*. Stanford: Stanford University Press.

Plato. (1953A). *Phaedrus. The Dialogues of Plato*. Vol. III. D. J. Allan and H. E. Dale. eds. Oxford: Clarendon Press.

———. (1953B). *Symposium. The Dialogues of Plato*. Vol. I. D. J. Allan and H. E. Dale, eds. Oxford: Clarendon Press.

———. (1992). *Republic. The Republic of Plato*. Indianapolis: Hackett Publishing Company.

Rawls, J. (1971). *A Theory of Justice*. Cambridge, MA: Harvard University Press.

———. (1993). *Political Liberalism*. New York: Columbia University Press.

Rorty, A. O. (1980). "Explaining Emotions." In *Explaining Emotions*. A. O. Rorty, ed. Berkeley: University of California Press.

———. (1991). "Rousseau's Therapeutic Experiments." *Philosophy* 66: 413–434.

Rorty, R. (1998). *Achieving Our Country: Leftist Thought in Twentieth-Century America*. Cambridge, MA: Harvard University Press.

Rosen, S. (1965). "The Role of Eros in Plato's *Republic*." *The Review of Metaphysics* XVIII(3): 452–475.

Rosenblum, N. (1987). *Another Liberalism: Romanticism and the Reconstruction of Liberal Thought*. Cambridge, MA: Harvard University Press.

Rousseau, J.-J. (1953). *The Confessions*. New York: Penguin Books.

———. (1960). *Politics and the Arts: Letter to M. D'Alembert on the Theatre*. Glencoe, IL: The Free Press of Glencoe.

———. (1979). *Emile: Or, On Education*. New York: Basic Books, Inc.

———. (1985). *The Government of Poland*. Indianapolis: Hackett Publishing Company.

———. (1987). *Discourse on the Origin of Inequality. The Basic Political Writings*. Vol. 55. Indianapolis: Hackett Publishing Company.

———. (1992). *Discourse on Political Economy. The Collected Writings of Rousseau*. Vol. 3. Hanover, NH: Dartmouth College, University Press of New England.

152 • Bibliography

———. (1994). *On the* Social Contract. *The Collected Writings of Rousseau*. Vol. 4. Hanover, NH: Dartmouth College, University Press of New England.

Santas, G. (1988). *Plato and Freud: Two Theories of Love*. Oxford: Basil Blackwell.

Saxonhouse, A. (1976). "The Philosopher and the Female in the Political Thought of Plato." *Political Theory* 4(2): 195–212.

———. (1984). "Eros and the Female in Greek Political Thought: An Interpretation of Plato's *Symposium*." *Political Theory* 12(1): 5–27.

———. (1992). "Democracy, Equality, and *Eide* in Plato's *Republic*." *American Political Science Review* 2: 278.

Scheman, N. (1993). "Anger and the Politics of Naming." In *Engenderings: Constructions of Knowledge, Authority, and Privilege*. New York: Routledge.

Schott, R. (1988). *Cognition and Eros: A Critique of the Kantian Paradigm*. Boston: Beacon Press.

Scolnicov, S. (1978). "Reason and Passion in the Platonic Soul." *Dionysius* 2: 35–49.

Shklar, J. (1969). *Men and Citizens: A Study of Rousseau's Social Theory*. Cambridge, MA: Harvard University Press.

Simon-Ingram, J. (1991). "Expanding the Social Contract: Rousseau, Gender and the Problem of Judgment." *Comparative Literature* 43(2): 148.

Singer, I. (1984). *The Nature of Love*. Chicago: University of Chicago Press.

Smith, R. M. (1985). *Liberalism and American Constitutional Law*. Cambridge, MA: Harvard University Press.

Solomon, R. C. (1984). "Emotions and Social Choice." In *What Is an Emotion? Classical Readings in Philosophical Psychology*. C. Calhoun and R. Solomon, eds. New York: Oxford University Press.

———. (1993). *The Passions: Emotions and the Meaning of Life*. Indianapolis: Hackett Publishing Company.

———. (1995). *A Passion for Justice: Emotions and the Origins of the Social Contract*. Lanham, MD: Rowman & Littlefield Publishers, Inc.

Spelman, E. V. (1988). *Inessential Woman: Problems of Exclusion in Feminist Thought*. Boston: Beacon Press.

Spelman, E. V. (1982). "Woman as Body: Ancient and Contemporary Views." *Feminist Studies* 8: 109–131.

Spragens, T. A., Jr. (1981). *The Irony of Liberal Reason*. Chicago: University of Chicago Press.

Spragens, T. A., Jr. (1990). *Reason and Democracy*. Durham, NC: Duke University Press.

Starobinski, J. (1988). *Jean-Jacques Rousseau: Transparency and Obstruction*. Chicago: University of Chicago Press.

Stearns, P. N. (1994). *Americal Cool: Constructing a Twentieth-Century Emotional Style*. New York: New York University Press.

Tamir, Y. (1993). *Liberal Nationalism*. Princeton: Princeton University Press.

Trask, H.-K. (1986). *Eros and Power: The Promise of Feminist Theory*. Philadelphia: University of Pennsylvania Press.

Tuana, N. (1992). *Woman and the History of Philosophy*. New York: Paragon House.

Vlastos, G. (1973). "The Individual as Object of Love in Plato." In *Platonic Studies*. Princeton: Princeton University Press.

Walzer, M. (2002). "Passion and Politics." *Philosophy & Social Criticism* 28(6): 617–633.

Weiss, P. A. (1993). *Gendered Community: Rousseau, Sex, and Politics*. New York: New York University Press.

Weiss, P. and A. Harper (1990). "Rousseau's Political Defense of the Sex-Roled Family." *Hypatia: A Journal of Feminist Philosophy* 5(3): 90–109.

Young, I. M. (1990). *Justice and the Politics of Difference*. Princeton: Princeton University Press.

———. (1996). "Communication and the Other: Beyond Deliberative Democracy." In *Democracy and Difference: Contesting the Boundaries of the Political*. S. Benhabib, ed. Princeton: Princeton University Press.

Zerilli, L. M. G. (1994). *Signifying Woman: Culture and Chaos in Rousseau, Burke, and Mill*. Ithaca, NY: Cornell University Press.

Index

A

Abstract rationalism, 76–77
Action. *See* Political action
Agathon, 50
Alcibiades, 63, 65
Alienation, 106
    problems of, 97
American Cool: Constructing a Twentieth-Century Emotional Style, 12
Anderson, Charles, 27
Angry part of soul, 41
Apathy, political, 125–126
Apology, 64–65
Appetite, passion, distinguished, 16
Appetitive part of soul, 41
Aristophanes, 49–51, 68
Aristotle, 6, 18

B

Beauty
    commonality of, 52
    understanding of, 52–53
Beliefs, judgments, infusions between, 128–129
Body
    femininity, disparagement of, relationship, 69–70
    objectification of, 102–105
Brock, Rita Nakashima, 95–97, 102, 106–107, 114–115

C

Calhoun, Cheshire, 15–17
Capitalist societies, culture of, 111–112

Caring, enthusiastic, 13
    passions, relationship, 6, 11–20 (*See also* Passion)
Carson, Anne, 37
Character of passion, 28–29
Choices, political
    role of passion in shaping, 7, 121–133
Christianity, role of, 100
Citizens, education of passions, 29, 65–67, 121–133
Cognitive theory, 15–17
Community
    emotional commitment to, 124–125
    passion for, 71–92
    political, 122–126
    role of passion in, 9, 39–92, 121–133 (*See also* Passion)
Compassion, reason, relationship, 75
Conceptions of good, 32–33
    variations in, 32–33
Confessions, 76
Conscious principles, natural impulses, distinguished, 116
Cravings, respect for, 114
Crimes of passion, 13
Crito, 64
Cultural influences on reason, 14–15
Culture, nature, relationship between, 79

D

D'Agostino, Fred, 26–27
Daly, Mary, 95
Damasio, Antonio, 17
Defiance, expression of, in display of flag, 2

153

154 • Index

Democracy, 121–122
  conversation of, 129–130
  epithumia in, 62–67
  passion for, 130–132
  practice of, 131
  taking account as core of, 130
Democratic society, education in, 29, 65–67,
  121–133
Desire. *See also Epithumia;* Eros
  beneficial, 47–48
  change in Plato's views, 60–61
  conceptions of, 40–42
  erotic, incorporation of value judgment, 42
  limitation of, as key to happiness, 45
  lower, higher forms of, distinguished, 48
  necessary, unnecessary, distinguished, 46
  power and, 44–45
  public, private, contrasted, 85
  rationality, opposition between, 41–42
  reason controlling, celebration of desire,
    contrasted, 59–60
  tyranny by, tyranny of others,
    relationship, 44
  unchecked, as root of injustice, 43–47
  for wisdom, 47–48
Desire for good, as source of eros, 50–51
Dialogues of Plato, 62–67
  participants in, social class represented by,
    61–62
Dimen, Muriel, 105, 111
Diotima, 63–64, 68
  Socrates, dialogue between, 49–53
Discourse on Political Economy, 74, 83–86, 88
Discourse on the Origin of Inequality, 9, 71–81,
  84–86, 90
Display of flags, psychological aspects of,
  1–4
Dominating behavior, 102
Drama, role in education, 69

E

Education of passion in democracy, 29,
  65–67, 85–88, 121–133
Egocentrism, 74
Eide, 68
  knowledge of, 52
  recollection of, 56–57
Emile, 75–76, 80, 84, 86–87, 89–91
Emotions. *See also* Passion
  cognitive theory, 15–17
  myopic, 17
Empowerment, achievement of, 129–130
L'Encyclopedie des Sciences et des Arts, 73–74
Enthusiasm
  concept of, 15
  passion as, 12–16, 20 (*See also* Passion)

Enthusiastic caring, 13, 22
  passions, relationship between, 6, 11–20
Epistemology, Platonic. *See* Plato
Epithumia, 18–19, 40–42, 54, 57–63, 66–67
  dangers of, 42–48
  defined, 8, 41
  eros, contrasted, 57–58
  gendered associations of femininity with,
    68–70
Epithuymetikon, 41
Eros, 18–19, 40–42, 111–119
  association with women, reciprocal
    dynamic of, 112–113
  as beneficial madness, 55–56
  blessings of, 48–59
  conception of, 8, 11–20, 96–99
  defined, 8, 41, 51
  devaluation of, 99–101
  empowerment by redirection, 109–111
  epithumia, contrasted, 57–58
  in feminist theory, 93–120 (*See also*
    Feminist theory)
  gender difference, 106
  gendered association with masculinity,
    68–69
  idealization of, 113–116
  lack of, 49–50
  link to reason, 49–71
  mythical genealogy of, 50
  orientation toward normative ideal, 19
  passion, 8–9, 39–70
    for good, 39–70
  patriarchal society, 114–115
  in Platonic theory, 8–9, 39–70 (*See also*
    Plato)
  political contribution of, 64–65
  power of, 105–111
  problem with, 54–55
  reason, opposition between, 113
  repression of, 101–105
  sanctity of, 114
  as source of desire for good, 50–51
  supranormal phenomenon, 55–59
  ubiquitous nature of, 51–52
  variation in concepts of, 70
Eros the Bittersweet, 37
Erotic knowledge, empowerment with, 93–120
Ethical behavior, unethical behavior,
  distinguishing factor, 20
Exclusion of women, passion, from public
  sphere, parallels between, 81–82

F

Factions
  passion as root of, 23–24
  problem of, 31

Index • 155

Fairness, justice as, theory of, 31–33
"False self," "true self," distinguished, 115–116
Fanaticism, passion and, 20
Federalist Paper No. 10, 23–24
Federalist Paper No. 15, 3
Federalist Paper No. 49, 31
Federalist Paper No. 55, 25
The Federalist Papers, 31. *See also* individual
  Federalist Paper
Femininity. *See also* Feminist theory
  body, disparagement of, relationship
    between, 69–70
  gendered associations, 68–70
Feminist theory, 117, 122, 125–126, 133
  alienation, 97, 106
  association of eros with women, dynamic,
    112–113
  body, objectification of, 102–105
  Brock, Rita Nakashima, 95–97, 102,
    106–107, 114–115
  capacity for judgment, integration of eros
    and reason, 118–119
  change, necessity of, 111
  Christianity, role of, 100
  conscious principles, natural impulses,
    difference between, 116
  core self, link to our own, 94
  Daly, Mary, 95
  debilitating, nature of, 98
  deepest cravings, respect for, 114
  Dimen, Muriel, 105, 111
  dominating behavior, 102
  eros, 95–96, 111–119
    conventional conception of, 96–99
    devaluation of, 99–101
    empowerment by redirection, 109–111
    estrangement from, 105
    feminist conceptions of, 94–96
    gender difference, 106
    idealization of, 113–116
    power of, 105–111
    reason, integration of, 118–119
    repression of, 101–105
    sanctity of, 114
  erotic, refusal to acknowledge, 104–105
  erotic knowledge, empowerment of,
    108–111
  "false self," "true self," distinguished,
    115–116
  feelings, abuse of, 114–115
  "feminist eros," concept of, 95–96
  good, link to, 95
  Goodison, Lucy, 109–110
  Hartsock, Nancy, 95, 99–100, 108
  Heyward, Carter, 95–97, 100, 102, 107,
    112, 114–117
  human nature, assumption of, essential
    goodness, 115

invulnerability, cultural model of, 102
Johnston, Jill, 95
Kant, Immanuel, 100
late-modern industrial capitalist societies,
  culture of, 111–112
life force, 95
Lorde, Audre, 93–95, 97, 99–100, 104–106,
  108–112, 115, 118–119
masculinity, cultural standards, 100
Moraga, Cherrie, 95
Morgan, Robin, 95
natural impulses, conscious principles,
  difference between, 116
natural phenomenon, ethical ideal,
  conflation of, 115–116
negative desire
  recognition, 118
  treatment, 118
objectivity in philosophy, displacement of
  forbidden eroticism, 103–104
opposition between reason and eros,
  perpetuation of, 113
oppression, 99–101
passion in, 9, 93–120
patriarchal society, distorted eros, 114–115
people
  link to, 94–95
  treated as objects, 104–105
Plato, 68–70
popular association with women, 98–99
power, dynamic of, 106–111
powerless, alienation condition of, 107–108
public spheres, private spheres, dichotomy
  between, 98
rationality, Western, 100
reason, eros, opposition between, 113,
  118–119
repression, 99–101
Rich, Adrienne, 95
Rousseau, 81–82
sadomasochism, 107–108
sadomasochistic sensibilities, 117
sanctity, language of, 108
Schott, Robin, 98, 103–104
self, social influences on, 115–116
sensuous world, link to, 95
sexuality, 97–100
Sister Outsider, 93
structures of power, shaped by
  relationship to eros, 107–108
Trask, Haunani-Kay, 95, 102, 108, 114, 116
"true self," "false self," contrasted, 115–116
violence, 97, 106
Western masculinist thought systems,
  98–101
work, politics, separation from, 97–98
Ferrari, Giovanni, 58–59
Flags, display of, psychological aspects, 1–4

156 • Index

Free Public Reason, 26–27
Fundamentalism, religious, 30

G

Gendered associations
    of *epithumia* with femininity, 68–70
    of eros with masculinity, 68–69
Gender inequality. *See* Feminist theory
General will, 84–86, 88
Good
    conceptions of, 32–33
    desire for, as source of eros, 50–51
    passion for, 39–70 (*See also* Eros)
Goodison, Lucy, 109–110
Gore, Al, 123–124
Gorgias, 64–65
The Government of Poland, 73, 82–84, 86,
    124–125
Grassroots political movement, passion and, 126

H

Halperin, David, 41–42
Hamilton, Alexander, 3, 23
Happiness
    identification of good with, 51
    limitation of desire as key to, 45
Hartsock, Nancy, 95, 99–100, 108
Heyward, Carter, 5, 95–97, 100, 102, 107, 112,
    114–117
Hirschman, Albert O., 25
Hobbes, Thomas, 24
Holmes, Stephen, 22–23, 26
Hume, David, 6

I

Ideals
    passion, link between, 123
    political, 122–126
Industrial capitalist societies, culture of,
    111–112
Injustice, 23–24
    unchecked desire as root of, 43–47
Innovation, political, stifling of, 36–37
Intention, in enthusiasm, 16
Interests, transformation of passions into, 26–28
Invulnerability, cultural model of, 102

J

Johnston, Jill, 95
Journeys of soul, parable of, 56–59

Judgment
    beliefs, infusions between, 128–129
    capacity for, integration of eros, reason,
        118–119
    in enthusiasm, 15
    passion, infusions between, 128–129
    requirement of feeling in, 17
Julie, 80
Justice
    as fairness, theory of, 31–33
    increase in potential for, with education of
        passion, 132 (*See also* Education)

K

Kallipolis, 63–64
Kant, Immanuel, 24–25, 100
Knowledge, erotic, empowerment with, 93–120

L

Lack, as source of eros, 49–50
Lange, Lynda, 81
Legislator, role of, 86–87
Letter to D'Alembert, 86, 90
Liberalism, psychological premise of, 22. *See
    also* Liberal political rationalism
Liberal political rationalism, 8, 21–38
Locke, John, 22–23, 25
Logistiken, 41
Lorde, Audre, 93–95, 97, 99–100, 104–106,
    108–112, 115, 118–119, 125
Love of self, 74
    reason, contrasted, 74–78
Lycurgus, 65–66
Lysias, Socrates, dialogue between, 53–58

M

Madison, James, 22–25, 31
Madness, 43
    eros as beneficial form of, 55–56
    marginalization of passion, 22–28, 36
Masculinist thought systems, 98–101
Masculinity. *See also* Feminist theory
    association of eros with, 68–69
    cultural standards, 100
Matthews, Richard, 31
Maturity
    complex paradigm of, 128–129
    conventional Western paradigm of, 128
Mill, John Stuart, 22–23
Moderation, 46–47
Moraga, Cherrie, 95
Moral sensibility, 33–34. *See also* Passion

Index • **157**

morality of association, 34–35
morality of authority, 34–35
morality of principles, 34–35
Morgan, Robin, 95
Morgenstern, Mira, 91
Mythical genealogy of eros, 50

N

Nationalism, 13–14, 30, 125. *See also* Patriotism
display of flag and, 1–10, 13
Natural impulses, conscious principles, distinguished, 116
Natural phenomenon, ethical ideal, conflation of, 115–116
Nature
culture, relationship between, 79
ideology of, 90
state of, modern society, contrasted, 78–80
Negative desire
recognition of, 118
treatment of, 118
Newell, Waller, 65
Nussbaum, Martha, 15–16, 60, 63

O

Objectivity in philosophy, displacement of eroticism, 103–104
Opinion, acquired, 54, 57–58. *See also Epithumia*
Oppression of women, 93–120. *See also* Feminist theory
Overpowering nature of passion, 13–14

P

Parable of journeys of soul, 56–59
Passion
appetite, distinguished, 16
character of, 28–29
of citizens, education of, 29, 65–67, 121–133
for community, 4–6, 9, 71–92 (*See also* Rousseau, Jean Jacques)
conception of eros, 8, 11–20
in contemporary feminist theory, 9, 93–120
defined, 11–12
for democracy, 130–132
democratic education and, 121–133
derivation of term, 11–12
education of, 29, 65–67, 85–88, 121–133
as enthusiasm, 12–16, 20, 22

enthusiastic caring, relationship, 6, 11–20
eros and, 8–9, 39–70
exclusion from public sphere, 81–82
in feminist theory, 9, 93–120 (*See also* Feminist theory)
for good, 39–70 (*See also* Plato)
ideals, link between, 123
inclusion of reason in, 15–18
judgments, infusions between, 128–129
kinds of, 8
in liberal political theory, 8, 21–38
link to reason, 8, 11–20
marginalization of, 36
as object of political process, 27–28
omission as topic in political theory, 26
overpowering nature of, 13–14
political choices, role in shaping, 7, 121–133
in political community, 9, 71–92
politicization of, 83–85
in politics, 1–10
praise of, 74–75
as problem, 23–26
problem reason must correct, 27
public, private, contrasted, 82–85
public institutions to control, 23
rational components, 16–17
reason, 11–20 (*See also* Reason)
contrasted, 80–82
dichotomization of, 14
dichotomy, 3–4
link between, 8, 11–20
politics, relationship, 10, 121–133
relationship, 8, 11–20, 75
role in politics, 9, 39–92, 121–133
Rousseau's terminology of, 72–74
of self-interest, 82–85
sentiment, distinguished, 17, 73–74
transcendence of, 82–83
working with, 127–130
The Passions and the Interests, 25–26
Pateman, Carole, 81–82
Patriarchal society, distorted eros, 114–115
Patriotism, 1–10. *See also* Politics
Pausanias, 68
Phaedrus, 8, 18–19, 39–42, 46–62, 124
Philia, 40–41
Philosophy
contribution to politics, 64 (*See also under* specific philosopher)
tension with politics, 62–64
Plato, 4–6, 8–9, 18–19, 39–70, 88, 92, 122–124, 133
Pleasure, lower, higher forms of, distinguished, 48
Poetry, role in education, 69
Political action, 121–133
Political apathy, 125–126

158 • Index

Political choices, role of passion in shaping, 7, 121–133
Political community, role of passion in, 9, 71–92
Political contribution of eros, 64–65. *See also* Eros
Political implications of flags, 3–4
Political importance of education in reason, passion, 29, 65–67, 85–88, 121–133
Political innovation, stifling of, 36–37
Political instability, 24–25
Political Liberalism, 27, 32, 35
Political rationalism, 8, 21–38
   liberal, 121–133
Political theory. *See also* Passion
   liberal, treatment of passion, 8, 21–38
   omission of passion as topic in, 26
Political unity, role of affect in, 77
Politics
   epithumia in, 62–67
   passion in, 1–10, 30–35, 39–92, 121–133
    (*See also* Passion)
   philosophy
     contribution to, 64
     tension with, 62–64
   positive aspects of passion in, 3–4
   practice of, 65
   reason, passion, relationship, 10, 121–133
   role in community, 9, 71–92
   separation of women from, 97–98
Positive aspects of passion in politics, 3–4
Power, structures of, relationship to eros, 107–108
Powerlessness, alienation condition of, 107–108
Private desire, public desire, contrasted, 85
Private passion
   public passion, contrasted, 82–85
     public reason, contrasted, 80–82
Private spheres, public spheres, dichotomy between, 98
Psychoanalysis, feminist, 6. *See also* Feminist theory
Psychological premise of liberalism, 22
Psychology, political. *See* Passion
Public desire, private desire, contrasted, 85
Public passion, private passion
   contrasted, 82–85
   opposition between, 82–85
Public service, 65
Public spheres, private spheres, dichotomy between, 98

R

Rationalism, 87–88. *See also* Reason
   abstract, 76–77

   criticism of, 74
   liberal political theory, passion in, 121–133
   political, 8, 21–38, 121–133
Rationality, 100
   desire, opposition between, 41–42
   desire conquering, falseness of, 54–55
Rational part of soul, 41
Rawls, John, 8, 22, 27, 29, 31–35
Reason
   compassion and, 75
   connotations of, 15
   cultural influence on, 14–15
   desire and, 59–60
   education in, political importance of, 65–67, 121–133
   eros, opposition between, 113, 118–119
   inclusion of passion in, 15–18
   link of eros with, 49–71
   opposition of passion to, 13
   passion
    dichotomization of, 14
    dichotomy between, 3–4
    politics, relationship, 10, 121–133
    relationship, 8, 11–20, 75
   Rousseau's terminology of, 72–74
   thought and, 15–17
Reasonableness, human capacity for, 34–35
Reason and Democracy, 26–27
Religious fundamentalism, 30
Repression of eros, 101–105
Repression of women, 99–101. *See also* Feminist theory
Republic, 8, 39–48, 51, 53, 59–62
Rich, Adrienne, 95
Right object, direction of passion toward, 83
Rorty, Amelie, 15, 73–74
Rosen, Stanley, 62
Rosenblum, Nancy, 24–25, 28
Rousseau, Jean Jacques
   theory of passion, 4–6, 9, 23, 71–92, 122–124, 133

S

Sadomasochism, 107–108
Sadomasochistic sensibilities, 117
Schott, Robin, 98, 103–104
Self, social influences on, 115–116
Self-determination, increase in potential for, with education of passion, 132
Self-interest, passions of, 82–85
Self-love, reason, contrasted, 74–78
Sentiment, 33–35. *See also* Passion
   passion, distinguished, 17, 73–74
Sexuality. *See also* Feminist theory
   preoccupation with, 99–100

Index • **159**

reduction of women to, 97–98
Simon-Ingram, Julia, 81–82
Sister Outsider, 93
Smith
  Adam, 22–23
  Roger, 27
Social Contract, 9, 71–72, 76–81, 85–87, 92
Social contract theories, 23
Social influences on self, 115–116
Socialization, 90–91
Socrates, 39, 42–43, 45–58, 65–66, 124, 130
Solomon, Robert, 15–17, 127
Sophrosyne, 46–47
Soul
  enslavement of, 43–44
  journeys of, parable of, 56–59
  parts of, 41
  structure of, 60–61
de Sousa, Ronald, 15–16
Spirited part of soul, 41
Spragens, Thomas, 26–27
Starobinski, Jean, 75
State of nature, modern society, contrasted,
  78–80
Stearns, Peter, 12
Structures of power, relationship to eros,
  107–108
Symposium, 8, 18–19, 39–42, 46–62
  definition of eros, 18–19
  difference from other dialogues, 39

T

Taking account, as core of democracy, 130
Temperance, 54

A Theory of Justice, 31, 34–35
Thinking, role of feeling in, 17
Thought, capacity for, 15–17. *See also*
  Reason
Thrasymachus, 65
Thumoeides, 41
Trask, Haunani-Kay, 95, 102, 108, 114, 116
"True self," "false self," contrasted, 115–116
Tyranny, 43–47
  by own desires, of others, relationship
  between, 44

U

Ultra-nationalism, 30
Unethical behavior, ethical behavior,
  distinguishing factor, 20
Unhappiness, desire and, 45–46

W

Walzer, Michael, 126
Weiss, Penny, 90–91
Western masculinist thought systems, 98–101
Western paradigm of maturity, 128
Western rationality, 100
Will, general, 84–86, 88
Wisdom, desire for, 47–48
Women, treatment of. *See* Feminist theory

Y

Young, Iris Marion, 81